PAPER VIEW

PAPER VIEW

The Best of the *Sunday Times* Television Reviews

A.A. Gill

Weidenfeld & Nicolson
LONDON

First published in Great Britain in 2008
By Weidenfeld & Nicolson

1 3 5 7 9 10 8 6 4 2

© A.A. Gill 2008

A CIP catalogue record for this book
is available from the British Library.

ISBN-13 978 0 297 85449 4

Typeset by Deltatype Ltd, Birkenhead, Merseyside

Printed in Great Britain by Clays Ltd, St Ives plc

Weidenfeld & Nicolson

The Orion Publishing Group Ltd
Orion House
5 Upper Saint Martin's Lane
London, WC2H 9EA

The Orion Publishing Group's policy is to use papers
that are natural, renewable and recyclable products and made
from wood grown in sustainable forests. The logging and
manufacturing processes are expected to conform to the
environmental regulations of the country of origin.

www.orionbooks.co.uk

This book should be dedicated to my dad,
but on his behalf I offer it to his grandchildren,
Flora, Ali, Louis, Hannah, Edith and Isaac,
for whom the argument 'is television a good or a
bad thing' is laughable and irrelevant.

Contents

Acknowledgements

Behind the screen of this book is a very good production team: Celia Hayley, the editor who is responsible for the way the book reads; Alan Samson, Lucinda McNeile and Carole Green at Weidenfeld & Nicolson; Helen, Adrienne and Patricia at the *Sunday Times*; my amanuensis Michelle Klepper; and agents Grainne Fox and Ed Victor.

Introduction

I'm writing this from a hospital bed. It's the first time since I was born that I've been a patient in a hospital. I'm going to have a small operation of convenience. I'm not nervous. I'm rather excited. I've been lying here for a bit wondering why I'm not more frightened. I'm not in pain and my life is not remotely threatened, but still, I have to undergo a general anaesthetic, sharp invasive tools will be plunged into my innards; it's not wholly without risk. But in truth, I have this keen sense of anticipation. I don't want to miss anything, and I know why. It's nothing to do with medicine, it's because of the telly. I've never been in a hospital bed before but I know loads about hospital beds. I know how to behave, I know what's expected of me, because I've seen it on television.

This is a hospital room. It is also a set. The nurses and porters and doctors all fit neatly into my personal narrative. They have also seen a lot of hospital on television and have learned their lines. We all do little scenes from *Emergency-Ward 10*, *Dr Finlay*, *Grey's Anatomy* and *Carry On Matron*. I know my role as a patient because I've seen so many patients. Nothing since the discovery of antisepsis and the two-tone siren has done so much for the practice of medicine as the television has. In fact, there is a television in the room with me now. It's an essential bit of hospital kit. Actually, there are two televisions; one has *Casualty* on, the other one has me. I'm attached to it; it's broadcasting my heartbeat. I'm a television station – not very interesting in itself, a bit of a plot cliché, the screw of dramatic tension. We all know what to expect from the disembodied line hiccuping across the screen. How often has this TV been used on the other TV as a denouement to tie up loose plot? I've always thought there should be an award for animating objects on TV, the familiar character props of drama … And the nominations are ... the bedside alarm clock, the missed phone, the rearview mirror. So, here I am, watching my heartbeat on television, confident that I'm in the hands of people who are all word perfect, who have been cast to fulfil their stereotypical callings. And most importantly – there must be pathos in hospital dramas – I know that statistically I'm unlikely to have the sheet pulled over my head, mainly because I don't have a backstory and no one in here loves me. Hospitals on television are the homes of happy endings and that is one of television's greatest gifts. To give the audience a constant stream of happy-ever-afters. In fact, that may be the greatest gift of all civilisation. Fade to black.

It's not just hospitals and policemen that television has manipulated. It's everything. No piece of human exchange, no corner of the possible world, hasn't passed through the periscope in the parlour. It never ceases to amaze me how many people still come up to me and say, 'I don't know how you manage it. I don't know how you do that for a living. Staring at that godawful box. There's absolutely nothing on.' I could have called this collection *A Life with Nothing On*. A sneering out-of-hand dismissal of television is the one cultural prejudice that can still be delivered without inverted commas. The intellectual orthodoxy that forbids the watching of TV has remained remarkable consistent since it was black and white and 405 lines. It states that by its very nature television is stupid, vain, coarse, small-minded and embarrassing. It diminishes the great and elevates the negligible. It makes the clever look fools and fools appear clever. It leaves nothing of value behind it, only a general sense of thwarted aspiration and fearful insecurity. At best, it's a stickily sentimental pacifier for the masses, and at its worst the adulterator of art, the bad culture that drives out good and poisons the springs of originality and inspiration, reducing everything to grinning, shrieking gratification. It'll also ruin your eyes, posture and table manners. This is the embroidered homily, the embossed litany and brailled health warning of the middle-browed, the badge of belonging and the catechism of the hardback intellectual. That includes a great many of the people who make, commission and appear on television, and like most tenets that are universally held by people who should know better, it's arrant and utter cretinism, a fearful cry from those who think there's already quite enough civilisation to be going on with, and couldn't we please have a moratorium or at least a breather while the slowest children catch up?

If it's any consolation, this is precisely what they said about the novel. It's the medium they dislike. They hated printing, and oil paint, and pianos, and opera, and atonality and recording on wax cylinders and on iPods, and organs in church. They waved their hands in horror at photography, cinema, colour, folk, skiffle, jazz, rock, pop and rap. And now, of course, at computer games. We know only two things with absolute certainty about the rise and fall of civilisations. First, that they can only move one way, and second that the people who claim to be their staunchest defenders always want to stop them in their tracks. Saying there's nothing worth watching on television is like saying there's nothing worth watching on Western civilisation.

I am the same age as television. Mass broadcasting kicked off with the Coronation in 1953. It was the first television event that stimulated the purchase of television sets. It nearly didn't happen (not the Coronation, sadly, the broadcast). The prelates were against it. This was a church service. Men might watch it in pubs. Possibly with their 'clorth ceps' on. But the BBC made some tasteful promises and as Elizabeth was crowned, so was the telly. In the same year 68 per cent of Americans watched Lucille Ball give birth to a fictional son on *I Love Lucy* whilst on the same day she had a real son, Desi Arnaz Jr. A weird premonition of reality TV. The BBC produced the first station identity symbol, called the bat's wings. It's a spookily authoritarian graphic. In 1954 ITV arrived, and so did I. The BBC began the world's first regular news broadcast and my father joined the corporation. He went there to do the new course for directors and producers and went on to work for Schools and Arts Programmes which he did for the rest of his life. He'd been in the RAF during the war and he'd been part of the Occupying Forces in Germany. The evisceration of Europe and the inability of the great old Überculture to prevent it posed the most pressing intellectual question for the post-war century. He didn't take up his place at Guy's to study medicine; instead, he went to Edinburgh to read philosophy and psychology. For him broadcasting was more than a new medium, it was a new start, a new way of making things better, a vision that was so compelling and accessible and watchable, unencumbered by tradition or heritage, that it would mean that no one would ever again be able to say, 'I didn't know, I was never told.'

Television was the way and the means to show everyone to everyone. My dad never lost his belief that the only salvation for humanity would be through culture, or that TV was the defining culture of his age. It's often said that the BBC was a construct of Lord Reith: traditional, imperialist, with the Victorian attitudes of rectitude and improvement. Reith laid down the BBC's relationship with the government and its position in the Establishment, and the tone of the wireless. But television, its demeanour, its inquisitiveness, its philosophy and its defining unwritten manifesto was made up by young men like my father, most of whom had been junior officers in the war, most of whom were university educated in the arts which they never ceased to revere, most of whom were Socialist and most of whom fervently believed that whatever we'd been doing before the atomic bomb hadn't worked, and wouldn't work again. There had to be a new way to describe the world and what it felt to be part of it, and first go they came up with a medium that had a language which would be effortlessly welcomed and accommodated around the world. It was broad and flexible enough to fit a bewildering variety of forms, formats, genres and conventions that had no hierarchy and no snobbery. I am the first television generation. Everything I know I learned from the box. Every opinion I have is informed by it. I passed no exams, I have no degrees, and when the *Sunday Times* asked me if I'd like to do the television column, I grabbed it with both hands. Everything that is anything happens on television. If you're not watching, you're not part of it. I've switched on the box pretty much every day for fifty years and each time I'm impatient with anticipation. There is a twinge of excitement.

FICTIONS

Cops

Prime Suspect

When I got this job, they said, what do you think you need to be a good, insightful, even-handed, tough but fair television critic? Oh, passion, I said. Passion and commitment, insight and love, and a lively interest in popular culture. A working knowledge of the history of the medium, a pretty shabby social life and a sofa.

If they asked me now, I would say the first requirement was a bottomless bucket of facile things to say about policemen. Review television and you will meet more policemen than the Krays. By the time you get to your thousandth bending the rules, trouble at home, sex in the office, prematurely balding, cynical but senti-mental, go-go-go merchant, you really start earning your wages. What else is there to say about policemen? 'Hold on, Alpha Alpha Garbo, I am just checking. The answer is negative, over.' There is nothing. Not a single original amusing thing left to add to the long march of coppers, and that is because there is not a single amusing, new or original thing being made about them on television.

We've done comedy cops, realistic cops, social philosophy cops, parody cops; we've done parody of parody cops. But policemen stopped being individual in about 1982. Since then, it has been like watching classical kabuki. The sets are the same, the costumes are the same, the dialogue is the same, and there are only three plots. It is comparing like with like and giving marks for handbrake turns. There is only one thing left that can deal with policemen: allegory. I am going to finish this once and for all, in a metaphorical sense of course. No more Mr Simile Guy.

Prime Suspect (ITV) last week was the fifth *Prime Suspect*. Five. They've done this story five times. The cast changes, the crime varies slightly, but the story is just the same. Allegorically, *Prime Suspect* is not about a leathery senior policewoman fighting misogyny, her own sexuality and obsessive tunnel-visioned ambition. It is really about a leathery prime minister fighting misogyny, her own sexuality and excessive tunnel-visioned ambition. It is the biography of Margaret Thatcher. Helen Mirren is Margaret Thatcher. Prime suspect, prime minister, geddit?

The first *Prime Suspect* was so successful because we were living in the middle of the Thatcher years. Nobody had ever made a drama that explained why we both loathed but were entranced by this dictatorial, barmy, sexually radiant woman. All the political satirists went head-to-head with her, threw cartoon ridicule, hurled insults at her and went down like plastic *Belgranos* in her wake. The name-calling and mud-slinging made her more mysterious and enigmatic, added to the sense of Thatcher as unstoppable force of nature. Only a silver ballot would do it.

Prime Suspect used the allegory of a police station – what better for the Thatcher Cabinet? And a Britain populated with child abusers, prostitutes and deviants – how very much like Thatcher's view of us. Mirren got closer to explaining what Thatcherism really was than a decade of *Newsnights* and *Spitting Images*. And when she got her kit off, there was that same creepy-crawly horror that you would feel if *Hello!* printed photographs of Margaret having her toes sucked by David Mellor.

Now, five series and one-and-a-half administrations later, the Thatcher years have an uncomfortable poignancy. *Prime Suspect* has followed the Iron Lady into a peripheral dark limbo – for the sake of allegory, appropriately called Manchester. Mirren, like Thatcher, has lost it. She is a shadow of her former self, she has gone off like a Catherine wheel that spun off its nail. It was a sad end to the longest-serving policewoman this century. Next week, class, we are doing Pets Win Prizes, the allegorical dissection of John Major and which giant centipede will make it over the obstacles to join the ERM.

James Nesbitt is wonderfully watchable: a sort of potato-faced, balding George Clooney. But not in a million years do I believe in him as an Al Pacino-style undercover detective with a borderline psychosis and a merry wit. Indeed, we were told he had had to choose to have his little daughter executed by the IRA, and we said: 'Get away.' We might swallow that sort of monstrous Wagnerian background for Edward Woodward, or even John Thaw, but not cuddly little James. He can't do haunted and he can't do tough. And, sadly, every police-man has to get tough at some point. Nesbitt manages to look like he's threatening a fridge for letting the milk go off. If he touches a gun, it instantly becomes a water pistol. If he ever has to handcuff anyone, it'll look like chaining a bike to the railings, and probably a bike with stabilisers.

Poirot

Like Fisherman's Friend, there ought to be a cough lozenge called the Detective's Friend. It would be sweet with a bitter aftertaste. It should salve, but it would never de-solve. The Detective's Friend always leaves you with a lump in the throat. There is a no more emotionally crippled bunch in all of fiction than the detective's sidekick – from Watson to Morse's Sergeant Lewis, from Batman's Robin to Secret Squirrel's Mole. The whole point is they never got the point. They're the last to know.

He has to sit in railway carriages and promenade tearooms and say: 'Remarkable, but whose was the footprint in the herbaceous border?' The Detective's Friend lives a sad tweedy life being patronised from a great height. And, of course, he has to carry the revolver; the detective is never going to risk the nightmare of having to kill someone. There ought to be a support group therapy session for Detective's Friends. A psychiatrist should say: 'After breakfast I want you all to meet me in the saloon and sit in a circle and I'll tell you what's wrong with you.' 'Remarkable, how on earth did you work that out?' they'd all say in psycho-frantic unison.

The Identikit for the classic Detective's Friend is that he should be a bachelor of about the same age as his mentor but a slightly lower social standing. And while a detective is light and air, in-tuition and imagination, the sidekick should be earthbound and stoical. You don't need to be doing a redbrick deconstruction thesis to work out that the detective and his friend are Yin and Yang, male and female. They actually go together to make up one person. The detective gets all the court cards of character, the friend all the rest in spades and hearts. One of the reasons detective fiction seems populated with cardboard men is because they are all cut in half, and it's why they have such a strong sense of homosexuality about them. 'Holmes, there is an evil sense of homoerotica lurking here.' 'Yes, Watson, it's because we're both in love with the same person: me.'

The saddest of them all is Hastings, Poirot's better half – his very name redolent of south-coast loneliness, solid white cliffs and English tragedy. David Suchet and Hugh Fraser are both utterly splendid in the television incarnations. Together they make up a complex character that manages to rise above the obsessive period production values. Hastings is such a painfully inept, emotionally vulnerable chap I could hardly bear to watch him in *Murder on the Links* (ITV). The subplot had him falling in love with a stock femme fatale. It left me gasping in desperate embarrassment. Hastings is out of his depth in a teacup of liquid lust. In the last shot of the film, Poirot pimps the devious girl for his desolate friend and the credits roll on the two proto-lovers kissing on the prom. It was more than I could stand. You just know that Hastings is bound to be a really dreadful kisser. And when you imagine him in bed … I'm afraid I had to put my fingers in my ears and hum tunelessly. So there's Hastings schoolboyishly snogging, waves crashing, orchestra bowing their strings with vibrato. And we get a cutaway shot of Hercule watching them wistfully with a touch of sadness, and we know who Hastings should really be clasping in his manly arms. The crime that dare not speak his name. The one mystery Poirot will never uncover. ''Astings, I want you to come to my bedroom. I will reveal all.'

The plot was the usual convoluted, belief-stretching dross. Sensibly, the production didn't dwell on it and concentrated in-stead on the look of the thing. The direction does master a David Lean-style swank. Every passing extra was weighed down with immaculate detail. Every distant tennis racket and bicycle clip was just so. This is a very dangerous route for a series with a weak plot to take, because all too easily the whole thing can drown in a swamp of spats and the right type of golf ball. But the combined characters of Suchet and Fraser save it with elegant, believable, surefooted performances.

The whole thing is so terribly gay. They are the Colefax and Fowler of television detectives. And finally, if Poirot is so good at clearing things up, why on earth hasn't he had his piles seen to? That walk, really.

Into the Blue (ITV) wasn't so much full of red herrings as written by red herrings. It was shot on Rhodes, cleverly disguised to look like the Isle of Wight, and staggered along with all the elegant, subtle grace of a muddy tractor.

Cop Shows

Spooks and now The Ghost Squad. Are they trying to tell us something about modern policing? They most surely are. Cop eras on the box have always been bellwethers, if not for the state of society, then for the way society views its state. Voltaire, or someone impersonating a French philosopher, said that you judge a country not by its palaces, but by its jails. And you can judge the collective concerns and fears of the sofa-bound nation not by the quality of prizes and guests on game shows, but by the crimes and punishment on its police shows.

This is familiar territory for media studies in Midlands universities. We start off with Dixon of Dock Green, avuncular simplicity and the happy 1950s. Actually, we should start with Dick Barton and the Edwardian, Hannay-rip-off gentleman detectives at the beginning of broadcasting. Following Dixon, there was Z Cars, Softly Softly and The Sweeney. And then all those American imports, such as Kojak and The Rockford Files. Then there was The Bill, and Lynda La Plante, and Cracker. Then American imports that swapped chummy homoeroticism and violence for forensics. Now we've got Spooks, which has just finished a successful run, and The

Ghost Squad (C4), which is just hitting its stride. Both series are about guardians of our safety who aren't there, who aren't there for us, whom we can't see, can't call, who won't do anything to help, don't walk the streets and don't pick up the phone.

The assumption that we have the best police force in the world underwrote all British police series. Well, it doesn't any more, because I don't get the feeling any of us assume we do any more. And the new police dramas have unerringly understood this. *The Ghost Squad* is about the useless crookedness of the regular police, but unlike its predecessors, it is morally ambivalent. There appears to be precious little difference between the poachers and the game-keepers. Or, as George Orwell (who started off as a policeman) might have said, there is no difference between pig and man.

The Ghost Squad, which has upped the gritty reality in terms of swearing and behaviour, but is still a long way behind *The Sweeney* in terms of overt violence – and is really not much worse than *Little Britain* – owes its success to a pithy script and juicy characterisation. Last week's episode had a particularly vile and explosive gang of feral girls, who were marvellously like a chorus from *The Bacchae*. Gangs of kids are now much more chav-some and current than the stocking-headed, broken-nosed blaggers and lags of *The Sweeney* and *Softly Softly*.

Television cop shows have stopped being about the public at all. It's a sign of how we see the police in real life, and if I were Home Secretary and adept at reading the social semiotics, I'd be very, very concerned. Then again, who am I kidding? The Home Secretary is Charles Clarke, and he probably thinks a semiotic is a type of Czech submachine gun.

Blue Murder (ITV), the latest detective show, was exhausted before it began. Caroline Quentin is the detective trying to juggle single mumdom with murder. If I tell you that the most exciting bit was her making breakfast for the kids, you may get some inkling of the extruded torpor that was this programme. Dull is too short a word, boring too hectic. Sitting through this made a coffee enema seem an attractive alternative; indeed, if you find yourself watching future episodes with someone who says they're just going to put the kettle on, for Christ's sake don't say you fancy a cup. Quentin is a good actress: she does harassed normality really well, indeed so well it's like watching the woman over the road do the housework – and why would you want to do that if you have a telly?

Doctors

'What is sin?' inquired the delirious man with third-degree make-up as if he really wanted to know. 'Well, I'd say sin is a moral evil in a religious sense,' Raymond Massey replied, with his comfortable Mount Rushmore gravitas, in that voice that always sounds as if it should have an echo. St Peter is probably Massey's understudy even as we speak.

This is a deathless (literally) extract from *Dr Kildare*. Doctors and patients don't have conversations like that on *Casualty*. The one irretrievably moribund victim of the electric hospital has been God. Television medics have striven for years, worked inhuman hours to overcome and eradicate the curse of the divine from mankind, and now, finally, they've succeeded. God is seen only occasionally, huddled in the waiting room, as a secondary symptom of some more important sickness. Religion rears it ugly buboes as Christian Scientists refusing blood transfusions for their children, or as tired, sad, deluded Catholics who struggle with abortion. Faith has been cured by antibiotics, mystery seen through by scans, prayer vanquished by cosy corridor homilies, morality replaced with ethics. If a patient came round demanding to know what sin was in any of the current medical soaps, he'd be told quick as an ECG that sin was National Health cuts, opted-out hospitals or an acronym for some piece of equipment.

Docs on the Box, BBC2's Sunday evening of old doctor programmes, showed quite what a radical theodectomy our humanity has sustained. *Dr Kildare*, the Genesis of medical dramas, looked truly bizarre. It could have been Jacobean. The sets were utterly stark; there was none of that whirligig and roistering we associate with TV doctors. The show had hardly any medicine in it. It was all about morality: doctors were not so much medicinal as priestly.

In fact, if they had turned their collars round, the whole thing could have been set in church. And, oh, there was that truly weird Richard Chamberlain, one of the creepiest creatures to appear on the box outside of *Star Trek*. He just oozed sticky campness, camperama, camperamissima, campola. To post-modernise, with the innocent veil of the 1950s ripped aside, it was obvious he was desperate to leap from the medical closet dressed as matron and take Massey's temperature the *Carry On* way.

Compare *Dr Kildare* with *MASH*, the longest-running US show in the history of the universe. Somewhere in the world, every hour of the day, Radar is monotonously repeating: 'incoming, incoming.' *MASH* famously has the highest quotient of gags per medical procedure, and the longest unbroken Groucho Marx impersonation ever undertaken, by Alan Alda. That it was a watershed show for the modern medical genre is a given. It put the opera into operations. All that joking around the table, the banter. These were the first doctors to start their sentences with 'Hey'. Other 'stand-back' dramas may have stolen the mask and badinage (nurse, will you badinage that ankle) but, for the viewer, the real innovation was that it did away with the patient. The wounded became merely anonymous bags of blood. It was the doctors we sympathised with, not the injured. They didn't even have names, most of them didn't have faces. So when Hawkeye performed some life-or-death procedure that went wrong, it was his angst with which we sympathised.

The medical drama has changed from a chapel, with doctors the interpreters of divine fate, to a pit-stop, with doctors playing mechanics on bits of broken machinery. And so it has remained. The patients in almost all medical dramas speak only to give tongue to symptoms. Their embarrassment and distress, their pain and loss, are there to give the doctors drama. When a surgeon breaks the news: 'I'm terribly sorry, but we did everything we could,' it is the man in the white coat we feel for. The camera lingers on huddled misery for an embarrassed, decent moment, but then it's out of there. Incoming, stand back.

This alters the viewer's perception: it changes us from being a patient in God's hands to being the doctor playing Rubik's cube with ethics, time, money and a tatty love life. And it is rather disturbing, unpleasant, belittling and dehumanising. As *Z-Cars* and *Softly Softly* and the go, go, go dramas that followed changed the behaviour of cops, and probably robbers, nature following art, so I'm told, the medical show has influenced a generation of doctors, made them jokier, cooler, harder. But, more importantly, it has changed patients and changed us. We now go to the doctor's full of diagnosis and jargon, expecting the gofer behind the desk to fill in the prescription we saw last night because, of course, we want to be the curer, not the cured. Just listen to yourself next time. You'll use all that spurious call-a-cut-an-abrasion, a-skin-an-epidermis speak. You'll play out the corridor consulting scene. The language of medical drama has a religious parallel. In *Dr Kildare*, the dialogue was momentous, but English. It was a Presbyterian sermon. Now, it's that shouted plainsong of expertise, a tongue spoken only by the initiated. It's like listening to a Latin mass: comforting rhythms but unintelligible, the modern religions of chemicals and technology.

The third ancient medical show to be brought out of cryonic suspension was *Dr Finlay's Casebook*. I have a soft spot for the old doctor here, no, a bit higher, oh yes, just there. My mother was in dozens of them. I remember watching her when I was twelve at school. She played a gypsy having a baby. It must have been the first time anyone gave birth on the BBC before their watershed, and it was the most embarrassing moment of my life. *Dr Finlay's Casebook* wasn't so much a blood-and-guts series as a medical whodunnit. You had to piece together the symptoms and make a correct diagnosis before Dr Cameron got there.

I'd sussed this one within five minutes. 'Ergot poisoning!' I shouted at the screen. From wet rye – caused mass death and madness in medieval Germany. 'You're severely weird,' said my outreach voluntary carer on the other end of the sofa. 'How on earth do you know about ergot?' From the telly, of course. If anyone ever asks you what the greatest advance in medicine has been this century, have no doubts: the answer is that box in the corner.

Children

Teletubbies

Last week there was an episode of *Teletubbies* (BBC2) called *Naughty Lady, Yellow Cow*, which sounds like a Russ Meyer film. I'm assuming you won't have seen *Teletubbies*, and trying to make its truly spooky weirdness live for you is difficult. But here goes. The *Teletubbies* are small dancers dressed up as coloured fluffy aliens with blank, deeply frightening plastic faces that blink. They live in hyper-reality, a grassy landscape that vaguely resembles pit-village land reclamation, with real rabbits and plastic flowers. They meow and giggle, with candy-floss voices. Oh, and they have a television in their tummies which is switched on by a big windmill.

The Teletubbies live in a bunker underground, with a metal rottweiler Hoover and a crematorium-sized toaster. The naughty lady was real-ish – she appeared on the gut-television, speaking to a group of ethnically correct children: 'I'm going to be naughty, now.' She then apparently suffered a short epileptic fit before telling a story about a naughty yellow cow which was her favourite friend. It was a story only in the loosest sense, as it was bereft of beginning, middle or end, and utterly plotless. The cow was yanked off on a piece of fishing gut and reappeared in a hideously badly made prop teapot.

This is only scratching the surface of this truly bizarre programme. Overall, it was, well, like … Imagine not sleeping for three days and then taking acid in a Japanese toy shop with Virginia Bottomley. Who knows what children make of it – but they don't pay the licence fee or whine to the *Daily Mail*. What is truly awe-inspiring about *Teletubbies* is that it was made not just by people who are apparently drug-free but who have done research, questioned study groups, actually thought about it. The question we should be asking isn't what effect does children's television have on our children, but what effect does it have on the people who produce it?

At last week's international convention on children's television, a Scandinavian kiddies TV producer laid into the Teletubbies' deconsonanted, monosyllabic muttering for impeding children's language development. Oh, righto. But what I want to know is: in Norwegian, how could they possibly tell? It begged the question: what has Scandinavia ever done for children's television? Sorry, my mistake, there was *Noggin the Nog*. And it raised the blissful image of the Teletubbies made by Ingmar Bergman.

TINKY WINKY: The sun is smiling. It mocks me.

LAA-LAA: Have toast.

TINKY WINKY: How can I eat? It is sad.

LAA-LAA: Where's Po?

TINKY WINKY: Black death.

LAA-LAA (wailing): The rabbits, the rabbits have black death!

TINKY WINKY: Now I have to play chess with the vacuum cleaner for my soul.

DIPSY (comes in covered in snow and sacking bandages): Teletubbies say there is no God. Life is a meaningless tread-mill of misery and hugs.

Closing shot: Teletubbies silhouetted against blasted skyline, dancing with a man carrying a scythe to tune of 'Have You Seen the Muffin Man'?

An American producer defended the Tubbies by calling the Scanda broad 'an ignorant slut'. He then went on to explain that slut didn't mean the same in America as it does here. (Ignorant is presumably pretty international.) All of which rather proves the point that being brought up on a televisual diet of *Blue Peter* and *Sesame Street* doesn't necessarily mean you're a well-rounded human being who can talk peace and love to the rest of the world, although you can probably make a slut out of an old loo roll and sticky-back plastic.

Overall, the international convention on children's television has been gloriously bad-tempered and intemperate when compared with, say, the international sales conference of pornography producers, which is a vicars' tea party – often quite literally. And it proved a point that can't be stated too often: it is not television's job to turn children into wholesome adults, and getting educated doesn't necessarily make you a nice person. Just because you knew what was through the round window when you were four doesn't mean you won't break into someone else's when you're fourteen. Watching television doesn't necessarily make you anything.

> The new *Jackanory* offered us John Sessions telling a story with all the usual Mummy-pleasing boredom that comes with danger-free adventure, non-violent conflict, lovable baddies, victors without victims and judgement-free denouements. Sessions is a man whose constant gurning runs the emotional gamut from gay surprise to camp shock. He does accents like someone flicking through the options on a car navigation system.

Puppets

Television has made stars out of some pretty weird, talentless and undeserving people and things – look at Carol Vorderman – but possibly none so strange as puppets. You would think that in a rational, normal and sensible world, one of the purposes of television would be to put an end to puppets, like eradicating polio or the plague. But, by some hideous mutation, puppets jumped mediums: the box actually gave them an extra lease of what passes for life if you've got somebody's fingers up your back passage.

As a last farewell to the silly season, Channel 4 offered us *Zippy and George's Puppet Legends*. I am slightly too old for this camp pink hippo and the acid-yellow bondage-head to have been part of my formative years, thank God, so I can regard them with dispassionate shudders of disgust. All puppets are the stuff of nightmares. In this programme, the ones of my infancy were bundled together in a single black-and-white category that looked as ancient and bizarre as Edwardian newsreel and as terrifying as Nosferatu.

How can even a two-year-old coming out of rationing have been entertained by *Muffin the Mule*? It was so badly made, painted with a toothbrush and apparently manipulated by arthritic members of the British Limbless Ex-Servicemen's Association. And who thought up the Woodentops, who were half naked all the time and did nothing but fall over? Or Pinky and Perky, who actually played the Palladium live, for Christ's sake, and put out umpteen albums in those speeded-up harpies' voices? Then there was the utterly incomprehensible Bill and Ben, like something nihilistic and bipolar in the nursery written by Beckett, *Endgame* for the under-fives; and all the variations on stick-your-hand-up-a-sock – Sooty, who didn't even have to speak, Roland Rat, Basil Brush and some gopher-chipmunk thing from kids' Saturday TV. Sadly, they didn't manage to find a space for Lamb Chop, who really was a sock with Shari Lewis's fist up it.

Collectively, puppets come on as creepy child-molester familiars. They have a malevolent power. It goes back to our cultural Dark Ages; they are homunculi and voodoo dolls. They are innately evil, receptacles for ill will, jealousy, revenge and psychopathy. Animated dolls given life and voices are playing with our basic fears from the very edge of civilisation. Letting them loose on children is smiling cruelty. Worst of all are the ventriloquists. Zippy and George offered us the desperate Emu and that green bird in a nappy. From which locked-ward-therapy session did that thing spring? We weren't shown Archie Andrews or Lord Whatsit, or Spit the Dog, which was a small mercy. Number one of the top ten was Kermit, a puppet so benign, he barely had a character at all, the Alec Guinness of puppets, a Method sock.

This programme was dingily produced and written with all the wit and pizzazz you can extract from a thing with a fly for a gob. And I realise that what we really wanted was to see a programme about the bottom ten men to devote their lives to puppets, from Harry H. Corbett to the serial sidekicks of Basil Brush. It's a life that must strip away any sense of self-worth and leave the practitioners with an empty loathing for children and the fundamental fear that your right hand might actually find out what your left hand's been doing.

In a parallel universe, exactly the same programme as *George and*

Zippy's Puppet Legends was put on earlier in the week by Channel 4. It called this one *The Death of Celebrity*, and put Piers Morgan in charge of it. It barely managed to keep a straight face as it described itself as a documentary about the slurry of vacuous, no-hope celebrity that is invading the media, although it didn't mention Morgan by name.

Really, this was just another exploitation of human glove puppets, those feckless kids with overdeveloped egos and no embarrassment gland who discover that if they mess about in public the way they used to do in bus shelters, then lots and lots of leery old men will come out and take pictures of them, and pay them money to do it. The show followed the hackneyed Fleet Street path of wallowing in muck while pretending to condemn it. It used all the trappings and conventions of the reality shows it claimed to be decrying – a top ten, talent auditions and surprise guest judges. And, of course, it has the traditional reality presenter, a fading star looking to clutch at a new career. Just as Ulrika Jonsson takes up tabloid journalism, so Piers Morgan turns up as a light-entertainment presenter. It's a fair swap.

This is the Morgan who made a grubby living first as a relentless gossip columnist, then as a star-struck, cloth-eared tabloid editor. He took a swing at the people he had invested his career in chasing, paying and bullying. As a format, this is beyond irony. There is no qualitative or cultural difference between Morgan and the kids he seemed to take such lurid pleasure in kicking, except, of course, that they had the excuse of youth, and he doesn't. Though, in fairness, it must be said that Morgan has sharpened up his light-entertainment persona, being alternatively cravenly sycophantic and Tourettishly rude, bellowing with pre-emptive laughter at his own jokes. It became obvious that Piers Morgan has become Basil Brush, with his own hand up his behind.

Cartoons

There's a continuing debate over the domination of children's television by cartoons. On one side, it goes: cartoons are a passive stream of noise and movement that make little or no demands on children. At best they're bland, at worst they're violently nihilistic. They teach kids fantastically annoying catch-phrases, funny voices and that if they cut someone's head off, it will grow back. On the other hand, the argument goes: 'Wah, wah, goo-goo, bang-bang, aaarrrggghhhh!!!! Lighten up!'

If you have ever been left in charge of small children for any length of time – and any time is lengthy – you will know that toddlers live in hamster days. For them twenty-four hours is the equivalent of an adult month. And you will also have discovered that cartoons are the single greatest invention of the twentieth century. I don't think there's been any research into how long a child will remain utterly static in front of the television, but my guess is that it could well be into their thirties.

Because of their odd history and the even odder people who draw them, cartoons have evolved a peculiarly lawless and amoral narrative language. Originally they weren't made for children at all. So although cartoons are now, almost without exception, aimed at an audience that can't wipe its own bottom, there still lurks the adult wish-fulfilment and surreally violent dreamscape. This means that they can so often be seen on two levels – as slapstick and as theatre-of-the-absurd metaphor.

Which brings us to the BBC's new *Walking with Dinosaurs* (BBC1). A brontosaurus of a series that has a heavyweight, glossy, marketing look that can be sold around the world, as if the continental drift had never happened. But when all is said and done, and an awful lot has been said and done, this is just a cartoon. It may have been constructed with state-of-the-art modern technology and state-of-the-art prehistoric palaeontology, but it's still Krazy Kat with knobs on and no jokes.

The first question it posed was: 'Who is this for?' Dinosaurs are the enduring obsession of children, and the series was prefaced with a screening of *Jurassic Park* – which seems to imply they expect a young audience – but the narrative is straightforwardly Bristol-nature-documentary of the anaemic Discovery Channel type. Perhaps it is aimed at the Cro-Magnon market: children in adult bodies or, as they are technically known in television marketing parlance, Americans. The reconstruction of big defunct lizards is fantastic. I watched with my two children. They were rapt, if not rapturous. One of the technical things that makes it all very impressive is the depth of feel. In cartoons, everything is equally in focus. These computer-generated images have a sharpness in the foreground and the background softens, as with a real camera. But the excitement of seeing dinosaurs walk rather like photorealist paintings lasts about five minutes. After that you need a story. Here, I am with the creationists. What God created in Genesis was the story: 'In the beginning' begs a middle and an end. The plot of dinosaurs is: big scaly bugger comes and eats other scaly bugger, then evolves. This may be *EastEnders* meets *The Taming of the Shrew* to your palaeontologist, but it won't sustain the rest of us.

My children grabbed at a peculiarly unprepossessing badger thing as their hero. It suckled its young and mated for life. (How do they know? They found fossils with wedding rings? Do the males have particularly bent ears and garden sheds?) The line between science and Disney is tricky, and they have settled on the side of worthy and educational. But there are universally acknowledged truisms about dinosaurs that are pure dinomorphism. Carnivorous ones are all cunning psychopaths, and herbivorous ones all passive and dull. Experience tells us that it's not necessarily so. Would you rather face a bull or a poodle?

Although *Walking with Dinosaurs* was long on death, it was peculiarly squeamish about birth. The badgers may have mated for life, but the big lizard didn't seem to mate at all. And how did a stegosaurus do it? How did a female brontosaurus put up with four excited tons on her back, getting down to the short strokes? Has anyone considered that dinosaurs might have become extinct because the female had the longest headache in prehistory?

I indulged in a spot of regression last week and had another look at *Blue Peter* (BBC1). Weird. It was like *The Twilight Zone*, or Miss Havisham's drawing room. Nothing's changed at all. It's exactly as I left it twenty years ago. They're still collecting bottle tops, and India ought to be knee deep in water with all the wells *Blue Peter* has dug over the years. Watching it reminded me of why it is so important that children see as much television as possible. When you grow up and the conversation flags, you can just say, 'Oh, remember John Noakes?' and everybody is suddenly talking at once. 'Remember Shep and the *Blue Peter* garden that got vandalised and the mug holder that broke?' You see, if you didn't have a television you're not part of it, you're out of the loop. Children's television is cultural bonding. We are all sticky-back-bonded by Peter Purves. The presenters have changed. Well, they would. Peter, John and Val were definitely uncles and aunts to the nation. This new lot are brothers and sisters, or boyfriend and girlfriend. The two perky lads were prime toy boy. I have no idea whether *Blue Peter* attracts the same audience it used to. Maybe it's just watched by grannies in old folks' homes and the unemployed reliving happier days. But it's very comforting to know that when a troupe of Moravian boy scout kazoo players comes to visit, there's somewhere for them to go.

Just William

I've got a little list. Like Ko-Ko in *The Mikado*, I've got a little list, and none of them would be missed. It's a bit more than a little list, actually, it's a blueprint for a cultural spring-cleaning. When I'm director-general I'm going to organise a surprise picnic for the most loathed and loathsome TV funsters. The charabanc will jaunt into the country. Brucie will organise the singalong, dozens of great communicators in horrible blazers will sway to 'Tie a Yellow Ribbon'. Gaggles of alternative comedians will keep everybody's ribs tickled until we reach the field. Out they'll scamper, gamboling and communicating happily.

From the edge of the wood, there will come the faint jingling of harnesses. From the shadows, a ragged line of light cavalry will appear. They'll start at the trot, the horses' breath pluming, the tips of the men's sabres catching the light. The ghastly fleshy denizens of the box will look up, startled, meat-paste sandwiches hanging from expensive dental work. The terrible truth will dawn. And as the cavalry breaks into a canter, they'll start running. Esther will be cut down under the steel-shod hoofs, Danny Baker will kneel and beg, Tony Slattery will pretend to be somebody else. But my orders are absolute, no mercy. There will be no survivors. The whole epic will be witnessed by families whom I force to stand and watch. These are the most appalling parents, the ones you meet at PTA meetings, the ones who leave dinner parties early, the ones who pay with book tokens in W. H. Smith. They're the parents who don't have a television for the sake of their children. After the massacre, their kiddies will be forcibly removed and sold into slavery as light-entertainment studio audiences.

Not having a television for the sake of your children is the ultimate brutal smug philistine snobbery. 'We think it's important they should read books.' 'We think it's important they use their own imaginations.' 'We think it's non-participatory and sedentary.' I think the argument for not allowing your children to join in the culture of their contemporaries ought to be grounds for fostering. The sort of parents who forbid their children to watch television are the type who insist on speaking French at table, offer carrots as treats and make boys play with tea sets. It is arrant elitism to suggest that books are better or more culturally important than television. Or that ten minutes being imaginative with a cardboard box, a felt-tip pen and a stick is of more use than Deputy Dawg. Ninety per cent of everything I ever learned that was of any interest or use I got from television. The children who spend their evenings reading might have vocabularies that impress aunts, but they can't speak the language of their friends.

Generally, I shy from reviewing children's TV because it wasn't made for me, and if I like it, almost by definition it has missed its mark. All those weekend pop and slapstick magazine shows leave me aching with boredom. But then they should. I don't want to read *Paddington Bear* for pleasure either, or eat fish fingers for dinner at 5.30 p.m. I can, though, still tell the dread hand of 'worthy children's television', just as I could when I was six. These are the programmes that grown-ups thought I ought to like, the ones that were improving. In my day, they were usually historical adaptations of Edwardian books or they involved kindly gentlemen on barges who knew about badgers. I think that pederasty and appalling acting have sunk most of them.

One hardy perennial of the we-think-this-is-good-for-you children's television re-emerged last week. William is back. As the last two Williams inflicted Dennis Waterman and Adrian Dannatt on us, you'd have thought they would have put a stake through the little scamp's blazer and buried him at a crossroads, but no. I watched in amazement as naughty ancient William went through the frogs, mud-on-the-carpet, vicars, toffs-in-toppers, stinky-girls and soppy-old-tongue-sarnies routine yet again. Who is *Just William* (BBC1) made for? Who is supposed to be watching? Real kids have just plugged into *The Bill* and MTV, so what are they supposed to make of pre-decimal pocket money? 'I've just bought a tub of Ecstasy for half a crown.' 'What's half a crown?' I imagine that a lot of people at the BBC are very pleased with William. It's quality television. Yet Richmal Crompton was a second-rate, patronising, humourless writer fifty years ago; all the television adaptations of her *oeuvre* have been well up to that standard.

The line between what is, and is not, children's television is far vaguer than it was when I settled in front of *Picture Book* and *Twizzle*. The most popular children's programme now is *Neighbours*; I would imagine that within twenty years there will be no children's television aimed specifically at kids between five and eleven. They will go straight from cartoons to soaps (and barely notice the difference). The big should-we-let-them-watch-it? programme at the moment is an American import called *Mighty Morphin Power Rangers* (Sky One; ITV). Flora Gill, aged three (well, very nearly four), adores it. I watched an episode last week. I'd love to be able to tell you what happened, but translating cuneiform would be easier. There were these kids who miraculously turned into superheroes, yet were also somehow dinosaurs and sometimes one large robot. They had powers that sometimes worked and there was a bit of a love story and some comedy and some singing. I know this sounds unlikely, but the villain was called Oyster Man. How do you make a villain out of an oyster? Well, you give him two large nipples that squirt plastic acid. And that's as much as I could glean. There obviously was a plot, but the programme is cut so fast and so much is assumed to be known that it was way over my head. I'm not being ingenuous. I really couldn't follow it. But it made perfect sense to Flora, so I asked her to do the review: 'It's really good because they fight the baddies who want to break the world and they always win.' Then she karate-chopped me. Well, as a parent, that's a comforting moral message. Far better than William, which is all about bribery, burglary and lying. Being able to karate-chop is quite an achievement at three, nearly four.

Costume Drama

Middlemarch

It is a well-known fact that a woman in possession of a good job is searching for classic romance once a week, and, if it's really good, she might like it repeated on Mondays. There's something about a man with a really stiff collar.

Middlemarch (BBC2) has really hit the prime-time G-spot of the middlebrow. They're just gagging for it. Hampstead living area/ dining rooms are all a-twitter with the sheer gorgeousness of it all. Ladies with professions toy with mixed-leaf salads as their bosoms flush and heave and they try to outdo each other in euphoric recall. The only argument now is whether or not it is just brilliant or simply superb. *Middlemarch*, to these professional women, is what the Chippendales are to their secretaries.

Dutifully I have been sitting and watching it and, dear reader, let me tell you I have never been so bored in my life. No, I tell a lie: I once spent a night in the cells at Earl's Court police station that was more boring, but only just. I watched and tried really hard to see what it was about costume drama on the BBC that, to use a phrase on everyone's lips, made the licence fee worth it. Why does the collective critical ability disappear when some girl in a crinoline sits down at a harpsichord and sings the nineteenth-century version of Chas and Dave? What is it about a shot of a National Trust house with a horse on the gravel that makes the whole semi-detached country reach for its Bafta?

I sat and tried to imagine if anyone would have spent all of Wales's licence fee contribution making this series if Tristram Major-Drama had come into the Television Centre production meeting and said: 'That George Eliot needs a little kick in the gusset. Why don't we make the whole story contemporary and set it in a Liverpool cul-de-sac and get rid of the horses and hats and have cars and shell suits instead? And then it will be relevant. It'll be about National Health Service hospitals and council housing. A sort of cross between *Brookside* and *Casualty*.'

The answer is, of course, they wouldn't dream of any such thing. What would costume drama be without costume? Just drama, just another story and a pretty thin story at that. No, Tristram would have been sent back to *EastEnders* before you could say Trollope. The fact is, dear reader, that's exactly what *Middlemarch* is: a cross between *Casualty* and *Brookside*, with production values. And it's played at half-speed. The whole thing crawls along in first. This is a prerequisite of costume drama. It's got to be very slow. The participants have to deliver arch, unbelievable bits of dialogue and then there has to be a long pause while we take in the wonder of it all, as if we were suddenly special-needs children who had to be given time to catch up. Most of us manage to follow *Noel's House Party*, which is four times as complicated and moves at tabloid speed, with one eye shut. But when the BBC makes costume drama they seem to forget that some of us have seen television before, and what's more, most of the ecstatic viewers gripped on the sofa have read the book so they know how it ends. Can you believe it, they actually know who gets the girl. Although, why anyone would want the sanctimonious old trout is beyond me.

And there's the clue to why costume classics are such a hit with the corduroy-and-hardback set. Nineteenth-century classics, particularly the ones written by women, are an adolescent illness. They afflict almost everyone who stays on at school after the age of sixteen. Very, very few of you ever pick up a Penguin Classic after the age of twenty-three. But while you're in the grip, they're completely debilitating.

Girls get classics badly. Serial classic reading happens when young things are particularly vulnerable. Jane Austen and the Brontës et al. invade the cerebral cortex at about the same time as loss of virginity, chronically painful crushes on English teachers, and membership of Greenpeace. This heady cocktail, combined with a first really disastrous haircut and getting sick for the first time on Bailey's Irish Cream, causes lasting romantic damage. Most people grow out of it, and bury Mr Rochester and the rest, deep in their subconsciousness, under mounds of Martin Amis, Graham Greene and unfinished Booker Prize-winners. On the face of it, they lead normal lives but, like malaria, the nineteenth-century novel lurks, a dormant bacillus. These poor creatures will always be prone to bouts of classics and the BBC knows it.

Costume drama reinfects grown-ups with adolescent classics. They relive the most emotionally taut decade of their lives. It's a sort of fever. The excitement, the heartbreak, the intensity. The BBC brings the costumes, the audience brings the drama, and all critical facility is lost. Just the sight of a Royal Shakespeare actor in pince-nez renders them pimply putty again.

Now, gentle reader, you may be wondering how it is that I and one or two others, like characters in *Invasion of the Body Snatchers*, managed to avoid being infected with classics (I should say here that the BBC classics start in 1740 and finish in 1914: Gilgamesh and Gawain don't have the same effect). Well, it was just good luck really. When we were at our most susceptible, our most prone to classic contagion, our hands dawdled over *Middlemarch* and we saw the portrait of George Eliot and thought: 'Don't fancy her much.' So we picked up George Orwell instead.

And George Orwell is a lifelong inoculation against all the romantic costume drama the BBC cares to throw up.

Set in a grim Nottinghamshire mining town, *Sons and Lovers* (ITV) is the story of a thwarted, battered Methodist wife and her stony-grim ambition for her sons. In great part it's D. H. Lawrence's auto-biography, a remorselessly unsentimental and disparaging view of a working community. In this production, though, they've done their best to brighten the loathing by adding a dollop of sentimentality and making it by far and away the cleanest, neatest, dearest little pit village you've ever seen. There's no soot, no grime and apparently they were too poor even to afford rubbish, though their china's very nice. Outside it's all rural bliss, just perfect for moping, fornicating and getting consumption in.

Georgians

Three hundred years after the sack of the Roman Empire, when Europe was well into its dark age, people who lived near Roman ruins imagined that they had been built by an extinct race of giants, superhumans. I know how they felt. I feel the same way about the Georgians. I mean, how did they make all that furniture, all those tables and chairs and sideboards and stuff? When they were bored with ordinary furniture, they made gear that had no known or conceivable use – davenports, pembrokes, break-fronted side cabinets, secretaires, folding commodes, reading stands with concealed card tables, and whatnots. 'What you making, Jude?' 'Dunno, it's just a sort of whatnot.' They ran out of names before they ran out of furniture.

Where the ancient Egyptians are remembered as being a civilisation obsessed with death – 60 per cent of the population were employed in sarcophagus- and pyramid-selling – the Georgians were a people with a furniture fetish. When they weren't turning out linen presses, they were dancing – stupid, insipid, childish hop, skip and jump dancing – or they sat on the chairs they'd just varnished, boring each other rigid. I know all this because I've seen it on television.

This is how the Georgians will be remembered: as tedious, skipping joiners, and Jane Austen's *Emma* (ITV) was the most trippingly tedious Georgian of the lot. Her *raison d'être* was social woodwork. She was a nuptial joiner, and I desperately – more desperately than I've ever felt anything for a long time – wanted to screw her into a mahogany coffin with scrolled finials, fluted pilasters, bas-relief acanthus and a fold-out bureau plas. And bury her. In all the fiery, clamorous, pounding, ferrous Industrial Revolution that finally drove a steel spike through the marquetry heart of the awful Georgians there is not a single engine powerful enough to dig a pit deep enough to bury bloody Emma in, for still she stalks the earth. She is horrible. The television film was utter purgatory, like watching a dramatisation of the *Antiques Roadshow* written by Hugh Scully. If you want to know what the Georgians were really like, just watch the furniture experts on the *Roadshow*, those spraunced and pinched plonkers with marbled hair and patinated jowls pulling ancient drawers off old widows' ball-and-claw feet and getting all arch about their lovely dovetails. That's the true voice of Georgiana.

Back to *Emma*. The production was as predictable as a church service: the Christmas-card carriages, the lingering establishing shots, the fifteen reaction cutaways for every one bit of twee declamatory reception-room wit, the reverential editing and more dolly track than Intercity for the obligatory walk in the gardens. Here were all the careful National Trust accoutrements and clutter. You could imagine the museum handlers waiting just out of shot to rush in and rescue hairbrushes and cake stands.

The story of Emma is, of course, vomitously dire, a moral husk of a tale larded with empty snobbery and vain civility. Emma is a role model for girls as Oliver Reed is for boys. The original It girl whose crass attempts at genetic engineering fall apart when everybody settles happily into their allotted social strata, a result that is pitifully obvious even before the opening credits have faded into a swoon of Barbara Cartland watery silk. I managed to stay through to the bitter saccharine end only by imagining complicated and explicit humiliations for each member of the cast.

All my life I thought it was a good thing that we won the Napoleonic Wars. Now, I have doubts. In fact, I'm beginning to wish that the Mongol hordes hadn't been stopped at the gates of Vienna and had rushed on across Europe to ravage and lay waste Bath, Cirencester and Swindon for five hundred years.

The main attraction of *Wives and Daughters* (BBC1) is some bint called Molly, whose ups and downs, ins and outs, we are supposed to follow with lachrymose rapt attention. Personally, I wanted to punch her lights out. She made Pollyanna look like Rosa Klebb. Is there no end to the low-fat little madam's goodness? I screamed. Molly trips hither and yon to comfort dying people, until just the sight of her on the threshold makes you think you've got an incurable illness.

Trollope

There used to be an annoying bit of coquetry that single girls would simper at prospective mates. 'I could never love anyone,' they'd sigh, 'who didn't love ...' There would then follow: Leonard Cohen; *Now, Voyager*; Gerard Manley Hopkins; the Grampians; or toasted marshmallows. I remember one miserable night sitting on the end of a rapidly cooling lustful bed, one sock on and one sock off, professing my undying admiration for Pooh, Piglet and all their work, like a star pupil in some Cambodian re-education camp. Generally, when girls started with the 'I could never love anyone who didn't ...' bit, you knew, 3–1, it was going to be Sylvia Plath. That bloody *Bell Jar* must have been responsible for more coitus neverstartus than every happy-clappy abstinence evangelist in the country. This is a completely female thing. No man would ever say: 'I couldn't love anyone who didn't love *Tintin, Bravo Two Zero, Grand Theft Auto*, Millwall, midweek lock-ins or lesbians.'

But I think, late in life, I've discovered that I've got one. It's negative, of course. I don't think I could love anyone who loved Anthony bleeding Trollope. Trollope is the best reason I can think of for remaining illiterate. It's not that he's a bad writer; there are dozens of bad writers. He's a properly appalling writer, a man who could write, but did awful things with words. He's a literary virus. Scan the first page of any tome of his clerical hokum and you can feel your mental files being shredded, your head turning to mush.

People who read Trollope don't read anything else. He and they share the defining characteristic of the true bore: a disdain for their audience. Trollopeans proselytise and congregate in covens, as if they are a wacky weird sect. Even by Trollope's standards, *He Knew He Was Right* (BBC1) is pretty lethally tedious, quite apart from having the worst title ever conceived. Nobody has actually finished it: it's 1,000 pages of tortuous, mimsy whingeing. Andrew Davies, the adapter and amanuensis to the Victorian dead, may well have pastiched the whole thing. Nobody would be any the wiser, except that it has the authentic cold hand of moralising cruelty and lascivious sentimentality that is Trollope's leitmotif.

The story is essentially a reworking of *Othello*, except without Iago or any credible motivation. This jealous husband is played as a whiny, wet, irrational nag, and his wife, who we're told is strong and independent, comes across as an equally irritating, boneheaded victim. Everyone else comes out of the BBC Dressing-Up and Colourful Characters box. Yards and yards of sub-Dickensian bonkers old ladies and bumptious, *Great Expectations*-style young men. Nobody in this production is remotely believable as the characters they are supposed to be playing, which, given that it's Trollope, may be a blessing. Still, the first episode has elicited the usual handful of brittle little articles in the arts pages telling us how Trollope is a great author for today, and how everyone should be made to read him before being allowed to vote, marry or open a bank account.

Last week's offering was *Sense and Sensibility* (BBC1), written by one of those shrew women who have heritage-trail gingerbread and chintz named after them. It's about – well, you know what it's about. It's what they're all always about: selling teenage virginity for cash and crenellations. The most astute deconstruction of every plot nuance and character trait in the Austen or Brontë novel can be found in Noel Edmonds's *Deal or No Deal?*.

In this case, a widowed mother and her three daughters find themselves in reduced circumstances and fret terribly about whose box to open and what on earth they're going to do with themselves. 'Get a f***ing job,' a million viewers shouted at the unheeding screen. You're strapping girls – go and do something productive and useful instead of spending the entire day sitting about like empire-line fungus, sighing and preening and self-obsessing and wondering if you can make your hymen stretch over 11,000 acres and 20 grand a year. Nobody with a surname in Austen country has ever had a job. Nobody does anything except not eat meals, leave cards, walk aimlessly, not read books in arbours and twist their limbs elegantly. They have the least possible fun at dances and, finally, marry a house with a view.

Why does anyone think watching this is an enjoyable way to waste an hour?

Victoria and Albert

Against all my better judgement and a lifetime's supine experience, despite years of bitter disappointment with costume drama and historical reconstruction, given my innate loathing of dressing-up-box telly, I was strangely elated by the idea of *Victoria and Albert* (BBC1). This, after all, was the big one, le grand fromage. For a generation, television has pussyfooted around the old lady with an antique bazaar of Victoriana, adapted novels and adventures, whiskers and sepoys. It's as if the old girl was just too big for the small screen.

But now the BBC have given it a go, and again, against my better judgement – which I'm well aware is what you pay me for – I rather enjoyed it. Well, half enjoyed it. Derived a sniggering pleasure. Needless to say, for reasons that had nothing to do with the ones the producers intended. To start with, you have to remember that *Victoria and Albert* wasn't made for you, and certainly not me. It may have been on our televisions, about our shared history, and acted by familiar friends from our glittering entertainment family, but it was actually made for foreigners. In a very Victorian sense, the BBC is turning out cheerful shoddy for its vast dominions, like Sheffield tin trays sent to Rangoon and Kampala, for an expanding empire over which the repeats never set. The BBC has seen that its future lies in the past, a past that must be accessible to fourteen-year-old Minnesotans, Karoo herdsmen, lascars from distant docks and snug families of leather-chewing eskimos.

So it was that Victoria and Albert presided over no recognisable country. They stalked the corridors of an endless Gormenghast: it could have been Ruritania or Utopia or, indeed, Minnesota, for all we knew. This was a love story set not in a time and a place but in the ethereal metaphysics of television. An elastic electric nation, where every Sunday is fancy dress and of which every human being can be a citizen or, in this case, a subject. Freed from the dull responsibility of historical accuracy, answerable only to frock and wig, Victoria was allowed to become a strange cross between a *Blue Peter* presenter and a cairn terrier. Not an altogether unbeguiling or unintriguing bit of genetic modification, and indeed, who's to say that the old bat wasn't actually like that? She may well have been half Vanessa Feltz, half walrus. As it was, her little polished button eyes constantly glinted with puckish hysteria, as if she'd just spied the last Bonio in Albert's pocket. Or she'd show us how to construct a Great Exhibition out of dispatch boxes and blotting paper.

Her husband was a somewhat less interesting combination of sideboard and Richard Chamberlain. He spent most of his time wandering from room to room, trying to find a home. 'Perhaps he'd go over there by the window ... no, I think I liked him better by the mantelpiece ... perhaps we could stand him in the corner and hang hats on him?' The very idea that a bloke whose idea of amusement was organising window-cleaners and filling coal scuttles could be a great romantic hero was rather touching. Here was a chap who gave the world Christmas and then was out-acted by the tree.

Lark Rise to Candleford (BBC1): the very title makes you want to run amok with a rifle. These are names from toffee tins, full of rural whimsy. Episode one was the story of whether a hamlet (Lark Rise) was more or less than eight miles from the nearest post office (Candleford), told exhaustively over an hour, as if it were the discovery of the double helix or preparations for D-Day, with a sub-Hardyesque, turgid bosky-ness, if you can imagine anything sub-Hardyesque. And if fretting about the distance between hamlets weren't enough, it also featured Dawn French being the vicar of Dibley as a drunken, feckless leech on her neighbours – well, just the vicar of Dibley, in fact. It was a piece of casting that stuck out of the amiably adequate troupe of doll's-house thespians like a short, fat, loud comedian doing a turn in the middle of a dull costume drama.

Russians

I've been away for a couple of weeks, and, not having seen any television, I feel out of the loop. It's odd how the whole deal of daily tuning-in is rather like sharing sheltered accommodation with a lot of dysfunctional monomaniacs who've forgotten to take their medication. So you get back and go: 'Anything new, anyone died, any of the more chronic cases been transferred to cable, did you miss me?' After Uzbek TV, I must say I reached for the remote with more than the usual excitement. 'After the entire speech by the minister for big holes in the ground, we'll bring you traditional nomad wrestling from a packed car park in Samarkand, where the winner gets a Japanese television and the losers get their yurts burned. After that, an hour's folk-wailing, accompanied by one-string violin plucking.' No, no, all things considered, I was greatly looking forward to the best telly in the world. Telling indigenous folk out there that back here I was a television critic elicited looks of utter incomprehension. 'You call that a job in the West?' Well, almost. 'How does it work? A producer doesn't fill his quota, so you kick his door in at 3 a.m., denounce him before a people's tribunal, then send him, his family and friends to mine uranium with a spoon?' Oh, how I wish. And what do I find on returning?

Bleeding *Anna Karenina* (C4).

Suddenly, thirteenth-century wrestling looks appealing. I suppose it was only a matter of time before the great horde of book pillagers moved on to the Russian novel, having left English literature a smoking, barren wasteland, with only the wailing of unmarried second daughters to tell that there was once a vital, vivid civilisation here. 'Onward, my children, to truncate and adapt to the end of the known world!' But finding out they're already at the gates of Moscow can only fill cultured folk with dread. The endless ranks of costumiers and prop fetishists and unloved casting agents have started to pillage imperial epaulettes, samovars and fake fur.

The difference between the classic English novel and its Russian counterpart is that over here everyone wants to leave the city to live in the country, and in Russia it's the other way around. In fact, it was an old tsarist law that all novels, instead of starting 'Once upon a time', had to begin: 'Father, when shall we go to Moscow?' And within the first hundred pages (barely a third of the introduction) a girl has to say: 'Will there be balls?' Balls, my little otchki-otchka, there'll be more balls than you can handle, you'll be tripping over balls, big balls, huge balls, nothing but balls.

This adaptation was full of them, with that unbelievable dancing that you just know some woman whose day job is running the Historical Terpsichorean Re-creation Society has spent a happy day teaching a lot of luvvies to do (and they think TV critic is a weird occupation). The thesps will all have agreed that really it's very sexy in a restrained sort of way and much more erotic than four hours of garage on E. Watching this stuff is hell. What English and Russian nineteenth-century novels have in common is that they're all about getting married. Of course, the English versions were written with a snide, monetary cynicism, whereas the Russian ones are inscribed with sighs and consumption (in English novels, the disease of choice is gout; with the Slavs it's TB), but all this plot stuff is secondary to the real nastiness of the tics and dramatic clichés that are still the soggy home ground of Lit Hist TV.

They're all present here. So, for instance, every character must eat as if they're going to sit a test on it, being marked for Artistic Chewing. They can't walk and talk at the same time, they stroll in meaningful, poignant silence, and when someone finally plucks up the courage to say, 'Well, did you get the tickets for Moscow?', they have to stop to discuss it before moving on in silence until the next line. Can you imagine actually doing that in the street? Then there was the Object: there's nothing an actor in a stiff collar likes better than getting his hands on some bit of period kit and fondling it. So nobody just wears spectacles, they conduct with spectacles. Canes, whips, parasols, handkerchiefs, pokers, swords, hats, pocket watches, bells, bottles, books and bodices all get pawed and twitched as if their owners were nervous first-time presenters on the *Antiques Roadshow*. Costumes are inhabited rather than worn – the women in particular seem to move about in them like estate agents showing you round a very small flat. Altogether, it's too horrible.

This particular production was especially grim because Russians are especially grim. The abiding colours were grey with added grey. The look, for all its period rightness, was of a performance in a church fête bric-à-brac tent; and some very dubious casting made the story a panto performed by the cast of *The Bill*. They kept sighing about how handsome and beautiful everyone was, and we kept searching the screen saying, no, they're jolly well not. If Anna and Vronsky aren't grade-A-beddable, crawl-over-broken-glass must-haves, then the whole gloomy charade means nothing. And they weren't; they wouldn't have turned heads on a tram in Gorky.

If you don't know the story, by the way, it ends badly. I trust that hasn't spoilt anyone's fun.

Bear with me while I tell you about a wedding reception I was at last week. I got rather a good draw for dinner. Usually I'm offered a distant aunt who's flown in from Cork without her hearing aid, and nanny. This time, on one side there was a posh-totty actress who specialises in costume drama of the dressing-for-dinner type, playing the sort of gel who looks splendid in camiknickers and pearls and says things like 'I have an awful feeling this will be the last summer of the old world, nothing will ever be the same again, Ralph. Let's get horribly horribly tipsy and dance, I want to dance and laugh and laugh and dance, ha, ha, ha, ha, ha.' Naturally, she was complaining about the slow, expensive and agonising death of period drama. 'You know it's just too, too beastly, will things ever be the same again.' Etc.

Nostalgia

You remember the bit in *Crocodile Dundee* when the great antipodean is transported to a hotel room in New York and his girlfriend points at the television and says: 'That's a television, magic box, conjures Dreamtime out of thin air. It's what we do instead of abusing wallabies'? And Croc says: 'Oh yes, I saw one once,' switches on and there's *I Love Lucy*. 'Yep, that was it.' Well, I've just had a Dundee moment. I turned on the set and there was *Brideshead Revisited* (C4). 'Yep, that was it.' Seeing *Brideshead* for the first time was one of those dead-Kennedy moments.

Cue colon-knotting music ...

I remember my first sight of Brideshead, glittering in the yellow evening sunlight, timeless and remote, yet somehow completely present and prescient. We none of us knew quite how important it would become, or with what nostalgia in the years to follow we would, each in our own ways, return to that honey-coloured memory, and think: did this really happen? Was I really here? For it was perhaps in that endless summer that I was perhaps first really happy and yet with the unknowing knowingness of youthful knowledge we rolled up the long drive, that insatiable, irresistible tune thumping in each of our breasts. The siren call of languor that was to mean so much to so many of us in our own private ways. Was I perhaps in some way aware of the shrill bat squeak of a kind of love? Probably. Was this then the enchanted sight of a kind of heaven, what we would perhaps in time call a golden age or simply perhaps gilded Thatcherism? Perhaps.

Brideshead is one of the twin totems of television drama, the binary shibboleths, if you will, or perhaps the iconic brace. The other pillar of excellence, the alternate jewel in the crown was, of course, *The Jewel in the Crown*. These were the Pelion and Ossa of hindsight television that are always being held up as examples of the sort of thing we have lost for ever, a honey-coloured Gale's golden age of drama that will never come again, now made impossible by Producer Choice or satellite or digital or just general all-purpose dumbing-down.

Well, they've both been reshown recently, and *Jewel* has grown in stature. Its largo pace and staggering performances, its expansive script and encompassing vision confirm it as a true masterpiece. But *Brideshead* ... I watched with growing disbelief. The series that sold a million teddy bears, that sent a thousand people to the property ads of *Country Life* looking for a rustic pile, that reduced a thousand thousand dinner-party hostesses to dementia searching for plovers' eggs. Oh my God, it's so awful, so utterly, risibly naff, so arch and mannered, so stuffed with appalling performances, with a script that needed an intravenous dose of syrup of figs or just a bullet.

The first thing that screamingly stuck its hand down the front of my Oxford bags was that it was so gay – howlingly, retentively, fumblingly, Dorothy-friendly homoerotic. I mean, we all knew it was a little fey, but I'd always imagined it was just a sensitive phase. This was as if someone had called a casting director and said, 'Look, we need a pair of irons.' 'Well, I can do you one – will you take an Anthony Andrews instead?' I just wanted to chuck a tapestry scatter cushion at the screen and bellow: 'For Christ's sake, snog him, and save us having to sit through another umpteen episodes!'

The acting is utter dross, with the towering exceptions of Nickolas Grace as Anthony Blanche and John Gielgud as Irons's father. In fairness, I can't really say that Irons himself acts badly, because he doesn't perceptibly act at all. He strolls and smiles, but I can say with even-handedness that he strolls badly and smiles horribly and that Marcel Marceau was his speech coach – his part could have been written on the back of a postcard in lemon juice. All the post-synch narration is so embarrassing, I nearly ate the sofa. Anthony Andrews, on the other hand, is just plain lost. He never shows the remotest sense that he's aware of what programme he's in, let alone which scene. His confused torment comes across as idiot stupidity. He's not struggling with demons, he's simply a struggling imbecile.

The straitening question is: Why on earth did we fall for this so heavily first time round? Well, the camerawork is solidly adequate, and there's that music, which is potent in a Noël Cowardish cheap way. But that's no excuse. I can only put it down to mass-hysterical avarice. *Brideshead* wasn't redolent of the 1920s, it was the Zeitgeist of the 1980s. We were all going for the burn, feeling the pain, filling our Filofaxes, passing on Wimpy lunch so that eventually we could aspire to this ghastly, snobbish, cultureless, tipsy, ivy-clad repressed nirvana without a working class, all claret and cufflinks and cardies and a nanny in every attic.

But we're over all that now, thank God. Every generation has to see things through the veil of its own time, and today *Brideshead* looks disturbingly like syrup-coloured perspiring dreams.

I've just been to see *Gladiator*. I know the jumbo screens aren't really my province, but a little cultural cross-pollination isn't a bad thing. *Gladiator* is relevant here because it was part of my obsessional quest to discover why I hate television costume drama so much. You see, I really rather liked *Gladiator*, and I can't see why I should so take agin one and not the other. Except, of course, for the perfectly obvious reason that Jane Austen has precious few pitched battles involving trebuchets and heads on sticks. And the Brontës are unforgivably remiss in the one-on-one mortal combat dept. In most literary adaptations, it's fair to say, there isn't enough blood inside or outside the participants.

But I think there must be a historical cut-off. Maybe I just don't like anything after the Hanoverian succession? No, I couldn't stand *Children of the New Forest*. Perhaps it's the Stuarts? ... Okay, anything pre-Plantagenet is fine. What surprised me, and I think most of the audience, about *Gladiator* was that if a chap's dressed in a beach towel and has a tin can on his head, we'll happily listen to any amount of truly dire dialogue. One of the nice things about the film was that although the special effects for swords-and-sandals have grown more lustrous over the years, the scripts remain as chronic as ever. I was particularly struck by the fact that it seems to be understood that all pre-1066 people spoke exclusively in rhetorical questions. Every sentence comes with both exclamation and question mark: 'Is this what Rome has come to!?' 'Have we not drunk our fill of blood tonight!?' 'Is this the dish I ordered!?' It must be quite difficult to write a whole film entirely in the declamatory inquiry mode. The only present-day people who still talk like this are schoolteachers: 'Is that the way we dress in school?!' And 'What do we do to boys who run in the corridor?!'

Thomas Hardy

Hardy makes you want to eat your own extremities. Whenever I pass through Hardy country, I pray for urban sprawl. The first thing you notice about this reworking of *Far from the Madding Crowd* (ITV), his most vacuously stupid book, is that he wrote bloody awful occasional music. The programme opened with the smelly root vegetable Oak seeing Bathsheba beside what looked remarkably like a South African rondavel, in a landscape that could have been the Natal midlands on a grey day. For one joyous moment I thought maybe, maybe someone has had a spark of imagination with a classic series and not just gone to the V&A costume museum and the National Trust. Have they, perhaps, please, crossed it with *Zulu*?

Imagine how glorious that would be. The stomping ululating Impi falling on Casterbridge market, disembowelling all those Gummidges in smocks ineffectually waving their crooks and stick-on beards; Bathsheba's farm, standing in as Rorke's Drift; Troy shouting: 'Front rank, fire!'; Colour Sergeant Squire thingy whispering, 'Do your tunic up, lad, now back to your mates.' It would be brilliant. In fact, we could have all of Hardy's beastly characters in there getting assegaied, and Tess finding out she's really M'D'Urberville and distantly related to Cetewayo.

Ah, but like most things in Hardy, it was not to be. It was more of what we've come to expect, morbidly slow, heavy on smouldering atmosphere, yards and yards of establishing shots and people walking over hills like itinerant surveyors to no purpose except to show off hills. And, true to form, it began with a carriage. The rule for costume drama, as I keep saying, is: If you take away the costumes, do you still have a drama? I'm sorry, but a plot based around a misdirected Valentine card would only just make a weak aside on *Emmerdale*.

When the Zulu option was cruelly discarded, I spent the weary hour trying to imagine a situation comedy where these three men shared a bachelor flat and all fancied that Bathsheba upstairs – *Men Behaving Slowly* or *The Middle-Aged Ones*. Troy and the Squire would be on the sofa arguing about whether to watch *Trooping the Colour* or *One Man and His Dog*, and then the disgusting Gabriel would come in and say: 'Sorry, mates, I dropped the lamb in the sink.' This is what I'm reduced to by costume drama – making up my own television programmes. Whoever said the box would be the death of imagination? If this is the sort of thing you like, then I'm afraid nothing I can say will stop you. More distressingly, it won't stop any of you making it either. Oh, and by the way, I think Brian Blessed played a haystack. It went up in flames with a characteristically over-the-top performance. Nice one, Brian.

I don't know what *The Chit Behind King Billy* means or refers to. It was the title of the first episode of *Lilies* (BBC1), a drama series set in Liverpool after the First World War. More than that, I couldn't say. I watched it intently, in the way a terrier watches a hole in the ground. Some of it I watched over and over, but it remains a Stygian hole. Nothing popped up. What, why and who they all were, and it all was, I haven't the faintest. I imagine it was some sort of Catherine Cookson, heart-warming, clogs-on-the-cobbles, abortions-in-a-bucket thing. But it didn't make a shred of sense. I understood only one word in three, and that might have been by Seamus Heaney in his books. There was this lad who, for reasons best known to himself, the writer and possibly one or two of the cast, tried to gas himself. But they managed to get him out of the oven just in time. He came round looking sick and confused and not altogether happy at having been forced back into the second half.

I strongly identified with him.

Rhodes

'And a cast of thousands!' the extravagant glossy press brochure promised at the end of a breathless list of production boasts. Ten million pounds! A decade in the making! Scope! Panache! Vision! Derring-do! Oh, come off it. Really, a cast of thousands? Who do they think they are? Cecil BBC DeMille? Nothing irritates like a Tristram trying on Hollywood's hyperbole.

Rhodes (BBC1), the epic story, started with everything against it and then they made it all worse. *Rhodes* – contentious history! *Rhodes* – a drama about imperialism and racism! *Rhodes* – we spent more of your money on this than anything, ever! *Rhodes* – played by the short, dark bloke from *The Professionals*, the English Starsky, or perhaps it was Hutch! Rhodes – the vision, the dream, the great big hole in the ground! One concentrated volley from the critical irregulars should have seen this off. *Rhodes* – a target so big you can't miss!

Actually, funnily, against all the odds, it was not that bad. Of course, it very much depended on what you thought you were watching. Personally, I don't care if it is good history or not. Television drama is not a primary source of historical research. If they want to make a chap a three-foot mulatto transvestite with a lisp, I don't care as long as it's entertaining. Never let a few facts stand in the way of a good story. But an epic? Television is not an epic medium. Huge amounts of money and production values tend to clutter the screen and divert from the intimate them-and-us's of a drama. Tristrams always want you to see every inflated pound, so there are a lot of extravagant panning shots with authentically costumed extras wandering pointlessly in the middle distance, slowing up the narrative.

For some opaque reason, the producers decided the story should be told in flashback, with old Cecil being reminded of his past by a thoroughly bogus and absurd femme fatale. Here we were comfortably back in risible television costume history. All the hoary old tricks of costume scene-setting were embarrassingly trotted out in a way that bore no relation to any known, or likely, human conversation. 'So, Rhodes,' the fatale said, in an accent that sounded as if she had had Russ Abbot as a voice coach, 'you had a great dream of building a railroad from the Cape to Cairo,' (points to map). 'This is Africa, I believe, a continent just south of Europe, and then you found diamonds and gold.' (Points to ring.) 'And black people. Ah, I see a picture of a black person, so that the viewers at home know what we are talking about.' It was simply dreadful. She did all that am-dram costume-walking. Walk, walk, walk, stop. Hand up on door jamb, turn head, open mouth. 'You see, I know all about you, Mr Rhodes. Ha, ha, ha, ha. I've read the script. But, still, you are an engima. Please explain yourself from the beginning. Hee, hee, hee, hee. So that we can get out of this scene with a flashback. I don't think I can laugh at nothing again.'

Historical-epic laughter is one of the most chilling sounds on television. The fatale did a lot of it, hysterically waiting for the director to shout 'Cut'.

Ruddy Tiny Tim, ghastly little toad, complete waste of a perfectly good crutch.

Poliakoff

Some years ago, André Previn made a small and forgettable programme that asked a memorable question: what happens to an orchestra if the conductor leaves halfway through? Previn said what he thought his purpose was, and the first oboeist said what he thought his point was, and they all got going on something big and Mahlerish. After ten minutes, André walked, taking his point with him, and what happened? Nothing – well, nothing discernible. The orchestra continued until it got to the end, then it stopped, all pretty much at the same time as Mahler. What was interesting was that within the format was the seed of reality TV.

Reality shows are always about getting people to do things: shepherds to be hairdressers, rugby players to wear bikinis, chairmen to be receptionists. Actually, what I want to know is, what happens if people stop doing things? What, for instance, would happen if the referee walked off the pitch during the Cup Final? If the Chancellor of the Exchequer went into hiding the day before the Budget? If a writer left in the middle of a drama? Well, I think we got a hint of the last one in *The Lost Prince* (BBC1).

I really didn't know what to make of this until I thought of it as a dozen characters in search of a plot, and then it became an elaborate game. I imagine everyone was sent three lines of character outline and a huge dressing-up box, then introduced to a lot of other actors, and everyone had to find out who everyone else was and whether or not they were related, without ever asking a direct question. If, inadvertently, someone said, 'I'm the Crown Prince of Schleswig-Holstein,' you were out and got assassinated by Serbian anarcho-syndicalists. Perhaps the concept of *The Lost Prince* wasn't a Peter Brook workshop, but if it wasn't, what on earth was it? Well, it was long, but not quite as long as the teaser preview ads that have been promising its arrival for weeks. And it was gaudy. I'm sure the publicist said 'Lavish' or 'Splendid' or 'Replete with the grandeur of a bygone age'. What it looked like was *Changing Rooms* does David Lean.

The story, which I only guessed at, thanks to the previews, was of this little-known prince, born to George the Something and Queen Whatsit, who was epileptic and died young. It was the brainchild with learning difficulties of Stephen Poliakoff, who is trumpeted by the BBC as one of the very, very few above-the-title authors. I go on all the time about the lack of class writers on the small screen, about how they are marginalised, under-funded, rushed and squashed into crass formats, so I should welcome the breadth of largesse and liberty that Poliakoff is given. But, you know, I've always had my doubts about him. It's not that he's a bad writer, he just doesn't write for television. What he does is deconstruct semi-resolved novels into semi-resolved scripts. His scenarios have an Escher-like complexity, his characters are forced to exist in endlessly convoluted situations, like the ridiculous *The Tribe*, or the credibility-defying picture library thing, *Shooting the Past*. If they or the viewer stops for a minute to question any of the givens, then the thing collapses into a migraine of plot props.

In *The Lost Prince*, Poliakoff took a historical moment and built it into something disjointed, scaffolded, cold and unbelievable. I didn't for a moment think that this was remotely what pre-war court life was like, and a fine cast was set adrift on sets that dwarfed or obscured them, searching desperately to glean some thread of character from their random utterances. Miranda Richardson reverted to being *Blackadder*'s Queenie. Michael Gambon just looked as if he couldn't wait for someone to shout 'That's a wrap', and Tom Hollander did Mr Angry, presumably because his beard glue itched. It's difficult to criticise child actors, but the whole production rested on the shoulders of Prince John, who never seemed to know what he was doing or saying, or why, and was directed with all the sensitivity of a Prussian brass band, so that, terminally, you didn't sympathise or even particularly like him. Ultimately, this huge, wasteful, shuffling, clumsy, unfocused programme wasn't so much the emperor's new clothes as the emperor wearing all his clothes, and the closet, at once.

Soap

Soap Opera

I don't have a lot of time for soap operas, and it gets me into trouble. A tabloid television critic has accused me of intellectual snobbery and dereliction of duty because I don't review them on a regular basis. I must say I have a sneaking admiration for colleagues who manage to write about these incontinent sagas as if they were actually news stories, and I do see that being a TV critic and not liking soaps is a failing, like being a football fan but not supporting a team. But just the thought of having to start from scratch is so exhaustingly daunting. Those grim pubs and those rude-faced professors from the University of Life, and their chubby little scrubbers, just biding their time and exercising their shriekingly thin National Youth Theatre talents till they can be mercifully run over, shot, bludgeoned or consumed in flames, to rise phoenix-like again in Lurex Versace on *Top of the Pops*, miming an old 1970s hit with a techno beat.

It's the demands that soap operas make on their audience that repel me. All drama asks for something, some involvement, some cerebral graft, but only soap operas insist you hock such a huge amount of your life. I have a horror of lying on my deathbed with the fading light, tossing up the profit and loss of a fleetingly short existence: I saw Venice and Paris and Cardiff, I ate foie gras and cornflakes, I heard the Troggs play live, I read *Moby Dick*, I loved four women who loved me back and ninety-seven who didn't, and I spent five years watching soap operas, which included sixty-four marriages, eighty-four unnatural deaths, sixteen births, five hundred infidelities, a billion gallons of unfinished beer and an infinite number of people saying: 'I hate you, Trevor.'

Seen as a lifetime commitment, soap operas are frankly untenable, a pretty good earthly imitation of hell, where ugly, talentless, sad people repeat the same mistakes over and over; where the clichés and climaxes come on with all the diminishing surprise of a man running into your living room and shouting 'Fire!' at precisely 7.30 p.m. three nights a week and once on Sundays. No, I can't face it, not even ironically. Especially not ironically. That faux cultural slumming of seeing Corrie as some sort of elaborate camp drag act, or the transparent people-pleasing of Roy Hattersley (briefly the *Telegraph*'s TV critic), who would write about nothing else – a piece of cynical sycophancy and intellectual relativism. This from a man who to his eternal shame suggested that Salman Rushdie's *Satanic Verses* should not be published in paperback. The sad thing is that it's not the format of soaps that is intrinsically duff, it's the fabulously low aspirations of their practitioners. Like First World War generals, they're only interested in the attrition of an audience body count. The actual concept of a rolling drama written as it runs is something only radio and television can do. Such a missed opportunity. As operas, soaps are all gratuitous Gilbert and Sullivan meets Wagner, and not anything like enough Mozart shacked up with Benjamin Britten. I'd stay in to watch *Don Giovanni Turns the Screw*.

I did, for strictly professional reasons, watch *EastEnders* (BBC1) last week, an episode that had been trailed in the press as a particularly Wagnerian denouement to some fetid plot. A pair of Polytechnic of Life graduates played out a melodramatic sub-Peter Shaffer drama of threats and bluff, in a story that was put together with rivets. What it violently reminded me of was the old *Thirty-Minute Theatre*, often mythologised as being a cornerstone of the golden age of TV; actually, most of it was pretty clunky and heavy-handed, depending on some inelegant twist at the end, as did *EastEnders*. It was a salutary reminder of how far drama in general has moved and improved since the 1960s, and how fundamentally soap operas haven't. There is one thing soaps do well: they produce real proper baddies, proper Victorian moustache-twirling villains. 'I've come for the rent and you've got two options, my dear.' Television has become so remorselessly nice, everyone on it wants to be homey and helpful and loved. Of course, we still hate them because of their fawning sycophancy, and contrarily we adore a proper bastard, but only the most confident, or desperate, actor will play them. Everybody wants to be the nice guy. Television at the moment has a real dearth of figures you love to hate.

There is one, though, a perfect example of the genre, a JR for today, an alpha male prat: Dr Anton Meyer from *Holby City* (BBC1). The rest of *Holby* is pretty much placebo bilge, a Petri dish of benign homosexuals (there are, even by television standards, a disproportionate number of gays in this hospital), all of a flaccid ilk that should thoroughly put off a generation of schoolchildren from same-sex experimentation. But like a colossus, Meyer strides among them, a simply fabulous sex sod, above emotion, above intimate relations, the man whom God calls for a second opinion. He is the National Health Service's version of Mr Spock, the man in the surgical irony mask. The great joy of Meyer is that they've made him remorselessly horrid, but also remorselessly right. A man whose self-regard is only eclipsed by the bona fide reasons for self-regard. Generally, baddies are weak and wrong; Anton Meyer is annoyingly perfect. May he go on for ever, the Mephisto of the deadpan bedpan.

Bad Girls (ITV) wins the award for scrupulous honesty in the titling department. They weren't just bad, they were bad. I mean truly, truly BAD. Advetised as *Cell Block H* meets *The Governess*, it was more *Grange Hill* meets *Home and Away*. No, what it was really like was Eldorado without the sun. Prison dramas have an enduring allure for television and you can see why – plenty of scope, the high jinks, bundles of character, no outside filming. They have all the soap values magnified, and a captive cast equals captive audience. But not this lot, hopeless recidivists to a woman. 'Hasn't your character been in every dreadful lazy drama for the past ten years?' 'Yes, guv, but society was to blame.' The governess herself suffered terribly from La Planteism, a condition that sadly now affects all women with straight hair cast in improbable positions of power over men. The girls may be banged up for a whole series, but I expect the audience went over the wall before the first ad break. Oh, for that little tent of blue that prisoners call the sky. Which, incidentally, was where *Bad Girls* belonged.

Coronation Street

So, forty years of *Coronation Street*, then. Only forty? My, it seems longer than that. Didn't *Coronation Street* take over where *The Odyssey* left off?

Coronation Street has had approximately sixty weddings, and Lord knows how many deaths by every conceivable illness, accident and act of God. Everyone who could be unfaithful has been, and still there's no denouement. Or, as the Americans put it, closure. Soap operas are like endless foreplay: you begin by being titillated and excited, then too late you realise they've no intention of going the whole way. Soap operas are far and away the most successful invention of the small screen – perhaps its defining invention. All over the world they draw the biggest audiences. In Brazil they change governments. In America they prevent them changing their government. And it's a given that all our politicians must proclaim an undying adoration for The Street: all prime ministers have to be photographed with a pint in the Rovers Return. The clip of Margaret Thatcher walking through the door like a triumphant bailiff was particularly surreal.

Despite what all the clever Tristrams come up with, however sophisticated and expensive television has become, and however many breasts it shows, *Coronation Street* is still invariably top of the ratings. And that's a remarkable achievement, though not necessarily one the audience should be very proud of. *Forty Years on Coronation Street* (ITV), the compilation birthday programme with added eulogies, was instructive, if rather puzzling. It crooned to the converted, it assumed we all knew who everyone was: like supermodels, the characters are only referred to by their first names. Their fictional lives are recounted like family histories.

There are three accepted facts that have attached themselves to The Street. One, that it is comedy; two, it's the home of the finest acting on television; and three, it's the Ark of the Covenant for the secular religion of working-class goodness. Well, as an outsider and non-believer, let me tell you unequivocally: it ain't a comedy. I know this because I've noticed it isn't funny. Not just not a little funny or occasionally smirksome – it isn't amusing at all. They showed funny bits, and they weren't. As for being the RADA of the small screen, it's not that, either. The characters are as wooden and phoney as the set; it is home to some of the longest-running, most hopelessly misguided thespians outside of church halls.

As for the working-classness, I've said before that the class struggle now exists only in TV fiction. Out here on the other side of the screen, it evaporated into fitted kitchens and holidays in Florida years ago. What we have in its place is race relations, which is why newsreaders come in all of God's limited palette and their accents are all regional but panglottally, politely middle class. In case you've got any doubts, that's a good thing. The abolition of the working class, all class, is what Karl Marx and Clem Attlee devoted their lives to.

Which brings us to Frank Skinner, who was one of the breathless sycophants of Corrie. Now, precisely how sick are you of Frank Skinner showing off his working-class credentials like a drunk at the bar flashing his tattoos? It's pathetic. Apply the elephant test. If it looks like an elephant, sounds like an elephant and there's half a cwt of steaming manure on the floor, it's probably an elephant. If you are a celebrity stand-up, chat-show host, whatever, earning a mobile-phone number, chances are you're as middle-class and aspirational as the rest of us. Your great-great-grandfather may have been Keir Hardie's mate and a Victorian son of toil, but by no stretch of the imagination does that make you a Victorian.

It's perfectly clear that working-classness has always been defined by economic status, education and health – it's a lifestyle thing. Skinner's lifestyle is about as working-class as a Surrey gymkhana. Now he wants to claim spiritual kinship with the Rovers Return, presumably because it gives him a licence to be a bit of an imp, an iconoclast, to puckishly stand apart and mock, without being compromised by success and moral relativism. And that, frankly, is the steaming pile of elephant's doo-doo. It patronises the audience.

Which is ultimately what I think of *Coronation Street*. It portrays a type of life that doesn't exist now and probably never existed. Its small devoted gay audience sees it as camp irony, but the true irony is that it does chime very nicely with an Establishment view of fantasy England. It's just the other side of the Pennines from John Major's warm beer and church bells and the Prince of Wales's bucolic village. They all come from the same Edwardian children's book.

That's not to say that there isn't a bottom of the pile: there's always a bottom of the pile. But that's not the old working class. That's the miserable, angry underclass who have failed their middle-class eleven-plus and who don't have any of the cohesion, confidence or self-reliance that the Lancashire workers in Corrie imply is their birthright. That's not just patronising, it's a three-times-weekly mean trick. *Coronation Street* illuminates fewer home truths than *Star Trek*.

Crossroads

You've got to admit there's something heroic about *Crossroads* (ITV), something that raises it above the sum of its parts. While most artistic enterprises strain for excellence, its ambitions have never glanced beyond surviving into next week. It's a broadcast version of an underpass busker, a collective televisual Norman Wisdom: it's not clever or funny or dramatic or pretty or anything much except an unimaginative way of spending half an hour. It's unfair to compare it with other programmes. It's more comparable with, say, having a colonoscopy in front of a class of first-year medical students or being told mid-Atlantic that there's absolutely nothing to worry about but you're going to make an unscheduled landing on Tristan da Cunha. Those are experiences beside which *Crossroads* seems positively benign and almost enjoyable. When it was put out of its low-grade depression and cancelled some years back, I think I can speak for all of us when I say there was a palpable sense of loss – something dear and dysfunctional had been ripped from our lives – because, while we're a sophisticated nation that can produce great art and culture that can furnish the world's galleries, theatres, couture salons and pop charts with cool Britannic excellence, we can also still make and endure *Crossroads*, proving perhaps that indeed we are a liberal, pluralistic society prepared to offer a home and acceptance to the culturally bereft and aesthetically crippled. Surely this is the measure of a great civilisation.

Like a gimpy Lazarus, *Crossroads* returned, only to be put straight back into the hospice for terminal plots. But now, once again, the old motel has been resuscitated, patched up and sent out into the cold with new implants. I can't tell you what a joy the new place is. I can't tell you because it's immune to criticism. It's also impervious to acting, drama, taste or any of the more rudimentary rules of narrative. The daytime Tristrams promise that this is going to be *Dallas* with room service, which frankly traduces even the last series of *Dallas*. What they've done is give it yet another new set, which I'll get to in a minute. They've also added Jane Asher. Now, adding Jane Asher adds a touch of class, doesn't it? Jane oozes class. In fact, you could probably bottle her ooze and sell it as eau de cologne. You can tell she's got breeding just by looking at her teeth and the arrogant porcelain arch of her demeanour.

We meet her first being added to water, lying in enough bubbles to remove even the most stubborn stain. She's drinking champagne and admiring her leg – like women do on telly in telly baths. Always admire one leg. When was the last time you examined a singular leg in a meditative, vain sort of way? When she gets out of the bath using both legs, she discovers a burglar in her jewel box. 'I'll have that towel,' he says. Oh, be still my beating loins. Jane drops the towel, and we can see, we can see, we can clearly see she's wearing a G-string and that's how much class our Jane has: knickers on in the bath. It's all right, though, because the burglar turns out to be her husband, who's only come to rifle her drawers.

Not bursting into peals of helpless laughter during this and every other scene demands the highest professional qualities from the cast. Either that or they've been given industrial quantities of Botox. All other professional thespian talents are utterly unnecessary, because even Stanislavsky leading a battalion of Oscar-winners would blunt their Method on this script.

The point of the new *Crossroads* is really the mise-en-scène. It's not so much a set, more Laurence Llewelyn-Bowen with malaria. It's way beyond taste, style or even irony, it's soft-furnishing porn. To get the full benefit of *Crossroads*, you have to see it as coursework towards a doctorate in camp. In fact, I wouldn't be at all surprised if it hasn't been made solely to give Graham Norton an endless deep pile of material.

Middle-Class Soap

Castles (BBC1) is a new umpteen-part drama that they're threatening to make into a soap opera. It's being sold as the first-ever middle-class serial. Now, it's written somewhere in the small print of the BBC's charter that soaps are not allowed to show a family gathering that doesn't end in tears, and I think there's a clause that says at least one person must be having an affair. Sure enough, after forty years of marriage, Grandpa was getting a little illicit legover. Thirty seconds of listening to Grandma and a million viewers were shouting the big question: 'What on earth took the old geezer so long?' Only illegal drugs and hard spirits supped from the bottle can have prevented him from planting her in bits in the garden immediately after the honeymoon.

The characters – and I use the term in the most loving Christian sense – behave as if they've never met each other before, particularly the ones who are living together. Grandma and Grandpa grew up during the war. He during the Korean, she the Crimean. All the couples are spectacularly mismatched, giving plenty of scope for fracture later on. But the one invaluable ingredient that *Castles* has got absolutely spot on, the one thing all successful soaps must have, is a writer who has mastered the complex Venusian language of non sequitur. People who wish to live for any length of time in the thin atmosphere of weekly drama have to learn to speak it fluently. So a typical exchange goes like this: 'Don't put the cake there.' 'You've got a new car.' 'On the sideboard.' 'What's the matter with

Mum?' 'Drink, anybody?' 'For God's sake, think of somebody else for a change.' 'Isn't this nice?' 'Oh, what a lovely cake.' 'Yes, it's a Mercedes. And it's having an affair with the sideboard.'

If you missed the first episode of *Castles* and don't want to be left behind, here's the entire, unexpurgated, hour-long plot. Grandma: 'You're having an affair.' Grandpa: 'No I'm not.' 'Yes you are.' 'No I am not.' 'Oh yes you are.' 'Oh no I'm not.' Daughter: 'Grandpa's having an affair.' Son: 'He's not.' 'He is.' 'He's not.' 'He is.' 'He's not.' Grandma: 'You are having an affair.' Grandpa: 'No I'm not. But I'll tell you something, I am having an affair.'

Roll credits.

And do you know what the plot's going to be in episode twenty? Of course you do.

In a business replete with ridiculous chippy twerps, Phil Redmond, the creator of *Brookside*, is twerp's twerp. He talks about soap operas, a genre that is to drama what ice-carving is to sculpture, as if it were epic verse and as if *Brookside* were Liverpool's *Iliad*. Is there anyone in the world more laughably embarrassing than an autodidact Scouser trying to sell you the Northwestern cultural canon like a bitter Mormon? *Brookside* was always the worst of the regular soaps because it was essentially fraudulent. It was Stalinist public service broadcasting dressed up as real life. It was cod-liver oil for the masses, one of those role-playing drama classes that are supposed to teach slow kids about racism and child abuse.

Monarch of the Glen

I can't imagine that more than a handful of people under seventy have read Compton Mackenzie. He's a cautionary tale of how the fashion and politics of literature can utterly obliterate a writer's reputation. Mackenzie was one of the most popular and highly regarded authors of his time. Today, he's barely readable. He is the Stephen King of whimsy. Mackenzie's particularly soggy furrow was soft, safe, easy listening with big, sloppy, feel-good endings. A bit like skinny-dipping with Susan Hampshire in lukewarm porridge. It's tartan Herriot with that particular brand of humour that has all but the merest smile effortlessly taken out. Needless to say, I adore him.

Monarch of the Glen (BBC1) is one of his best, but it has as much substance as a Seaforth Highlander's underpants. The story is ersatz Wodehouse transported to Brigadoon: old laird is deep in debt, ancestral pile and quaint nirvana estate are on the brink of being sold to (horror!) self-made men in trade who can't even shoot straight and who speak with disgusting industrial accents. Estranged son and heir reluctantly returns home from love and life in the real world to sort out the mess. Add the inevitable beautiful local schoolteacher – a cashmere ecowarrior and folksy radical activist. Naturally, she's feisty. In fact, she's probably called Kirsty McFeisty and she will, in episodes as yet hidden in the mist, have her feistiness channelled from the inappropriately sociopolitical into the more comely, making a nice home, and an energetic sex doll for the young laird. Which, in the wet and misty land of Mackenzie, is just how it should be. Chuck in a handful of local characters, all of whom are eccentrically two spoonfuls of mixed offal short of a haggis and would be led off with their sleeves tied behind their backs in any other location but this accordion arcadia, and you have a happy evening in that ends with a fly half's dive for the channel changer.

On every level, *Monarch of the Glen* is pretty horrifying. The teeth-aching whimsy has been enhanced by bringing the story up to date. The young heir is a trendy restaurateur, and there are wetbikes on the loch. But all the rest is still 1940s Powell and Pressburger, which makes the overall effect weirdly like an early episode of *Star Trek*. I haven't seen the final episode, but I will bet you all the oatcakes you possess that, in the end, the young man and the schoolteacher will turn the old castle (there have been McMogadons here for four hundred years – no, there haven't, it was built in about 1890) into a country hotel. Which wouldn't take much work, because that's what it already looks like. And everyone will be happy, there will be jobs for all, wearing tartan bow ties and pouring whisky macs down a thousand American tourists.

On television, Scotland is either shown as a Trainspottery tenement or this peaty hobgoblin simpleton's McTrumpton. Just by chance, the whole land-ownership and -use business is a serious and boiling concern north of the border. This gaelo-Surrey romance drives real Scots (as opposed to reel Scots) to the point of distraction. I wouldn't be a Tristram in Tobermory this weekend.

The Waltons

It's odd that, of all things, emotions are subject to fashion. They should be, after all, innate, untutored, spiritual. But it seems that the emotional responses valued by one generation can be forgotten or subjugated as inappropriate and embarrassing by the next. Take phlegm, highly prized by the early Georgians. Parky doesn't glance at his clipboard and say: 'My next guest has buckets of phlegm.' And whatever happened to sang-froid or swooning (which isn't the same as fainting)? All mothballed. We seem to be living in an ice age of emotional minimalism; the pandemic response of cool and its ugly sister, irony. Life's chicanes can be met with an all-purpose, imbecilic nonchalance, or an ersatz hysteria that comes with semaphored inverted commas.

I notice it on television. The emotional language available to dramas and audiences has fewer and fewer shades of nuance. If you look at American comedies now, they're almost entirely tennis-rally exchanges between brittle whimsy and mock fury. For a culture that spends such a lot of time talking about feelings and nurturing sensitivity, this limiting of appropriate reactions seems self-defeating.

If you saw the final ghastly death throes of *Big Brother*, you'd have noticed that most of these sad zoo creatures' angst comes from simply not being able to compose an appropriate emotional response to their phoney situation, or each other. They endlessly talk about honesty and accuse one another of being two-faced. Two-faced would be a monumental, Mount Rushmore improvement. I watched Davina McCall debrief one of the chaps who had been released back into the wild. She said: 'But it's just a bit of fun, isn't it?' Well, is it? I defy anyone to come to this programme cold, watch an hour and glean that it's even the slimmest sliver of a bit of fun.

I have a personal stock of old emotions that I keep as a solitary perversion for my own use. I wouldn't let them out in public. I'd be laughed at in an ironic, cool way. But I like to draw the curtains and indulge in pity. Pity is now so politically incorrect, you can probably be arrested for it. My all-time favourite emotion, however, is sentimentality. In a century, sentimentality has done a 360-degree volte-face, from being the finest human response to becoming an insult. If a critic wants to damn any cultural daub to oblivion, he just has to deem it sentimental. Sentimentality is a fugitive and Epicurean emotion. It lives solely in the civilised arts. To paddle or, indeed, wallow in sentimentality is one of the greatest cultural pleasures. Where would Victorian poetry, country music or black-and-white films be without lashings of sentiment? Very little else can make you sob with pleasure without actually laying hands on you.

Which is why I wanted to see *After They Were Famous: The Waltons* (ITV). *The Waltons* managed to inject more concentrated sentimentality into the eye of the viewer than any programme before or since. The person who watched this with me remained silent for ten minutes and then asked: 'Who on earth are these people?' 'That's John Boy,' I said. 'You must remember John Boy. "Good night, John Boy."' 'What are you talking about?' she replied, coolly. It's a shock to remember that *The Waltons* started in the early 1970s and finished more than twenty years ago. Well, for those of you too young or ironic to remember, it was, essentially, the American *Archers*, set during the Depression. Nothing much happened. But every slight plot posed a moral problem for a family member, which was solved with a mixture of kindly guile, family values and cod-liver oil.

I assumed, in a modish way, that the cast would be quite unlike their TV personas. In fact, they turned out to be just as winsomely whimsical, sugary and enthusiastic. It had all been one big happy family on and off set. Which was sort of spooky. I like sentimentality in art. I'm not sure I can cope with it in real life. One of the kids pointed out that the success of *The Waltons* had been due, in part, to it appearing during the Vietnam War. Someone else said it was the only drama that dealt with poor people. But its real joy was as a last sluice of hot sentiment. It wasn't just set in the past. Its emotional language was the end of a now-extinct feeling. The programmes that imitated it never managed to keep the irony out of their voices or resist sending themselves up. And that's the thing with sentimentality. It's Kryptonite to cool. The two can't exist in the same room.

Comedy

Laughter

The sound of merry laughter fills crepuscular drawing rooms. Down the closes, wynds and terraces of the nation, the tintinnabulation of jocund mirth skips. On high, God, distracted from gloomier and more pressing business, takes a moment to smile down on his blessed Albion and sighs: 'Ah, at least one small corner of Creation is happy.' But on the sofas and Parker Knolls, men, women and children in scratchy dressing gowns frown and point and mutter as one: 'What the hell are they laughing at?'

For all is not as it sounds. The carefree gales are a simulacrum, a horrible, humourless, disembodied joke; it is the canned variety, that thick oral sludge that demands you just add a comedy script written by two miserable bleeders in a suburban basement. Last week was the opening of the comedy season. At the BBC, a crack company of burly commissionaires march through the corridors bearing the venerable spool, shouting: 'Make way for Lord Reith's laughter!' and two men with orders to kill each other if either should go mad place it on the dubbing machine, and then the specialist applicator, the Master of the Humour, goes about his work. These practitioners are mythic, revered and feared, men who hold the ratings in the palm of their gnarled hands, known to Tristrams as the Jedi of the Watershed. It takes years of diligent study to become a Jedi; there are thousands of sad jokes, bogus situations, mono double entendres and phoney reactions to be learned by heart. I mean, given a typical sitcom, would you know where to put the laughter? How could a layman possibly tell? Where the laughter originated is hidden in the mists of time; it is said that it came from the episode of *Steptoe and Son* where Wilfrid Brambell eats pickled onions in the bath. It might have been a Morecambe and Wise Christmas special; some swear it comes from Vanessa

Feltz's first Weight Watchers' meeting. Who knows? Who can tell? All that is certain is that the perpetrators are long since dead. It is ghost laughter.

So used to the laughter track have we become that its absence is unnerving. Is this funny? Are we supposed to laugh? Am I smiling, or is it just wind?

Caroline Aherne's fabulously performed *The Royle Family* (BBC1) bravely does without its safety net. It is back with its cast of hideous characters who sit in front of the telly as a sort of surreal mirror image of us watching them. They have clichéd, brain-dead conversations that we smugly suppose are being repeated in every living room up and down the country except ours. It balances precariously on the edge between parody and mimicry and is so minutely well observed, and delivered with such monolithically straight faces, that it almost becomes the thing it is pillorying. Only occasionally does it fall into a comedy moment, and a piece of business or banter ring a false note as a flash of sitcom. Parody creeps up behind its subject and mugs it: it's funny. Mimicry is at best transiently clever. But part of the pleasure in watching *The Royle Family* is waiting to see how close they'll get without disappearing. I watched it without breaking into a smile, but I was laughing on the inside, which is, of course, the most satisfying place to laugh.

It's got to the point where I actually look forward with some ghoulish anticipation to the latest offering from Hale and Pace. Their latest doesn't disappoint. Well, it does disappoint, but in an utterly delicious way. Hale and Pace are to humour what infectious impetigo is to a first date. I am putting this as sweetly as I can. Their last three offerings have been cumulatively – I thought unbeatably – awful, but like the true troupers they are, they've managed to top them with this one. The concept (I use the word as they do, inaccurately) is a mix of skits, stand-up badinage and a quiz show. It has all the allure and anticipatory excitement of a strange washcloth found behind a youth-hostel sink. Hale, or perhaps it is Pace, only has one facial expression, and it is one too many. It involves leering at the camera, sticking his tongue out of the side of his mouth. I don't know about you, but my, how this works for me every time. I thought after the 800th viewing I might get a little tired of it, that the chuckle magic might wear thin, but no: No. 801 appeared and I slapped my raw thigh and shouted: 'Come quickly. Hale, or perhaps it's Pace, is doing that really amusing thing with his tongue. Again.' Hale and Pace scripts must constitute the longest suicide note in the history of light entertainment. Every one of them would have been enough to garrotte lesser careers. I've got a really good title for the next show, after this one is axed (trust me). How about calling it *Hale and Farewell*?

Comedians

As a viewing nation, we are inordinately proud of our comedians. The French may have cornered romance, the Scandinavians depression, the Italians enthusiasm, the Americans whimsy, the Belgians surrealism, the Japanese fury and the Germans guilt – but we do humour better than any of them. We have elevated humour to the highest pinnacle of human feeling, which is, in itself, funny, not least because, as far as the rest of the world is concerned, it makes a virtue out of necessity.

What is also funny, though only parochially, is that we don't take much pleasure in our humour. You don't walk around English cities chuckling: 'My, this is the land of laughter.' It may just be me, but I think that's because we don't really have a sense of humour. The English don't share jokes, they aim them, occasionally with accuracy, almost always with great force and malevolence. Consequently, we have managed to produce a pantheon of comedians who aren't funny. Some of the greatest aren't even remotely amusing. A few of the very finest are actually frightening.

One of the things I do to while away the time in doctors' waiting rooms or during foreplay is compose a top ten list of the greatest unfunny British funnymen. The order changes, though fighting for the top spot are the gigglishly challenged behemoths of Ted Ray, the Manchester United of lip rictus; Arthur Askey, a man who made you yearn for a swarm of killer buzzy-bees; Harry Worth (that shtick with a window made me want to stab my eyeballs with a mucky fork); and, of course, the vast black hole of hilarity that is Norman Wisdom. Close behind are Peter Glaze, chronic stalwart of *Crackerjack* ('Crackerjack!'); George Formby, a timelessly unfathomable enigma of gloom; and who could forget, even under therapeutic hypnosis, Terry Scott? Personally, though I know this is controversial, I would include *The Radio Ham* and *The Blood Donor*. I'm sorry, they're just not funny, they're weird and grim.

And Ken Dodd. Now, there's another one. I know there are those of you who say he's a comic genius, but then you're not funny either, or clever, for that matter. As a child, the sight of Ken Dodd would propel me behind the sofa with my fingers in my ears. He was terrifying. The Diddy Men and the tickling stick were the stuff of infant nightmares. Nothing I have seen since has made me think that first impressions aren't wholly sound. He appeared on a show called *Another Audience with Ken Dodd* (ITV), the only mildly amusing part of which was the title and the implication that someone had let him do this before. The *Audience With* series is becoming the memorial service for departed comics who don't know they are dead yet. Terrible old defunct music-hall fillers get to run through their own obituaries while an invited audience do syrupy platitudes of mourning.

The only hopeful feature is that these programmes have to be awarded at the end of a career, rather than when there are still acres to come. The audience in question was made up of the sort of small-screen personalities whose agents call *Celebrity Ready Steady Cook* on the off-chance that there has been a cancellation. Dodd himself is a hurricane of unfunnyness. He is humour-free, with a manic energy. The least amusing thing about him is that it's all so effortful. His act is like watching an old man have constipation against the clock. It's exhausting and mercifully fruitless. He can't resist gurning into a song, bringing a horrible epileptic life to a long-buried sentimental pub ballad. It would be impossible to try to explain the attraction of Dodd to anyone who wasn't born and bred British. Indeed, I've lived here all my life, and it passes me by. Sometimes, you know, I feel like a stranger in my own living room.

Ricky Gervais has been downgrading *Extras* until it sounded like his concept album. He is a man who speaks in so many layers of irony that he comes across as a sarky mille-feuille.

Liverpool

Now, Liverpool. Liverpool, a place so horrible they named it after offal and an oik's pub game that always ends in fights. I hate Liverpool with a dull, passionate loathing. When we finally get shot of Wales and it becomes its own little begging-bowl Bosnia, we should insist that they take Liverpool as a penance.

I should say, I have never knowingly been to Liverpool. Oh, but I know it, I've lived it. For thirty years, light entertainment has been one long advertisement for Liverpool. I know exactly what Liverpool is like. I know all about that 'we were poor but we shared what we had', the tearaway 'our kids', I know all about the gob and the crack and the repartee and the 'we were in and out of each other's kitchens' and the bits of thieving, but nothing criminal, the signing on and the singing for Brasso, I know all about the extended family loyalty and the sexual incontinence, and the leaving the kids with your Auntie Maureen, and the knockabout violence that doesn't mean anything, and the warmth of the pubs and the chip suppers and the crooning with your foreheads pressed together, and the click-clacking girls dressed to copulate on a Friday, and the religion of football and 'You'll Never Walk Alone' (or, as they sing it at Chelsea, 'You'll Never Work Again'). I've had a gutful of the smiling through the tears and the endless, endless, endless bloody chirpiness in the face of adversity. Oh, but don't I just know Liverpool. For television, Liverpool's long partial political broadcast started with *The Liver Birds* (BBC1).

The Liver Birds have a lot to answer for. They were two girls who shared a flat; one wet, the other perky. Both chronically annoying. In the chronology of sitcoms it was a watershed programme. Before *The Liver Birds*, sitcoms were vehicles for receding comics, middle-aged men with southern accents. *The Liver Birds* brought flat vowels and short skirts. It was the first germination of youth

TV. In the 1960s it was all rather daring and aspirational. Girls out on the razzle together, no grown-ups, nearly having sex, almost getting drunk. Set in a time when Gerry and the Pacemakers didn't make you think of open heart surgery. It wasn't a favourite of mine because, frankly, I was happy living at home and it wasn't very funny. But the relentless Scouse television mafia has decided to remake it. As if we cared. *What Happened to the Liver Birds*, unfortunately, is much as one might have imagined. They became fat and haggard and failed and lonely and broke and dim and, because they were from Liverpool, still tearfully, saggingly chirpy.

The new series makes the old one look like a comedy. Don't watch it if you're feeling under the weather or are alone with sleeping pills in the house. The first episode was the most suicidally depressing sitcom ever conceived. And it pointed up a great truth about the Liverpool in your living room. It's a place that worships, adores and yearns for failure. Its whole *raison d'être* is coping with a brave face and a smart one-liner, as you stand with ripped tights while life drives off, splashing you with muddy water. You couldn't have a Liverpool drama about success and wealth and elegance and sophistication, with a wine list and clean hair. It wouldn't be Liverpool. It would be somewhere else imitating the accents. Liverpool wouldn't know what to do with full employment and a win on the lottery. The sentimentalising of ignorance and poverty is one of the most nauseating things to be made party to. Liverpool has turned it into a municipal culture, a way of life and a lorra, lorra television. If Beryl and Sandra had come from Hove or Stoke or Aberdeen, they might have had a life, but coming from Liverpool they didn't stand a chance.

This week my favourite quote is from Dustin Hoffman. Now, there's a man who badly needs a twinklectomy. Trying to describe Billy Connolly's act, he hunted for exactly the right word, like Einstein trying to remember what comes after e=m. Finally, with exaggerated Method care, he came up with 'a depthful performance'. Depthful? He tasted it and saw it was good. And beamed sagaciously, as if he'd just said something very, very, well, very deep. Connolly's light biography, *Thirty Years of Billy Connolly* (BBC1), was a cautionary tale of a funny man who fell into bad company. He started among rough, violent, ignorant, drunk, Glaswegian shipbuilders and folk singers, and then moved on to film stars, celebrity presenters, Californian psychoanalysts and the Duchess of York. It was sad, really.

Friends

Among America's Tristrams, there's this piece of in-house slang: 'You know it's jumped the shark.' They say it often. It means that a series or sitcom has passed its sell-by date; has lost itself in success and longevity; is a dead show walking. The expression comes from an episode of the sitcom *Happy Days* when the Fonz had to jump over a shark, on water-skis. It was so ridiculous that when the producers saw it, they realised the game was up and the concept had become exhausted to the point of incoherence. As is often the case, a few days after I had had 'jumped the shark' explained to me, I serendipitously caught that very episode in the gloomy attic of American satellite repeats.

The image was indeed absurd: Henry Winkler on skis, in swimming shorts and a leather jacket, swinging about in front of the back projection. What was interesting, though, was the plot. It was set in Hollywood, and was about whether young Richie, the red-haired one with big ears, should take the chance of a lifetime and work in movies or whether he should go back to small-town college. Of course, he turns his back on fame and chooses heart-warming obscurity. The real joke is that the actor playing little Richie was Ron Howard, who went on to become one of the biggest directors in Hollywood.

What reminded me of jumping the shark was the hagiographic elegy *How Friends Changed the World* (C4). The shark-jumping moment on *Friends* was, I think, the appearance of Richard Branson. Branson's appearance on anything is a sure sign that it is nose-diving to cynical oblivion. And the star cameo in general is a sign that a sitcom has delusions above its situation. *Friends* had become a marketing opportunity, an in-house joke. The prolonged applause and whoops when yet another resting star surprisingly stepped through the door were a sign that the integrity of the original concept had been mortally holed below the watershed.

How Friends Changed the World was mostly back-slapping interviews with people who spoke in hallowed awe and genuflecting gratitude for having been allowed to inhabit the same space and time as Rachel's hair. It was plain how *Friends* had changed them. It had made them rich beyond belief or talent, curdled their critical faculties and destroyed any perception of cultural relativity. They seriously claimed that *Friends* had changed the language and the way we relate to each other; globally broadened and deepened the concept of family; heroically fought sexism and intolerance; become the manual and votive text for a generation; and possibly heralded world peace, prosperity and an end to ugly people. Throughout this bottom-licking post-mortem, the phrase 'would never be the same again' was used so often, I'm pretty certain the scriptwriters' salivary glands will never be the same again.

The answer to the question 'How did *Friends* change the world?' is: it didn't. It was entertaining for the odd half-hour, when we weren't doing anything else, and it spawned a haircut in Cheshire. Tristrams always snigger that the audience can't tell the difference between television and real life. I've always known this isn't true. Viewers can tell the difference between the telly and the spin-drier. It's the Tristrams who lose touch with reality, who think their creations are real, that they are electric Pygmalions. It's pathetic and it's sad. Which is what this programme was. Last week, an American television executive bounced up to me and said: 'God, it's a big week: the last episode of *Friends*. Fifty million viewers. Did you see it?' Well, no.

English Sitcom

Another report last week mildly slapped the BBC's limp wrist for its inability to make watchable, let alone funny, sitcoms. Their most successful offerings are all twenty years old: *Last of the Summer Wine* (of which we seem to have been imbibing the dregs since episode two), *Are You Being Served?*, *Only Fools and Horses* and *Dad's Army* (which will have to be called Great-Great-Grandad's Army if they rerun it for much longer). I really don't have the energy to go through the tired old arguments about why our sitcoms are so utterly dire. Everyone knows why situation comedies are dreadful. They're dreadful because they lack any confidence that they can be funny, and they're incapable of looking anywhere but at old sitcoms for inspiration and plot. And that's leaving aside the fact that they're all written by cynics on sedatives. I think we should just all agree to stop talking about them. Why don't we have a moratorium for, say, twenty years; like whales and tigers, we won't shoot any. Let a new generation think they've reinvented them. If you don't want to listen to me, just look at the three new ones that arrived last week. *Heartburn Hotel*, *Duck Patrol* and *Babes in the Wood*.

Where to start? *Duck Patrol* (ITV) ... oh God, I think I'm losing the will to live. Is there life after the grave for Victor Meldrew as a policeman on a leafy bit of the Thames? Of course there isn't. And nobody on the screen or off it remotely believes that there is. You can see it in their faces: this is a script that flung itself off a bridge in despair in Bray and was picked up three weeks later at the Isle of Dogs. Staggeringly banal, desperately ingratiating, stupendously turgid – hold on, I'd better pace the adjectives, I've got two more to go. *Heartburn Hotel* (BBC1) is a comedy about a DSS hostel in Birmingham, written by the man who did *Only Fools and Horses*. We get a bad-tempered old-git owner who goes round the human beanbags of his customers doing mildly racist and sexist one-liners that were old when they got to *Love Thy Neighbour*. His unlikely friend is a large Scottish teacher who can't get an erection. So that's the double entendres strapped on. And some pudding-like sack of kapok whose wife left him. None of it is remotely engaging or amusing.

The trick ... well, it's hardly a trick ... the glaringly obvious truth of sitcoms is that the audience have got to want to watch the characters, either because they love them or hate them or ever so rarely they make them laugh. You couldn't give a sucked Valium for any of this lot as performed or written. The desperate thing about characters in British sitcoms is that none of them bears a passing resemblance to anyone you've met in the past forty years. They all seem to be set in the past even when they're in the present. They get their comic characters from ancient Ealing comedies – fine in 1939 Ealing, but desperate now. It's like watching Japanese Elvis impersonators – they just remind you of how good the real thing was – only this lot do Bernard Bresslaw, Sid James and Alfie Bass impersonations. It's grim.

And finally, the much hyped, advertised and plugged, although not plugged enough, *Babes in the Wood* (ITV). Three girls who share the ubiquitous sofa in St John's Wood – they could have hailed from Shepherd's Bush and been *Birds in the Bush*, or perhaps from Battersea, where they could have been *Dogs from the Home*. Three bottle blondes who were supposed to be raunchy modern ladettes. Well, darling, they made the Liver Birds look like Mata Hari and Linda Lovelace. For a start, they've all got PMT instead of a character, and it's impossible to tell them apart, not that one would want to. Samantha Janus is cast as the men's magazine bit of phwoahh! totty, but on screen she makes waking up beside Hattie Jacques seem like a hornier proposition. There's a stupid one – well, a stupider one – and an angry one. Their foil, though without the implied sharpness or point, is that man who does bathroom-cleaner ads. The comic possibility in all these Babes has the dramatic breadth and nuance of Denis Norden's face.

American Sitcom

Ally McBeal (C4) is the latest American light comedy to knock hesitantly on your screen and say: 'Oh hi, can I come in, oh hey, you're busy, right, this is private, right, I'll call back later, no really, it was nothing, pretend you never saw me, are you sure I'm not interrupting, oh God, I feel so, look, really, I can do this another time if you're into something, you know, no, I don't mean doing you know, because obviously you wouldn't, but you know, I mean, hell, if you were, it wouldn't be any of my business, look, you know, there I go again, you never saw me, I wasn't here, I'm gone, history, oh God.'

Ally McBeal can go on doing this sort of thing for hours. They all can. Walking into a room in an American sitcom makes what Houdini did look minimal. Their scriptwriters must have competitions for who can keep going without a full stop longest. And they're very good at it. There were no surprises in this show and very few full stops. It was as polished and homogenised as every other sitcom. They mix the ingredients of insecurity, sassiness, cuteness and sentimentality with a bland assurance. The audience can lie on its back and have its tummy tickled, in the perfect confidence that things will never get rough or serious or make a grab for the rude bits.

You may or may not like *Ally McBeal* as much as, say, *Friends* or *Ellen* or that girl who is a cartoonist or the one who's a single mother, but it'll be simply caprice – because one's got a sharper haircut, or you prefer a dogged, permanently coitally interrupted boyfriend. To judge one from the other is like trying to say which carton of skimmed milk you prefer. Women in American sitcoms are all still Mary Tyler Moore. She's Dolly the sheep. They've never changed, never evolved. They still take fifteen lines and thirty facial muscles to get to a door. They still only kiss on the lips when they're saying: 'No, no. This is isn't going to work out. I find you terribly attractive but it wouldn't be right.' And they still close the door with their backs so they can face the camera for the reaction shot that looks like a kabuki audition and runs through every emotion known to Norman Rockwell.

I'm entranced by the moreishness of them, but also mildly disgusted that I can be continually grabbed by the same meagre, hollow lexicon of dramatic possibilities, all little filleted Aesop's Fables, morals without a dilemma. Years ago, Dennis Potter (Beatrix's boy) wrote a play about childhood, *Blue Remembered Hills*. The children were played by adults dressed in school uniforms. It was poignant and disturbing. *Ally McBeal* and its clones are the exact opposite. They are children pretending to be adults playing at doctors and lawyers, and lovers testing their pubescent sexuality out on each other, falling in and out of love with the terrible angst of a twelve-year-old and the intense faux-meaningful revelatory conversations of hyperexcited little girls. The sets are Wendy houses, and none of it is prickly or uncomfortable, because deep in the back of your head you know that when the credits roll, their parents come and pick them up and take them home in a big station wagon. 'Did you have a nice time, Ally?' 'Oh, it was amazing. Brad's in love with Skipper, and they're really serious, and I had to go to court and get this murderer off on a technicality. But it was all right because I talked to him after, and he's real sorry. And then we got a kitten in the office and Neil tried to kiss me and I think I might fall in love. But I've got to talk to Rhoda first. And what's for tea?'

It would be a mistake to try to draw any broader conclusions about the state of mind of America or Americans from these drama-less dramas. Over here in the old world, we still imagine that the bottom-line purpose of all play-acting is to reveal truth, to strip away, to be honest. American television has invented a quite different purpose. It's to obscure, to iron out, to simplify, comfort and offer security, whereas in real life we all know there is messy confusion, harsh decisions and uncertainty. It allows the viewer to indulge in half an hour's perfect regression with grown-up toys, and there's nothing wrong with that. I rather like it. It's just like: 'Look, I need to say this, help me out here, it's like, mortadella, no really, listen to me, it's, like, this Italy meat sausage thing, mortadella, mortadella is subtle and complex and is full of hard bits, and it's ancient and mysterious, well, it was taken to America, and we made it smoother and pinker and much, much more tasteless and now it's just a pale, mass-produced imitation that only Americans can swallow and you know what we call it, we call it baloney. Cute, huh?'

Dennis Potter

A big Christmas-telly must go to Father Helge Pettersson, who called for the banning of the poster advertising the *Shameless* Christmas special (C4), because it 'blasphemously' showed the cast in a tableau reminiscent of Leonardo's *Last Supper*. Father Pettersson took his ire to the press, which did the producers of *Shameless* the great favour of reporting exactly what he had said.

I see nobody has told the vicar where Leonardo or Caravaggio or, for that matter, Christ himself found their apostles. But it's the same every year: these godly Gradgrinds come to remind us all of the true nature of Christmas, want to have everything on television neutered or banned, then one of them vandalises the *Hello!* manger at Madame Tussaud's. We've heard an awful lot this year about legislation to protect faith, but we are in much greater need of a law to protect the rest of us from the officiously religious. As it happens, the *Shameless* poster was not a piece of theological kitsch, but a fair representation of the programme, which was a piece of theological kitsch.

Shameless is one of the best dramas of the year: barbed, honest writing, cleverly observed characters and sinewy performances. It is a situation comedy that, thankfully, resists trite situations and clichéd comedy. However, the Christmas special demanded a yuletide story and transformed this original piece of underclass-spotting into a sort of Tom Sharpe romp. The tale we got was Now That's What I Call Christianity, a compilation of all the New Testament best bits: births, expulsions, pogroms, rising from the dead, with the army standing in for Rome and the police for the Pharisees. Ultimately, we got a drunken Christ at a Last Supper, neatly, though confusingly, conflating Christmas and Easter. I assume we were supposed to make more of this than just a giggle, but as Brechtian social drama, *Shameless* shot its own turkey. The half-baked symbolism underlined its intrinsic weaknesses – a deep seam of sentimentality, a voyeuristic attraction for poverty, squalor and dysfunction. It walked a fine line between laughing with and at its characters, between decrying their situation and beatifying it. Its redemption is that it generally stays on the side of the poor and the angels, but this Christmas, it stepped over into farce.

I wonder what Dennis Potter would have made of *Shameless*. Actually, I know what he would have made of it. He used to sit in this chair. He was a very, very bad television critic. He suffered from the two terminal deficiencies of a wannabe reviewer: he didn't like the medium he had to watch, and he thought he could do it better.

I should qualify that: Potter liked the idea of television, he just hated what was on it. He and the other post-war, first-in-the-family university graduates who flooded the BBC saw television as a Fabian lending library with pictures, a means to educate and motivate the deserving working class. It was also a way of rationalising their guilt at having stepped up into the middle class. They made class and guilt television's abiding theme and became the new inverted Establishment, just as arrogant and insufferable as the old one had been.

The BBC is running a festival of Potter plays in the new year. Some of them are very good, like *Blue Remembered Hills* and parts of *The Singing Detective* and *Pennies from Heaven*; but a lot are pretty dreadful. The initially banned *Brimstone & Treacle* was dire, and the Orson Welles-ish hubris of *Blackeyes* was one of the most embarrassing things ever shown on telly. In the end, with his angry working-classness, his crippled hands and his cancer, Potter was an untouchable megalomaniac. After he died, having delivered his own eulogy to Melvyn Bragg, the BBC and ITV got two last posthumous plays that were beyond appalling. When they were broadcast, the Tristrams caught each other's eyes and thought: 'We must never let that happen again.'

Nigel Williams, whom I admire, made an *Arena* documentary about Potter, *Painting the Clouds* (BBC2), that consisted mostly of charming but unilluminating encomiums from his family. It wasn't just sympathetic, it was a Stalinist hagiography, a whitewash that failed to mention either of the posthumous plays and shrugged off criticism, interviewed no contrary voices and touched only briefly on Potter's demeaning and unsavoury sexual history, which would have been okay if Potter hadn't made it so central to his plays. If a writer makes his life his work, then his life should be examined contextually. This biography, whatever its original motive, looked like embarrassing pleading by the BBC on behalf of one of its own, with a bit of licence-fee hymn-singing on the side. I would far rather have had a biography and retrospective season devoted to Jack Rosenthal, who died recently and was a warmer, more humane playwright, someone who liked not only the medium he worked in, but the people who watched it.

Potter's subject was himself, which is fine, but he wrote about his life as if it were the only one that mattered, as if only his concerns were important. He was vainly, furiously solipsistic and, most damning in terms of the audience, he just wasn't very nice. If you are going to make your life your art, it helps if it's at least a bit likeable.

Actors

Actor

It used to be said that films made you rich, theatre made your reputation, and television made you famous. It was actors who used to say it. Rich, famous and revered is what thesps joined Equity to become. Actually, it's what I wanted to be, too. Actors in general are peculiarly dismissive of television. 'Theatre's the thing, dear boy.' All their training is theatre-based. They're grateful for the cheques, the regular work and the fan mail the box gives them, of course, but it's not their art, it's not the real thing. Television drama has traditionally acquiesced to this view of itself. The credits at the end of big telly productions used to have an announcer bumptiously saying: 'Upton Kilgore is a National Theatre player.' Or: 'Netta Cleavage appears courtesy of the Royal Shakespeare Company.' The stage manager of the Barbican never steps into the footlights and says: 'Dicky Pimple is currently appearing in a pantyliner commercial and three episodes of *Vet in a Puddle*.'

Television drama tends to use big theatre actors to give its costume dramas a touch of cultural class. There is a whole raft of theatre folk who will only appear on television in tights and a wig. They are invariably the duds in the production. Their mannerisms are mannered, their voices rise and fall like a starlet's knickers and they ooze an air of lazy patronage. This is all wrong. Anyone who has been to the theatre recently will know that television is where all the talent is. In terms of emotion, credibility and naked entertainment, if it's a choice between the new Harold Pinter or a rerun of *Minder* on UK Gold, there's really no choice at all.

The standard of acting on series such as *The Bill*, *Soldier, Soldier* and *Casualty* is incredibly high. Because characters on television become so real, so believable, we hardly think of them as being performances at all. And this, of course, leads to typecasting, which

is another reason actors dislike the small box. Their characters
become bigger than they are. I'm afraid I have suffered from this
personally. I was a child actor (that's the most embarrassing thing
I've ever written). I only did it once. When I was nine I played the
little boy in Brecht's *Caucasian Chalk Circle*. I was great, winsome,
touching, achingly poignant. That's what the make-up girl said,
anyway. I was so real, so wholly believable I just became a small
Manchurian orphan. But, sadly, I never got another part. I was
typecast. Agents and casting directors said sorry, and if they ever
turned *The Mikado* into a soap operetta we'll put you up for it,
but there's nothing at the moment. I was a has-been before I ever
was.

Channel 4 is running a short season on theatre and theatricals,
and it all rather smacks of the old self-deprecating genuflecting to
the boards. Here be real performing giants, proper culture. The
first programme was enough to put Cameron Mackintosh off setting foot in the theatre ever again. *Blow Your Mind See a Show: One
Man Show* (C4) was a master class given by Steven Berkoff. Let
me, your humble chorus, make it live for you. A sumptuous empty
black set, unencumbered by impedimenta save a *Mastermind*-style
chair, nothing to get between the genius and his thralled audience.
Lit by a single spotlight. There is a hush. Enter Berkoff, resplendent
in black vest and clown's trousers. A pause: we are in the presence
of greatness. The atmosphere is palpable. Berkoff starts to act. He
acts acting and then, gasp, he acts actors acting acting. The stage
is suddenly full of acts, life's an act, acting's an act, it's actorama,
actorissima, it's actuality. At home this audience was quite overcome and broke into spontaneous laughter. Never have I seen a
man make such an utter complete actor of himself.

I suppose in the theatre one might be able to suspend belief long
enough to watch Berkoff with something resembling a straight
face, but through the unforgiving lens it was impossible. The camera unerringly held up to ridicule every overblown movement and
every bit of stagecraft. There are few things in life that give as much
pleasure as watching a really self-important egophile blow his own
raspberry. Now, in real life Mr Berkoff may be a terribly sweet,

self-effacing man. He may be shy and retiring in the presence of ladies, he may have a streak of modesty as long as a tapeworm, but who could possibly tell? The real Steven Berkoff is buried under a luvvie mountain of drama. He is one huge act. The big finale was doing a bit of Oberon from *Midsummer Night's Dream* (or just *The Dream*, as we has-beens call it). It was simply the most ham-fisted, unintentionally funny thing this humble critic has ever seen. Shakespeare done to a bard. When it finished, I rose to my feet and woke the neighbours with shouts of bravo. The Tristram who commissioned and scheduled this deserves a medal. He is a man with nerves of steel, a man who knows no shame.

Felicity Kendal is an actor who is living proof that roses by any other name smell like roses. She just *is* the Felicity's Felicity. Felicity means bringer of happiness, huge happiness, unbelievable, vast, unending, soft, pink, infinite happiness, hip-hop, hoppity-hoppity, happy, happy happiness. And Kendal – a picturesque tourist destination that has given its name to a mint cake of such cloying sweetness, it makes your eyeballs bounce off your cheeks and your teeth scream for mercy. And isn't that just Felicity Kendal, little miss happy-sweet? Have you seen her try to do angry? It's like watching a toad try to do sexy. That moony face furrows up. You can sense her reaching down into the bowels of experience and dredging up yet more happy-sweet. Now come along, Felicity, try harder, you're really, really angry – good, fine, excellent. Now do it without giggling. If you really want a punishing brain-teaser for the weekend, try imagining Felicity Kendal's Lady Macbeth, particularly when she does her stern voice, where she lowers it a husky octave: it's like watching a hamster trying to retrieve peanut butter from the back of its cheek.

Please can somebody explain what the point of Sammy Davis Jr was. For a start he looks like the first draft of a character out of *The Lion King*. All that manic wall-eyed, finger-snapping, dooby-do stuff makes my skin crawl. It's so utterly without charisma. If you have any doubts about Sammy Davis, let me just tell you he's the person Bruce Forsyth based his stage act on. Yup, I thought that would do it.

Maureen Lipman

The Best of British (BBC1) is a cringe-making title. Anything that giftwraps itself in the flag is embarrassing. Would you watch a programme called *Best of Luxembourg*? The associations that come with Best of British are things like *Carry On* films, Marmite, Brasso, bread and dripping, last orders, morris dancing, Europhobia, the Blitz – or is the Blitz the Best of Germany? Anyway, Maureen Lipman seems to fit easily in there. She's someone I'd dearly love to see draped in a flag prior to being tipped off the end of a ship. The unimpeachable previewer for the *Sunday Times* said last week that no serious critic could possibly have a thing to say against Maureen. So, sadly, that's my credentials down the pan, because, for me, Maureen Lipman is the incarnation of a thousand cats sliding down a mile-long blackboard. She is lemon juice in the eye, she is chewing silver paper, she is a three-flush floater, sand in your socks and one blocked nostril.

I know this is irrational, a disproportionate reaction to a light comedienne going about her business (and boy, can she go about business), but I can't help it. I think it's that she's profession-ally Jewish. I despise, nay loathe, people who take the accident of birth as a defining characteristic, like Max Boyce. Why anyone would boast of being Welsh is a mystery beyond snooker and the Boycott/Trueman/Parky Yorkshireman. In fact, Lipman, born in Hull, had the choice of being either. She possibly felt there was more comic mileage in Jewishness – not Primo Levi Jewishness but Barbra Streisand's spinster auntie Jewishness, a sort of music-hall, chicken-soup and suffocating-interference Jewishness that only avoids being unpleasantly stereotypical because Lipman can claim it's home. In fact, it's as degrading and belittling as Stepin Fetchit's eye-rolling black servant.

There's no denying Lipman has ability and comic precision. She was good as the *ingénue* in Nell Dunn's *Up the Junction*, and also excellent in Jack Rosenthal's (her husband) *Evacuees*. He said the best thing about her as an actress was that she never showed the audience how hard it was to do what she did. She made it look easy and never milked applause. That was loyal of him and exactly the opposite of the truth. Lipman is a titanic show-off. Every mannerism, wink, aside, shrug and reaction is dipped in syrup and semaphored. Naturalistic she ain't. She does a shtick that disregards everyone else on stage. Her one-woman show *Live and Kidding* was one of the most archly manipulative, self-regarding, unfunny, creepy evenings in the theatre; and her performance in *Oklahoma!* was its one duff note, an extraordinary piece of casting that jarred with everything else. What was she doing on the prairie? You kept thinking she was going to slip into 'Matchmaker, Matchmaker, Make Me a Match'. It was Oyveyklahoma, the surrey with the fiddler on top. On her imitation of the divine Joyce Grenfell, Lipman said: 'It wasn't actually Joyce or me, it was another character, and I think it gained by being a bit of both of us.' What hubris: what Joyce Grenfell needed was a bit of Maureen Lipman. In the end, she's famous, like the PG chimps and the Andrex labradors, for a series of commercials. Cynical window-dressing to make the infuriating BT lovable. The phoney manipulation of style over veracity, and that's Maureen Lipman in a mezuzah.

Nick Berry is the actor – and I use the word in its most relaxed sense – who put the bla into bland. If he were a sandwich, he'd be processed cheese on Wonderloaf. Hold the pickle. He has as much presence, excitement and élan as an empty rabbit hutch. All of which naturally makes him the most popular romantic lead on television.

One of the great enduring attractions of male actors is hellraising. As a positive quality, it's only open to men. If women try it, they're talentless slags who sleep their way to the top. It's difficult to see why the offscreen behaviour of Harris, Burton, O'Toole and Reed should be so endearing. Of all human endeavours, getting off your face calls for the least skill, effort or training. But in the case of Reed and Harris, it was their great gift. Acting was something they did in between fighting, slurring their words and falling over. Usually their parts involved fighting, slurring their words and falling over, which, considering the amount of research they'd put in, they managed to do very, very badly.

Hellraisers (C4), the evocation of their tottering lives, revealed the truth that in retrospect they were very very boring. It was a very very boring programme. Listening to the veritas that vino brings is like listening to other people's dreams – unstructured rambling streams of unconsciousness that invariably finish with the unstated 'well you needed to have been there'. And, frankly, retro clips of Oliver Reed on *Parkinson* are becoming as tedious as reruns of Geoff Hurst's 1966 goal.

Dawn French

Sex and Chocolate (BBC1) was yet another of Dawn French's attempts to tell us that inside every thin person there is a gutbucket trying to get out. The plot, and I use the term as the Brothers Grimm would, was: teacher's assistant married to school janitor gets pursued by childhood boyfriend who is now world-famous fashion photographer and has had it up to here with bedding supermodels. I know, I know, you couldn't make it up. But look, this is political drama, so fat Dawn goes off to Paris where, lo and behold, Jasper Conran dresses her in a wedding frock and she traipses down the catwalk to oohs and aahs but manages to resist the photographer, even though he woos her with Willy Wonka's entire annual output. Dawn goes back to tearful janitor and cute, kooky family.

I haven't made it sound half as screamingly absurd and toe-curlingly ridiculous as it was to watch. Why, a nation asks, does Dawn French persist in trying to tell the public they don't know their own mind, that really they love blubber, and that if the great British bloke were offered two beds, one containing Kate Moss and the other Dawn French, they would pause only for a nanosecond, and go: 'Kate, Dawn; Dawn, Kate. I wonder ... Yes, yes, Dawn, my dumper-truck of lust, here I come, ready or not.' Oh please, you wouldn't even believe that on the Discovery Channel. French has many talents. Making men laugh at her is one of them; raising the beast in them is not. Whatever she says and however often she says it, fat is ugly. Watching fat people pretend to have sex is both funny and mildly disgusting. It isn't sexy – young, thin people are sexy. You can rail at me all you like, but I am just the messenger. It's not a conspiracy of homosexual designers and magazine editors, it's the way people are. They have opinions and preferences that are arrived at for perfectly good, social, aesthetic and behavioural reasons. Thin looks fit, lives longer, moves faster and can touch its toes. Fat wheezes, gets a rash on its thighs, tidemarks in its folds, can't see any of its knees and rolls over in shifts (for a full list see Ceefax).

The spindly narrative of this film collapsed under the dead weight of Dawn's agenda, which unattractively consisted mostly of rubbishing thin girls – a particularly unpleasant sort of feminism that disenfranchises sisters for being too attractive to men and therefore obviously dumb, anorexically loony and gullible. Dawn French offered up Dawn French and the epic, panoramic one dimension of her acting talent, which basically comes down to a cheesy grin and multiple dimples. Inside every fat comedienne there's a thin actress too exhausted to get out.

Archangel (BBC1) was a Robert Harris adaptation that dripped atmosphere and excitement. Of course, it had a plot that was too ludicrous to turn off. Daniel Craig was an English historian and Stalin expert, not unlike Simon Sebag Montefiore. Actually, as unlike Simon Sebag Montefiore as you can get and remain in the same species. Craig has Neanderthal confusion down to a T. He also does barely restrained aggression very daintily. Unfortunately, neither of these are characteristics you would normally associate with academic historians.

Joe's Palace (BBC1) was a long story about, well, nothing very much except an empty house. Watching it felt like eating unsweetened tapioca for an hour and occasionally finding a mouse-dropping. Poliakoff has a tea-strainer of an ear for dialogue, managing to retain what you want to spit out while losing what you want to drink in. I can only imagine that actors see his scripts as a sort of thespian commando course: horrid, but good for you.

Richard Briers

I've just thought of another person who can go on that very short list of TV personalities who are universally loved. Alongside the names of David Attenborough and Joanna Lumley you can carve Richard Briers. I can sense you are not convinced. Trust me. You love him really. Put it another way, can you find it in your heart to hate him? No, you can't. I know, because heavens I've tried. I've strained till the eyes bulge in my face, till my teeth stick out at right angles, till I've made involuntary rodent squeaky noises and the blood has sung 'Come into the Garden, Maud' in my ears. But I can't. I don't think it's humanly possible. It must be Newtonian law. A body travelling in a straight line can't hate Richard Briers. But we ought to be able to, he comes from a long line of deeply loathable characters. Those soft, smug middle-England, middle-class wry smiley comfort-fit chaps. Just remember with a quiver of revulsion all those others who have tripped over the fitted carpet and crazy paving of suburban microcomedy. The horror of Patrick Cargill, the vileness of Sid James. And don't even think of Hugh Lloyd, unless you want to return to chronic bed-wetting.

Briers is right up there with them, but somehow he manages to escape odium, and I don't really see why, but there you have it. That sprinkling of fairy dust, the beneficent blessing of Dame Drama that makes one man a national treasure and another a Lucozade enema. Even though he's repeatedly been seen in the company of Felicity Kendal (the Cadbury's Crème Rosa Klebb) he's still adorable.

He was given a living obituary last week in *Funny Turns: Richard Briers – A Good Life* (BBC1), where assorted greasepaint twinks got to throw their heads back and practise their RADA sycophancy in the hope that there might be some voice-over work in it. It transpired that Briers's entire career has been built on the ability to speak fast. Not, you might think, much of a talent, but then carnie folk aren't like you and me. Jimmy Edwards based an entire career on being able to grow facial hair, and it would have taken a pathologist to find Dickie Henderson's talent: 'Think champagne and you'll drink champagne' was his catch-phrase, which even by the standards of the genre, was utterly moronic. Actually, it works better the other way around.

Paul Scofield

In a week of lamentations, we had three deaths, three final curtain calls through the invisible fourth wall among those who put on the motley. The rude mechanicals must now cast aside Thalia's smiling mask to wear Melpomene's tragic visage: Anthony Minghella, whose shocking exit came just as his last film was about to be shown; Paul Scofield, a truly heroic actor. I watched the six o'clock news as the caster, some Autocue plug-in with a muted accent from semi-detached nowhere, arranged his face into that bland gravitas they keep for the latterly famous and freshly demised. He said: 'Today, a great and dearly loved actor passed away, best known for his portrayal of one of the old gits in *Last of the Summer Wine*, and the prison officer who wasn't the main one in *Porridge*. Brian Wilde will be greatly missed.' Then we saw a couple of unfunny clips and a hasty interview with a cardiganed denizen of decrepit sitcoms, and it was back to the studio, where the Noddy rote-reader added his own little 'Sadly missed', and looked up at the Autocue with a flicker of panic.

Oh no, there was another dead actor. What were the chances? He had peaked too early, already using up his famous-deceased face? So, he quickly slipped into the one reserved for announcing small tornadoes in Cornwall and said: 'Another actor died today: Paul Scofield, best known as that religious bloke in *A Man for All Weathers*.' There was a blurred photograph of Scofield from behind, as Lear, and it was back to weather or sport or an alsatian that was living in sin with a duckling. This happened on both ITV and the BBC early-evening news.

I don't often bellow at the television. I don't have to. I can do this instead. But I went properly radio rental – the complete Basil Fawlty, all on my own in the living room, screaming at the inoffensive, lick-spittle, Andrex-puppy newsmonger and the smiley, culturally relative, accessible, non-judgemental, multicultural, mouthwashed, soulless, fearful Tristrams who, in the final billing of death, had placed the man with two supporting parts in defunct comedies before one of the truly great post-war British actors.

This was not Wilde's fault, but not even his agent would claim he was a panoramic, life-changing talent. I know that, as both approached the pearly gates, Brian would have said: 'After you, old man.'

What made me, and still makes me, angry is that this cultural faux pas wasn't made on some kids' magazine programme or a funky satellite celebrity round-up – it was the six o'clock news. The biggest job in all news is setting the running order, deciding what is and isn't important enough to be broadcast. News is the one part of public broadcasting that can't be dictated by public opinion, but only by public service – not what we want to know, but what we should and need to know. And I know exactly why some young, pulsating gumboil of a know-nothing, sneery, cynical, bearded relativist thought a minor sitcom actor was more important than Paul Scofield. He thought it was a small, sniggering blow against elitism, hardback culture, the Establishment and snobbery – and probably fox-hunting, global warming and the invasion of Tibet. I've never called for anyone to be fired in this column, but this little prat should be. Not just fired – he should be handed over, naked and sobbing, to the Royal Shakespeare Company to play Yorick. I still don't feel any better.

Albert Finney is an inconsistent actor. He has produced some of the very finest performances ever caught on film. He has also hammed his way through parts like a mad pork butcher. Generously, fellow actors refer to this as having the guts to fail. What they really mean is that he shouldn't be given any excuse to go over the top. The character of Uncle Silas doesn't just give him an excuse, it gives him carte blanche and a bacon slicer.

The only two good things I have to say about *Raffles* are: Nigel and Havers. I know, I know. Like you, I've been tracing Nigel's career for some time, but have never had a clear shot. Now here he is, blinking and grinning in the headlights, that impish simpleton's grin on his face, and you know, I just can't find it in myself to pull the trigger. Even though I suspect he's a bloke who thinks genital piercing is where people who don't have stud boxes keep their cufflinks, that he probably gets out of the shower to pee, wears tanga briefs on the beach and has a dramatic range that makes a Buckingham Palace guardsman look like Lionel Blair, if we culled him, where would we find another one? You see, Nige, as he likes to be known, is the only person who could play himself, and he is rather a good television character (as opposed to actor). He's a small-screen David Niven and, like Niven, is best cast obliquely against type. Raffles was just too obvious. It hardly stretched him at all, and we'd all like to see Havers stretched – on a rack, preferably.

I know some of you think that Victoria Wood is innately funny. Unfortunately, you follow a trail along which I cannot follow. In my joyless life, humour and Victoria Wood have never reclined together on the same Parker Knoll. I hear she's been called the modern Joyce Grenfell, and although I'd cavil at the use of the word modern used in conjunction with Victoria Wood, I could go along with that. You could also say she's a blank verse Pam Ayres, or indeed the goy Maureen Lipman. All of these women merge for me into one long dire monologue about cellulite, bra sizes, intransigent stains and carrying shopping on to one-man buses. In fact, I have a suspicion that they are all secretly joined by having spent a night of passion in a discreet Elibabethan hotel with Michael Aspel.

Dames

So, I sat down to *Cranford* (BBC1) girded and gimlet-eyed, my modernist cudgel ready to bludgeon it to a silly pulp. Then, in the very first minute, Eileen Atkins gave me a look – just for a moment, a sideways look, more a glance, really, but it had such depth of character, such promise of interest and intimations of stories to come of hardship and parsimony, of steadfastness, piety, worldliness and a little kindness, all packed together in that one tiny gesture, like an apothecary's spice box – and I realised it was all up. I was hooked, gaffed, netted and filleted. Atkins could have me for her tea with tartare sauce. She is the cur's cods, the terrier's testicles, the business.

I will go further and declare that Atkins is the finest actor appearing anywhere in the world right now. There is, in her performance, a miraculous ability to project a complex subtext or emotion and motivation in her face and posture, while delivering words that seem real and immediate but, simultaneously, tell us something quite different. With the merest tightening of a lip or flickering of an eye, she raises doubts, opens lines of plot and is able to hold and impart contradictory emotions clearly and profoundly. To be able to do this isn't just talent or craft or practice, it is an intense sensitivity, an insight into the dilemmas of the human spirit. She is an era-defining actress.

And with her we got Judi Dench. To use a technical term, that was double bubble. Dench was the straight man, the feed, clearing space and giving time to Atkins. It was a performance of immense generosity, born from confidence and the understanding that to listen is as important as to speak; that a part isn't measured in how many lines you say, but in how many are said to you. Between them, they created scenes of bright brilliance.

Brian Blessed: Acting is too small a word for what he does; thespian is too small a word for what he is. Ohmygodwouldyoulookatthat would be too small a word for Blessed. He is to the stage what brutalist tower blocks are to architecture. He is a man in a periwig and grog-ram cape even when he's only wearing socks. His volume-control knob fell off years ago. A good deal of Tom Jones was shot down his throat. Blessed's mouth is a wonder of nature. You could fit the entire National Theatre, with revolve, into it. His gob ought to be next year's European capital of culture instead of Stockholm, which is a bland and meagrely appointed place by comparison. His talent, for want of a better word, comes in gargantuan regurgitated gobbets. I do think that for the sake of public safety, small children, people in wheelchairs, terriers etc., we might consider having it capped, or at least build a guard-rail round it with lifebelts.

Robbie Coltrane is a compulsive actor to watch as long as he doesn't have to kiss anyone. He's not good at kissing. He's like watching a dinosaur's bladder full of helium and haemorrhoids. He moves with an improbably uncomfortable lightness and grace and he does good punching. Have you noticed how bad actors have got at hitting each other? Most television fights these days look like German country dancing, but when Coltrane clouts someone you know they've been clouted. It brings to mind the great glory days of Dennis Waterman.

Caroline Quentin starred in *Von Trapped* (ITV): it's difficult to know where to start on this gloriously ghastly heap of a story about a hairdresser obsessed with *The Sound of Music*. Quentin had the look of someone sitting in a dentist's waiting room pretending to be somewhere else. She must have known she was straddling an epic turkey. I particularly enjoyed her subtle handling of the scene where her daughter informed her she was really a bloke, Von Trapped, in a girl's body. And had been shoplifting to pay for the operation. Quentin just turned her head and went to another place. It wasn't acting so much as composing the letter that would sack her agent. Sadly, what was missing from *Von Trapped* was Nazis. Why or why is there never a Panzer division around when you need one?

June Whitfield has beautiful reactions, really fine live muscular reactions. She can react where other actors just wait for cues. There's more movement, tone and training in her face than in Pamela Anderson's bikini, and I can't say fairer than that.

Rowan Atkinson was once BBC Personality of the Year. When hopeful journalism students on creative writing courses ask me for a definition of an oxymoron I always say Rowan Atkinson as Personality of the Year. Their little faces light up with recognition. He is regularly and ubiquitously said to be the reincarnation of Harold Lloyd, Charlie

Chaplin, several Marx brothers and Jacques Tati. I can only assume that the people who say 'Oh yes, Rowan Atkinson, isn't he the new Jacques Tati?' think that *Monsieur Hulot's Holiday* was introduced by Judith Chalmers.

Mark Rylance, the moonstruck actor/manager of the Globe, played Dr Kelly, the weapons inspector and dupe. Throughout the exhausting examination of his death and the circumstances that led to it, in the Hutton Report and in the real news, any sense of Kelly's personality remained stubbornly absent. In the brief film of him being unforgivably bullied by the Foreign Affairs Committee and in little bits of newsreel, he looked like a man hiding behind a beard and glasses, a birdwatcher lurking in a hedge. Rylance naturalistically played him as an actor hiding his performance in a hedge. He specialises in doing furrowed thought, and is one of the few actors who can do convincing thinking in character. This is a rare talent: most actors have trouble conveying thought as themselves.

Did you know Jamie Theakston is an actor? No? Well, as you were, he's not. He's just Jamie Theakston. But he's the reincarnation of Stanislavsky and Sir Edmund Kean compared to Amanda Holden. Admittedly, in her defence, the script was a lame – nay, crippled; no, dead – thing about a divorced couple who are really actually ... Oh God, who cares? It was obviously written by text message from a call centre in Bombay. But Holden is beyond horrific: her face simply doesn't listen to her mouth, so the voice is going one lump or two, but the maquillage is doing Hedda Gabler.

It's rather been Michael Sheen's week. Through the miracle of Sky DigiPlus, while I was watching *The Deal* (C4), I was also sitting right at the back of the gods for the glittering première of Stephen Fry's new film, *Bright Young Things* – or BYTs, as we BOTs have wittily ab-breviated them. As it happens, Sheen, who played Blair in *The Deal*, gives great nancy-boy-snorting-coke-off-the-cabinet-table-at-No. 10 in BYTs. I met him last week and asked if he was at all worried about being typecast. Simultaneously, he's also a werewolf in *Underworld*, but he's Welsh, so predatory, perfidious, camp, junkie lycanthropy is second nature, really.

You probably won't recognise Mr Sheen. Not because he's forgettable or because you've never seen him before, but because he has a rubber face, the ability to completely morph into a character. They always said that about Larry Olivier; that he could walk through Batley black-pudding market and nobody would shout, 'How's the bonkers missus?', 'Is it safe?' or 'What you done with the princes in the tower?' Today, it's rare for thesps to disappear into performances, because so much of screen acting is about branding and recognition and grooming for stardom. Now, I'm not Mr Sheen's agent. I only mention all this because he's a very fine actor and you should be seeing a lot more of him, or less, depending on how good he is.

Neil Morrissey was his usual lovable chronically hopeless puppy-man, but what he is most chronically hopeless at, you might already have noticed, is acting, comic acting in particular. I'm not entirely sure he could play himself. He has all the dramatic timing of a turnstile.

What I mind is that people keep writing sex scenes for Martin Clunes, It's those lips: whenever he puckers, it's like something Jacques Cousteau showed us from the deep. You can imagine the poor actress's agent calling to say: 'Darling, the good news is you've got the part. Bad news is, you've got to have your face sucked by the human lamprey.' Despite looking like a bagful of bouillabaisse, Clunes is a good actor for television. He's predictable in a comforting way, and one of the few thesps who can do completely ordinary, decent blokes. I expect his TV persona is closer to depicting his audience than any other actor's. He's decent, self-deprecating, confused and amused – a nice guy, a small-screen Jimmy Stewart crossed with an amorous haddock.

Actresses

For as long as any of us can remember, it has been a given that girls who appear on television must be as plain as pikestaffs. It's understood that an ability to act, present or stand in front of camera and point is incompatible with loveliness. This is a peculiarly puritanical, self-imposed English rule and a complicated part of the equation that makes up the Best Television in the World. We don't need to distract the audience with sensuality, tease it with totty. We've got professional performers, luvvies who look like slurry in a gunny sack but who can act beauty. Oh yes! Give them a couple of lines of decent dialogue and they can transform themselves into slobbering lasciviousness. We don't need oomph, we've got character. Character is a euphemism for 'perfectly safe in a Benghazi brothel'. Tristrams feel comfortable with presenters who look like the girl next door, and we must assume that they all live next door to plastic surgeons' waiting rooms. The rest of the world's television realised aeons ago that TV wasn't just radio you could read by. Yankee television is a swamp of gorgeousness. French and Italian television, which has the intellectual range of a pork chop, sticks pneumatic girls in front of cameras and tells them to jump up and down whenever possible. Only in Blighty would the troll trio from *Birds of a Feather* be marketed as sex symbols. Can you imagine what the show would look like if it were remade in Brazil? On the rare occasions when a complete Betty does get cast, you know for a fact you'll never see her again unless she puts on four stone and cuts her hair with a strimmer. Then, of course, you can't get rid of her.

Anyway, this week all that changed with Amanda Ooms, a seriously toothsome bit of totty whose very name sounds like an appreciative exclamation. Miss Ooms is Scandinavian-Dutch. Luckily the Scandinavian genes got to do the outside, leaving the Dutch ones to cope with the action. Ooms had to get her kit off. Doing this on British television is a cross between a martial art and clog dancing. There's a whole range of slightly awkward moves that actresses have to make so that the camera doesn't catch sight of too many bits. There's a lot of thigh lifting, knee swivelling and elbow blocking. I expect RADA does classes in pre-watershed stripping and bed work.

And then there was *Poldark*. Just to show that Ooms wasn't

a flash in the pan, we got Kelly Reilly, who was extraordinarily easy on the eye. The girl is a precipitously jutting coastline, and she smoulders like there's a pair of boy scouts down her basque rubbing themselves together. You could have toasted marshmallows on her reaction shots. And the heaving. Good God, man, the heaving. Nothing has heaved like this since the Battle of Jutland. It's a miracle the girl's not permanently seasick. Her horizon is the Roaring Forties in a D-cup. She's a menace to shipping, which is rather her point. Tousled young men kept panting, 'I've got a leaky lugger bobbing in a cove.' And all over the country men thought, 'Know what you mean, matey.' To be fair, Reilly doesn't do an awful lot of what Frances de la Tour would call acting – thank God. They'd have needed to write the script in bold type and give her binoculars.

Sci-fi

Star Trek

Be careful what you let your children watch. All those years, parents fought the weekly battle against *Softly Softly* and *The Professionals* because they were just too violent and your daughter might end up bringing home someone like Dennis Waterman. But they didn't have any misgivings about *Star Trek*. *Star Trek* was just a kids' adventure story, cowboys and Indians and disco lights and Velcro, wasn't it? No, it wasn't. Bad call.

Can you imagine the horror when the little mite grows up to be a Klingon – Dennis Waterman with a personality disorder and a migraine? For those of you who listen to the wireless, the Klingons are the intergalactic Indians – actually, they're Russians, but more of that later. Your adult Klingon looks like the unnatural progeny of Frank Bruno, Caliban and a Nissen hut, dressed up for a gay production of *Turandot*. To the uninitiated eye, they're pretty bog-standard aliens – a lot of prosthetics, grunting and elaborate water pistols. But to Trekkies, a Klingon is a thing of beauty and a misery for ever. There are Americans who have devoted their lives to Klingons, inventing a Klingon language, translating the Bible into Klingon. Being a committed Klingon impersonator, of which there are worrying numbers outside sheltered accommodation, makes collecting the tissue wrappers from citrus fruit or making brass rubbings of manhole covers seem reasonable and intellectually stimulating pursuits.

On BBC2's *Star Trek Night*, we were shown one of these acolytes dressing for a Trekkie convention. While attaching his huge and hideous corrugated-rubber headpiece, he let us into a little intergalactic style hint: 'See this, it's a lady's pantyliner. You stick it inside the headpiece, it's the best thing for absorbing sweat.' Now, there are times when, however boldly one sets out, there are places

I cannot go in a family Sabbath newspaper. I can take you to the edge of the joke, but you have to make it to the punch-line on your own. I'll meet you at the other side. Ready? Okay. What do you call a man with a sanitary towel on his head? ... And that, pilgrim, tells you just about everything you need to know about Trekkies.

Star Trek Night was a sad amateur shambles that fitted in perfectly with its subject. There was a dull quiz for Trekkies, where the prize should have been a life instead of two tickets for more *Star Trek*. There was a quick shufti around the science of *Star Trek*. Could it work? No. The real science was fascinating, but kept being annoyingly interrupted by B-picture special effects. And there was a history of *Star Trek* and the cultural importance of *Star Trek* that warp-factored belief. 'The gullibility shields are breaking up, Captain!' There were serious men who actually said to a camera that this programme was symbolic of the civil rights movement and that Captain Kirk was a dead ringer for President Kennedy. Oh really? And *Steptoe and Son* were thinly disguised impersonations of Harold Macmillan and Bob Boothby. Whoopi Goldberg came on and said what a life-enhancing social colossus Uhura had been, because she was the first black actress on television who wasn't a servant, when of course she was just a telephonist with a finger in her ear: 'Connecting you now, Captain.'

You don't need a doctorate in astrophysics to understand that science fiction is not about the future at all – it's about the present. It's basic humanities, current affairs and political philosophy for simpletons and misfits who can't cope with a complex and messy real-time world. Science fiction lends itself to conspiracy theorists and people who, if they can't see things in terms of black and white and good and evil, can't see anything at all.

Star Trek – and science fiction in general – was the cadet branch of the Green Party and all those henge-hugging Body Shop activists. It wasn't a cleverly camouflaged treatise on 1960s liberalism and human rights, it was the last spurt of the 1950s cop-and-saucer genre. It was about an insular protectionist society fighting a cold war against commie Klingons, a society that was alternately frightened of and patronising to foreigners, who saw it as their duty and hubristic right to inflict small-town Eisenhowerism on whomever they came in contact with.

Star Trek, like all sci-fi, was at its core conservative, dogmatic, reactionary and fundamentally philosophically terrified of new ideas, change and the future.

Cold Lazarus (BBC1): No hoary ancient futuristic cliché was left unsucked. Clothes in the future will be floaty nighties. Jewellery will be life-threatening. All cars will travel at a wobbly 5mph. The police will be blinkered with unlikely helmets. Chairs will move like Stannah stairlifts. All tables will have buttons that make things slide and pop, like the 1964 Ideal Homes Exhibition. The one thing we can all be absolutely certain about in the small-screen future, is that every rule of taste design and style will have been somehow forgotten. Nothing is ergonomically efficient: form never follows function. Potter's vision of the future is a stripped-down ersatz version of his gritty present. A joyless, bad-tempered, argumentative, self-abusing, ugly, dour place ...

Buffy the Vampire Slayer

On the face of it, *Buffy the Vampire Slayer* (BBC2) is the ponytail and mini-kilt version of *The X Files*, mercifully with its tongue and fangs firmly in its cheek. The rhythms of American high-school slang are as moreish and attractive as Damon Runyon's Broadway *Guys and Dolls*. She is also reminiscent of *The Addams Family*, one of my all-time favourite comedies. The problem, my problem, lies with the gothic Victorian origins of the vampire genre. Dracula and his clan are all metaphors for sex, specifically virginal girls' yearnings and their consequent sense of guilt. All the things that Rentokil's bloodsuckers are associated with: moral probity, crosses, holy water, the light of day and simple wooden stakes echoing the holy rood. Also, vampires have no reflections: being able to look yourself in the face is a sign of purity and innocence. And, of course, if you're bitten you don't die, you become one of them. Being unable to die is the final punishment, being excluded from

God's heaven. Vampires are high-cholesterol symbolism, and a high school should be a perfect modern environment for the old myth to rise again.

But Buffy gets coy about the true gothic sensuality and darkness that is the implicit nature of bloodsucking. What we are given is a Michael Jackson video cut with *Ferris Bueller's Day Off*, with added garlic. This is Pacific Rim Bram Stoker. It's Dracula written by Charlotte Brontë. It's plasma lite. Crosses are just another bit of Friday-night jewellery, holy water comes still or carbonated, stakes are broken furniture and sex is a hygiene problem. That said, Buffy and the rest of the cast are remorselessly easy on the eye. This is a high school where even the plain girls look like models for Victoria's Secret. And they're all remorselessly Anglo-white. If I were writing a communications studies thesis on Buffy (please don't try this at home), I might go so far as to say the allegory of vampirism has been subtly shifted from sex to outsiders. The monsters have the look of the underclass, the leather-jacketed, dangerous drifting denizens of street corners and recreation areas, the gangs of lost youth that prey on middle-class America.

Buffy's school is an embattled fortress of learning and the old Eisenhower American way of life, full of beautiful, clean, rich middle-American kids. It doesn't take a huge stretch of the imagination to see that this is how a lot of Americans view their current predicament, and there's no doubt where the real power lies. Pre-wedlock humping isn't the fate worse than death that keeps American mothers awake worrying about their daughters. It's crack and gun control and the waves of ethnic Visigoths that are taking over the heart of American cities, sucking the blood right out of the nation. And it's no great stretch of the imagination to set Buffy in the long line of separatist white xenophobia that is a continuing riff in American films and television. In fact, she has a lot more in common with John Wayne than she does with Peter Cushing. And she looks better than both in a miniskirt. If I were composing a redbrick seminar, I could say all that. But I'm not, so I won't.

Xena, Warrior Princess

Here's your thought for the day: I want you, as the blessed Loyd might say, to concentrate, cogitate and deconstruct: 'I believe that fate is an excuse for men with no destiny.' Look, to get the Nietzschean benefit of the thing, you really need to be dressed in a plastic breastplate with a lot of knobbles, a shortie Greek military kilt and a wig with a headband. It was said – no, it was emoted – with deadly seriousness by a chap in *Xena: Warrior Princess* (C5), a line of perfectly circular, basso profundo meaninglessness. It had no peer this week. It may be one of the greatest pieces of verbal gonads ever spoken – sorry, emoted. In fact, it could have been written by Peter Mandelson.

The whole of *Xena: Warrior Princess* might be Peter Mandelson does J. R. R. Tolkien. She's really getting into her stride, and what a stride. I can't recommend her too highly: really, I insist, run, don't walk. On the face of it, Xena is simply the modern distaff version of *The Lone Ranger* or *Batman*, with a dollop of *Highlander*. She's a Greekish brigand turned freedom fighter who stalks an imaginary land loosely based on pre-Homeric Ionia but much more like modern New Zealand, which by chance is where it's actually filmed. Xena is a vast, black-haired, flat-faced creature who in another life will probably become the lacrosse mistress at Cheltenham Ladies' College. She has a sidekick, a frontkick and a backkick, but the sidekick is a pert blonde whose job is to romantically and annoyingly get the team into trouble and, like most sidekicks, sorely deserves a jolly good kicking.

Both Xena (Lucy Lawless) and the blonde and, in fact, every other woman on the show, have huge bosoms. Xena's, of course, are the hugest, the ninth and tenth wonders of the ancient world. If you ever wondered what happened to the lost continent of Atlantis, it's straining to emerge from her corsetry. Xena's bosoms should have their own credits, they should have stunt doubles, hell, they should have their own Winnebagos. They already have their own fan club. Xena's bosoms are important not just because they are so evidently ipso facto important, but because they are the only things that differentiate her from the men. Mammaries good, man bad. In every other respect, Xena is a bloke, probably two or three blokes squidged together.

Actually, there is one other thing that indicates her sisterhood: her preferred weapon. Whereas all the men carry swords, spears, maces, clubs, etc., Xena, while proficient with the phallic masculine armoury, has her own unique device: a flan dish, a hollow metal Frisbee she flings to garrotte, disembowel, sever and emasculate. It hangs in front of her very short skirt. Now, you don't need to have a Ph.D. in psychology or to have undergone a course of Freudian analysis to understand the screaming symbolism of Xena's metal O, placed where real men just have a satay of useless gristle. It comes as no surprise that Xena, with her man-killing yonic emblem and blonde sidekick, is a huge lesbian cult in America. Or that a whole generation of Yankee boys is growing up to appalling dysfunctional sex lives and is more than likely to faint dead away whenever they come across a Dutch cap.

In terms of plot, drama, acting, tension and thrills, Xena is an utter dead loss, but then that's not the point. In demeanour and character, with her permanent scowl and blood-stained Frisbee, the overwhelming sense of Xena is of a woman afflicted with terminal PMT. She is a saga and epic lay of PMT. At the end of every programme, she steals away over the groaning bodies of men who have done no more than look at her bosoms the wrong way, on her trusty nag of a menstrual cycle. Every woman's fate, but also her destiny. Xena is camp. It's a knowing send-up of the superhero, *Dungeons & Dragons* genre, made so that trendy grown-ups can look over the heads of their children, who are the supposed audience, and wink knowingly. Camp is the most commonly overused characteristic of television at the moment. Camp is gay kitsch. Kitsch is a plastic model of the Pope set in fairy lights on a scallop shell. Camp is wearing it on your head and singing 'My Heart Belongs to Daddy'. Kitsch is a Germanic word that has overtones of political, sexual and religious deviance. But camp is just a chorus line of boys in high heels.

Camp works on television because it has no hard centre, no point.

It makes no demands. For the people who work in television it is a godsend, because it's so knowing. 'We know this is a pile of junk, rootless, forgettable, stuffed full of intellectual E-numbers, but we're doing it in a way that absolves us from responsibility.' Camp is irony for beginners. Camp is perfect for a medium whose makers intrinsically despise their audience. It's also perfect for people – and this includes 90 per cent of those who work in television – who culturally punch well above their intellectual weight. You don't really have to know or have read, seen or visited, or understood anything at all. You want classical Greece? Don't bother with Herodotus or Homer. If you've copped Ray Harryhausen's *Jason and the Argonauts* and Sophia Loren in a shift, then you are a camp expert. And what's more, you don't even have to be gay. Although camp grew out of the gay world's understandable desire to subvert straight culture and make it ridiculous, it's now been absorbed into that culture and belongs to anyone who wants to be thought clever but can't be bothered with the homework.

Golden Rose of Montreux

The Golden Rose of Montreux sounds as if it ought to be something from an Arthurian legend. 'And so it was that Sir Enfield, apparelled and caparisoned in the fairy armour of mummery, and having stood vigil at the Chapel of St Birt, did set out on his holy quest. From a high casement the Lady Yentob watched in silence and wove her schedules in patterns marvellous to behold. He would return with the marvellous Rose of Montreux to strew in her golden locks, or he would not return at all.'

What is the Golden Rose of Montreux? Has anyone ever seen one? And who gives them out? For as long as I can remember, British television has always won all of Montreux's roses. They say it's an award for international television, but I think we are the only ones they give it to, which must be galling for the director of light entertainment at Andorran public broadcasting. 'This year I think we've cracked it, we're in with a chance: Jurgen the Nitwit. He's big, he's fat, he's got a droopy moustache. A variety show with a difference from a scenic strudel bar, folk dancers in local costume. Paco the soul of Andorra, a great singer-songwriter hot from the Intercontinental Hotel's Glühwein Lounge, a few laughs, a few songs and a ventriloquist with a yellow goat. We've got it all. And Jurgen's catch-phrase: "Andorra? I can't get enough of her." We're a sure thing.' And then Harry Enfield goes and wins again.

There can be few purgatories worse than being a judge for the Montreux Television Festival. How many Class A drugs would you need to sit in a dark, airless viewing theatre with Judith Chalmers's simultaneous translation coming through the headphones? 'There was this Fleming, this Walloon and this Munsterlander on the Eurostar ...' for hours and hours? We occasionally catch glimpses of the boundless ghastliness of home-grown European television on holiday through the concierge's door and above the sticky zinc football bar. Being force-fed Danish documentaries on whale-blubber co-operatives, Irish junior tambourine contests and Portuguese investigations into organised salt-cod racketeering is more than the human brain can encompass. The horror, the horror. You want to know how bad it can get? One year Hale and Pace won, that's how bad. What I want to know is: what came last that year? If Hale and Pace are the crème de la crème, what could be the dregs?

Actually, the overall winner this year, winner of the Golden Rose itself, was a Canadian offering (that is how bad it can get). It was shown on BBC2: Yo-Yo Ma playing Bach to Torville and Dean. I'm not making this up. I've seen it. To say it was the worst arts thing on BBC2 in the past year would be unfair to the sterling depths plumbed by the Learning Zone, but by golly it was close.

Playing Bach to Torville and Dean is second cousin to reading Shakespeare to guppies. Ma said he has always been interested in crossing his art (cello plucking) with other forms to produce some mongrel hybrid. Now, there's a world of possibility here. Lieder sung to origami, operatic monumental masonry, mimed narrative verse. Expect it all at Montreux next year.

Cathy Come Home

Cathy Come Home is television's *Battleship Potemkin*, a pioneering classic that most people who are interested in the medium refer to in reverent tones, but few have actually seen. For the vast majority of you who aren't particularly interested in the medium, never speak in reverent tones about anything, but do watch a lot of the box, *Cathy Come Home* was the story of a young, poor mother who became homeless and lost her children because of a heartless and bureaucratic welfare system.

It caused an enormous fuss at the time, the 1960s. Directly as a result, the charity Shelter was set up and the law and the social services were changed. It was, as they say in the histories, a defining moment in the golden age of television.

I did see it, and I remember the shock of my mother crying, and the awful feeling of boiling injustice and fury as Cathy's children were taken away on a station platform. The anger and shock were due to a combination of things. First and foremost, it was brilliantly and sparsely written, and convincingly and powerfully acted. But then, so was a lot of television. The unique thing about *Cathy* was that it was conceived as a documentary and used the conventions of news footage: it was a sort of telly vérité, and the audience were quite unprepared for it.

I'm a bit cynical about golden ages – I think they glimmer in the retrospective cups of old men who reckon they don't get enough respect. But in the late 1960s a number of quite prosaic things came together to make television particularly powerful. There were enough televisions and little enough choice; a single programme could affect the whole country. And there was still an aura of conservative rectitude about broadcasting. We believed what we were told and trusted the people who told us. The audience were

still naïve about the way things were presented, the visual language
of television. Documentaries looked this way, drama that way. A
number of committed directors mixed them up, used the gram-
mar of fact alongside the vernacular of fiction, and hit the nation
between the eyes. It was exciting.

But the school of telly vérité was short-lived. You can't go on
producing the same trick and expect the same reaction. Drama
shot as newsreel has become the Handicam of *ER* and American
police shows. The audience now is media literate, even media cynical, and television is wary of a political fight. It compartmentalises
its output and labels all its programmes – this is a comedy, that's
a documentary – so there's no misunderstanding, no accusation of
bias or hidden agendas.

This makes for rather anodyne and bland programmes. Overall,
television has few beliefs. It cares, of course: it just doesn't have an
opinion. This political blandness is both its blessing and its curse.
The best television is opinionated, is angry, does want to change
things, and surely we're all grown up enough to be able to take on
board a little bias.

The reason the Tristrams sit so firmly on any passing fence is
historical, as was shown in the first of the documentaries, *Auntie:
The Inside Story of the BBC* (BBCI). This is a dullish, worthwhile,
long-winded programme, but it shows that in the early days, the
BBC came close to being taken over by government as an arm of
propaganda. Churchill, in particular, was mad keen to nationalise
the wireless during the General Strike, and he mistrusted the
BBC throughout the war. To protect its virtue, Auntie crossed
her legs and essentially did the job for him. It became the voice
of the Establishment. Ever since, the BBC has been scrupulous in
not rubbing vested interests' noses in their own mess without first
labelling it *Newsnight* or *Panorama* or *Question Time*. The commercial channels took their cue from Auntie. Every other medium has
a view, goes on crusades, takes sides. We know our newspapers,
magazines, theatres and cinemas are biased – in fact, we demand
it. Only television and the royal family think they are above politics
and hold opinions only on charities.

This documentary itself was a case in point. Scrupulously fairly, the BBC asked an outside production house to make it – transparent even-handedness. Actually, I'd rather have seen a committed bit of trumpet-blowing from the Corporation. The eternal guard against propaganda is not fair-play on-the-other-handism, it's choice. Today we have a huge amount of choice and we're going to get more. It is about time television took a view, nailed some colours to the mast, got angry again, left home.

FACTS

Batman TV

Powerful stuff, television – the most panoramic omnipresent medium of communication since Protestants got hold of printing. When it really got going in this country, in the early 1950s, the size and the scope of the spirits that had been let out of Pandora's box into the nation's living rooms came as a shock. The papers were full of thoughtful, clear-eyed, visionary pieces on the consequences, written by H. G. Wells types. Now soothsaying is a pessimistic art, so the predictions were universally dire. The really serious concern was for the teeth of the nation. (I'm not making this up.) The infant ration-white gnashers would be irredeemably skewed. A doctor wrote: youngsters habitually watch television lying on the floor with their chins resting on their hands (diagram). Prolonged pressure on the jaw would either drive the teeth back into the head or propel them at an oblique angle through the lips. Imagine the deleterious long-term consequences: who would take Albion seriously if it lisped and spluttered through bucked gobs? The Empire would collapse in derision.

Other serious double-breasted Mystic Megs at the time were making the easier prediction by describing what television ought to do. They came up with the famous and oft-bandied rubric: 'to educate, inform and entertain'. This, as it happens, is generally what television does; but it missed the fourth job TV chose for itself. The words carved in stone should have read: 'To educate, inform, and entertain and be Batman'. An awful lot of television is being a caped crusader, righting wrongs with a swift edit and a hidden camera, bypassing due process to fit into a twenty-four-minute slot, being policeman and hangman with a heart-warming wheelchair finale. It's the hard nut, soft centre that I find the most disgusting and unpalatable, be it Roger Cook puffing after men who graze on the remedially gullible, or *Rough Justice* with a Dave Spart bar-room lawyer second-guessing juries.

Batman television has done more than anything else to inspire a general sense of fear and mistrust and endemic injustice in the country. It has made mothers terrified for their children and suspicious of their husbands, old people fearful of everything, and social workers, teachers and doctors terrified to do their jobs. It nightly finds new things to beware of – the eyes of teddies, the handles of kettles, Boys' Brigade organisers and plumbers. It also implies, no, it shouts, that the law is an ass, that all civil servants are blind and stupid, that policemen are slovenly and dim, that courts are irrelevant. Only Batman television stands between the four horsemen of the apocalypse, timeshare salesmen, door-to-door insurance brokers, Pekinese abusers, Third World dodgy-doll dealers and your sofa. People involved in arguments with shop assistants no longer threaten to call the police, they call the ultimate enforcer: Esther Rantzen, Arnie in a frock, high priestess of Batman television. I put my head out of the window and shouted for Esther to appear in this column and answer some questions, but (pause; little crooked smile) she didn't have the courtesy to return my call.

Of all the studio-bound Solomons – Killjoy, Feltz, the Oprah wannabes – I find Esther hair and shoulders the most cynically, smugly, self-aggrandisingly unpleasant. Here are the facts (clasp clipboard, look at back projection screen). According to *Who's Who*, Rantzen is not a doctor, a lawyer, an engineer or a British Telecom operative, so she has absolutely no qualifications to be Batman, and definitely no diploma from Gotham City University to say she's a righter of wrongs. She is just a bird with an autocue who became famous for wearing Bar Mitzvah frocks and putting the *News of the World* on the small screen. That's life. Or, at least, life as Rantzen understands it.

Out of that grew *The Rantzen Report* (BBC1), where Esther wields the clipboard of justice on behalf of the downtrodden and vulnerable. Last week, she was taking up the cudgel for mentally-ill children in care. She has no mandate to do this. Then, like Hyacinth Bucket with a bee in her bonnet, she goes and publicly vilifies the healthcare workers she deems culpable. 'Name names,' she purrs at distressed studio interviewees with repellent relish. A name is broadcast, a photograph screened. A life is rubbished without appeal. Wide-eyed Esther hides behind the self-serving cloak of popular justice: 'They can always come and put their side of the argument.' But can they? Can a doctor or social worker unpractised in, and intimidated by, television defend his life's work in a two-minute biased interview with the chiffon crusader choosing the evidence and backed by a baying studio of the bitter and twisted? To me this smacks of television on behalf of Esther, a fundamental abuse of the power and the audience to use the camera as therapy.

It was without a trace of irony that Rantzen crusaded against bullies with the *Big Brother*, shop-your-mates-and-parents helpline. Batman television is the single biggest bully on the planet. It picks on the small and the weak, the stupid and the unlucky and the expedient, and it squashes them against the screen. The caped crusaders don't go after the Maxwells of this world; they go for sad dole cheats, shoddy electricians and lazy garages. The most galling aspect of all this is that you and I, the silent, unasked, unsolicited audience, give these backbenchers, late-night chat-show hosts, failed hacks and jumped-up studio managers their super powers. Without the might of millions of small screens, they're just a sad bunch of talentless continuity announcers. Rantzen should have a picture of Germaine Greer tattooed on her forehead so that every time she sees herself on a monitor she's reminded that you can be a committed, enthusiastic crusader on behalf of the downtrodden and still be intelligent, informative and entertaining.

It's just come to me. Television ruining teeth? It's her, isn't it? Esther. The soothsayers got it the wrong way round. It's teeth ruining television. Ah well, as Cassandra used to say, this vision thing isn't all that it looks.

Sport

Sportsmen

There's a Harold Nicolson story I dimly and inaccurately remember. Nicolson meets a chap with whom he was at school. A gilded youth, captain of the XV, XI, VIII, IV – probably the whole lottery card – firm of wind and limb, square of jaw. This Athenian paragon would exhort the runtish Nicolson to strive for the simple imperial virtues of fair play, teamwork, self-sacrifice and Christian exhaustion. Now, twenty years on, Adonis has become a down-at-heel lonely bore, travelling in ladies' underwear, who clasps Nicolson with a needy urgency, romancing over under-fifteen inter-house semi-finals and deathless hushes in forgotten closes, pulling out faded cuttings of match reports and litanising team-mates.

Although, as I say, I don't remember much of the story, the moral and Nicolson's steely, embarrassed disdain have the clarity of absolute truth. You should, he said, feel nothing but pity for the schoolboy hero, laurelled and harlequined in the colours of physical excellence. For his life has peaked before he's barely stepped on to the field. Everything for ever after will be anticlimax and a slow descent into disappointment and comparative failure.

As someone who had all the natural grace, ball control and co-ordination of a supermarket trolley, I draw great pleasure and comfort from all this. I will with a lofty sneer do almost anything to avoid sport on television; but I wouldn't miss *Sports Personality of the Year* for the world. Here the sneer grows into a grin and then a guffaw. It's the audience, you see. The collected jowly, puce-faced, vigorously shorn has-beens, the gala-event, round-of-applause anecdotalists who so warm the cockles of my sedentary heart. There is nothing so risible as set-aside sportsmen, their beefy hands clasping Sta-Prest knees, as they mumble pat-on-the-back bonhomie through crumpled septums for everyone and anyone.

All that old animosity, the desire to grind the other fellow into the dust, emulsifies into a sweet yoghurt of mutual admiration.

They all have the same microbic vocabulary of excellence, like politicians trying to find the correct phrase for a disaster. But their achievements now wiped from the record books by younger mono-syllabic muscle, the one-time heroes will turn up in any room with a plate of crisps and a microphone to polish again that moment when the ball did what balls do or the chin did what chins do. Wistfully, they mention that the game has changed. They only got paid three-and-fourpence, but the giants were more gigantic, not of course to detract from the brilliant lads of today. In every eye (except Jackie Stewart's, who doesn't have one – hence the execrable cap and windcheater), you catch the glint of jealousy and rage and more: of anger at business finished too soon. The actual moment of glory, the validation of their whole lives, was so fleeting, often just the stutter of a shutter, the ball in a hole, pocket, net, the raised cup, the tear; over so quickly that it can only be experienced in retrospect, an endless looped tape, your life stalled on permanent replay, turned into a thirty-second story that becomes as familiar and banal as a door key.

Every year, the *Sports Personality of the Year* is the one British sporting event that doesn't disappoint. It reiterates the great truth that all physical triumph is really a cruel practical joke on the road to failure. This being the *Sports Personality of the Century* (BBC1) they had to make it something special. And didn't they just. It was no surprise that Muhammad Ali won. We knew Jesse Owens wouldn't. He couldn't turn up to collect the prize. It had to be Ali's, because despite being hated, cursed and reviled as an 'uppity negro', a pinko, Muslim, unpatriotic loudmouth in his active years, Ali would elicit the greatest outpouring of toe-curling sentimental-ity, which when all is said and done is the most truly profound pleasure for the sportsman. Nowhere else in a zipped-up life can the adult male feel such unchecked, infantile, thumb-sucking emo-tion as during the great-moments-set-to-arias montage.

But the bathos turned to pitiful, mewing embarrassment. Not even through the rosy, uncritical, Kleenex-clogged eyes of television

sport could Ali be seen as anything other than a monumental disaster of a man. Some say it's Parkinson's disease and unrelated to
boxing. I don't believe that. Shambles like a drugged bear, shakes
like a leaf. The reiteration of his brilliance and the old footage only
underlined how truly, awesomely pathetic he is, sitting speechless
and confused, punched into a twitching simplicity, surrounded
by boxers all talking about what an inspiration he was, for all the
world as if the award were posthumous.

Ali was the best worst advertisement for sports and sportsmen.
Please, whose role model is he supposed to be? Who could say
to children: eat up your greens, or you won't grow up to be like
Muhammad Ali? The director live in his box lost his nerve and
produced a memorably shambolic confusion of pictures. It was as
if the camera wanted to get out of the room and away from this
desperate mocking of a sick man. Personally, I was stunned. I was
amazed, Brian, gobsmacked and speechless. So this, then, is the great
symbol of physical achievement in the twentieth century. No theatre
of the absurd could have come up with a blacker or bleaker
irony.

The rest of it paled beside it. The compilation best-of-the-century
clips were pretty dreadful, no top ten goals or putts, etc. Now the
BBC has hardly any sport of its own to show – it's presumably too
expensive to buy, say, motor-racing film from Bernie Ecclestone
or the Labour Party or whoever owns it – it all looked very thin
and half-hearted. What shone through was that Britain's sporting
decline has been a swan dive over the past century, and that at least
is a hopeful sign. When we can finally boast that we no longer
qualify for anything and that we're beaten at quoits by small Pacific
atolls and that we've reverted to calling sport by its proper name
– games – only then can we claim to be the most civilised and
sensible modern country in the world. Encouraging youngsters to
punch each other's heads, chase balls or run in circles for money
is really qualitatively and socially no different from urchins diving for coins. The fact that you think you're an altogether more
sophisticated and knowledgeable manner of fan changes nothing.
It just says a lot about you and delusions.

Finally, in the audience of flabby has-beens were Alan Yentob and Greg Dyke. What on earth were they doing there? Handing out oranges, perhaps? Between them sat a small boy – I hope the evening was a salutary warning for him to swap his season ticket for a library card. With luck he'd have seen enough of sportsmen and television executives not to touch either with a vaulting pole. I hope the poor lad's name wasn't Tristram. Come and be a journalist, son, it's a man's life and there's all the balls you could wish for.

Tennis

As I write this, the television is on behind me. This is what I can hear: 'Eurgh, plop, ahh, plop, eurgh, plop, ahh, plop.' If you didn't know, you might imagine it was Rolf Harris having sex with a Teletubby, but of course it isn't, unfortunately. It's the sound of a British summer. Like church bells and pigeons cooing and Judith Chalmers's thighs rubbing together, it's one of those ambient emotion-tuggers that brings a tear to an expatriate's eye and makes him think of home. It is, of course, the sound of a lot of foreigners onomatopoeically bashing balls. It's Wimbledon.

Just as tennis was probably the worst thing ever to happen to the English garden, so *Wimbledon* is possibly the worst thing ever to happen to British television. It is irredeemably, titanically, stratospherically boring. I'm sorry, I know you love it, but you're wrong. Trust me, I know about these things.

On the face of it, I grant you, tennis is seductive. It's a sport that might have been invented for television. The green bit fits into the screen nicely: you can see everything from one camera. The rules are simple enough to follow, the scoring is episodic and can be done on the fingers of one hand. There are only two contestants to remember. But it doesn't have that magic ingredient that makes a sport a game.

A game is a metaphor for love and war and life. Sport is exercise for the sedentary classes. All truly exciting games have one or two things in common: there is the risk or chance of inflicting physical injury (pulling your own hamstring doesn't count: I could do that changing channels), and they have to be about gaining or losing territory. Rugby, football, even polo are all games. Volleyball, tennis, ping-pong, golf and synchronised swimming aren't. (Quite obviously, cricket is neither a sport nor a game – it's a waste of time.) As a rule of thumb, all games worth changing into shorts for were played before the sixteenth century. Everything after that is a diversion for the middle classes, who happen to have been invented at about the same time.

Tennis is indelibly marked with the chintz stain of an insipid bourgeois mating ritual. It reeks of suburban Betjemanesque provincialism, of insecure snobbery and Edwardian Tudorbethan clubs with no blacks and no Jews, of knocking up with Joan Hunter Dunn. Nobody can inquire: 'Anyone for tennis?' without raising a tired titter. It doesn't matter how many Hitler Youth-style Slavs or how many right-on tantrums are thrown at Wimbledon, it's still just a weekend after-lunch flirty amusement where old fat blokes can pretend to be young thin blokes in front of girls. Tennis lacks the angst, the life-or-death commitment of, say, football. Nobody ever had 'Greg Rusedski walks on water' tattooed on their neck. Tennis isn't tears and blood, it's fake tan and Pimm's. And Wimbledon is the grand mosque of provincial probity, with its blazered officials, its uniform children drilled into obsequiousness, its Rotarian linesmen and Women's Institute genuflection to minor royalty – the whole blessed, ghastly little-Elgar-England pomp and peonies nastiness.

Television, of course, plays this up to the hilt: low-brow snobbery and extinct class are two of the most unpleasant things that television, and particularly the BBC, revels in. It's no accident that Auntie has let virtually all sport go to Sky except the Boat Race and Wimbledon (and Test cricket). The commentary is of an abysmal, amateur artlessness, of the sort that's only otherwise heard at the *Horse of the Year Show*. A succession of Peter Bowleses talk one-lump-or-two-balls to wannabe Penelope Keiths. All television sports commentary is, in a large part, stating the obvious, telling you what you've just seen. But tennis commentary reaches a nadir of asininity. The ball goes over the net, into the net, into the court or out of the court – what is there to say? Commentators are reduced to junior-sports-day sycophancy of the 'nice shot, well played' type.

I've just spent a day watching Wimbledon, trying to see what it is you all see, to understand what's so damned engrossing. The Peter Bowles man has shown me an unremarkable church steeple four times and told me what a wonderful church steeple it is. I've been shown a lot of tennis players' mums and/or Cliff Richard. Discussing the prospect of rain, Peter Bowles said: 'I wonder if Sir Cliff will be called on to entertain the crowd again this year. I sincerely hope not.' It was the only inadvertent piece of humour all day. What I have realised is that the repeated 'eurgh, plop, ahh, plop' has a sort of soporific fascination. There's a childish comfort in the moronic back and forth of it, and it becomes difficult to look away. I reckon after Wimbledon fortnight, a large proportion of the viewing audience must be showing signs of obsessive repetitive behaviour syndrome: that rocking psychotic bears do in zoos.

Des Lynam comes to every programme as if it might be his last, with his trademark insouciance. Many think this is a laid-back quizzical wit, while others assert that it's brain damage. Personally I've always assumed that he's listening to Classic FM through his earpiece and not really paying attention.

Winter Olympics

We happy few. In years to come we will be able with querulous voices to say: 'Yes, I was there!' And, with a rheumy eye and tremulous hand, raise high the bumper to toast the moment when, in a small way, the world as we know it changed for ever. Last Monday night will live as a milestone, akin to Nobby Stiles sans teeth lofting the World Cup in 1966. It'll be cousin to Garry Sobers skying the sixth consecutive boundary against Glamorgan, and half-brother of my own double-three that avoided Park Lane and won the family Monopoly challenge on that heady Boxing Day in

1972. The British women's curling team crowned their heads with laurel and mashed the Nips 7–5.

Curling has waited a demimillennium for this moment, and our braw Scots girls grasped it. I have no doubt that curling is going to be huge, vast, gigantic. Its first outing as an Olympic sport shows that it's a natural for television. The terrestrial box has been casting around for a new game to take the place of all that tired kicking, hitting, chucking and grunting that's been put offside by Sky. Curling is it. For those of you who haven't seen it yet, what a treat is in store, a sport for the millennium. Competitive housework in slow motion. Teams have to vigorously brush a kitchen floor half the size of a football pitch after a symbolic stone pot has been dropped; the pot has to end up in an RAF roundel called Home, having got across something called the hogline. The cleaning ladies shout 'Dirty hog' at the butterfingers and then sweep like billy-oh until everything's spotless at Home.

The overall effect is difficult to conjure, but it's a bit like those old advertisements where a cackling Scots daily scrubbed the lino 'in a Flash'. This is indeed a sport that every couch potato can identify with. The stroke of genius is playing it in slow motion. Slo-mo replays are a feature of all sports coverage: something happens, you can't follow it, so they have to show it again slowly, which breaks up the flow, which means you have to see everything twice. It's simply inspired to have a whole game that takes place at a snail's pace. I predict that, in no time, small boys will be pestering their parents for brooms, parks and pedestrian walkways will be spotless with practice, members of the Prodigy and Patsy Kensit will marry curlers, and large-chested naked women will streak on their tummies down curling pitches, very slowly. There will be slow-motion crowd violence and community dirge-singing. I can't wait. But I'll have to.

Which is not something I can say with my hand on my heart about the rest of the Winter Olympics. Has there ever, ever been a more tedious, boring, uncomfortable and soporific medium for doing anything in than snow? Where to start? Well, there's the ghastly clothes. You can always tell the intrinsic worth of a sport by its kit, and how can you take anything seriously that demands dressing up in a livid Babygro? It's like bad-taste fashion week with a 1-in-4 catwalk. 'And here's the Austrian in what is unquestionably this season's nastiest combination of all-in-one action painting.'

And can anyone explain why they don't have proper races? The only way skiing could possibly be watchable would be if they all started at once, like every other sport. A race that should take a minute takes an hour-and-a-half. Imagine if they did that with the real Olympics – ran the 100 metres one at a time. Actually, I have a theory about this: I think there are only four contestants and they keep going round and back and changing into new vile costumes. I mean, how can you tell who's behind those goggles? You've only got some Desmond's word for it that it's Gerty from Innsbruck and Olga from Minsk. They could both be Susie from Dollis Hill – except, of course, they couldn't, because Susie from Dollis Hill doesn't ever win anything, which is another good reason for not watching. If they had proper skiing games at the Winter Olympics we could get some medals: endurance braying, ski-pole baggage-handling ('Yes, the boy from Guildford's knocked over a family of Punjabis, poked out the eye of an unaccompanied eight-year-old and is going for the Qantas queue slalom'). We'd sweep the board at chalet-girl shagging.

After exhaustive research around the dinner tables of west London, I have finally found someone who has been watching the Winter Olympics for fun, with excitement and anticipation, as opposed to sniggering incredulity. Why? I asked; how? I asked. And the chap looked at me with glittering, faraway eyes and replied: 'Have you any idea of the size of thighs you need to ski over moguls?' I realised this was not in the spirit of clean-limbed competition, this was some weird, deviant deal. I'm not entirely sure what moguls are, but I quite like the idea of thick-loined Austrians with sticks on their feet bouncing over the supine bodies of Aurangzeb and Shah Jahan, in their bejewelled turbans, lying like sleeping policemen.

You may sneer at the mention of west London dinner parties, but they should be the natural home of Winter Olympic enthusiasm.

Everyone out here has fondue and Glühwein in their veins and padded Babygros and boots that look like they were designed by Dr Bovary in their wardrobes. After several nights' watching with growing disbelief, I have a number of questions that need an answer.

To begin with: why isn't gravity given a gold medal for almost everything, since it seems to do all the hard work? Why is there a style judge for the ski jump, which is, to the unpractised eye, simply controlled falling from a ten-storey window? And please, did any of these sports exist before we had nuclear watches that could measure quark time? Furthermore, how come, when sport is the competitive testing of human physical prowess, it's patently clear that with most of these, the human body is ergonomically unsuited to the ridiculous task asked of it? Competitors have to put on ever more absurd and ridiculous hats and limb extensions before lying, standing or being folded in half to remain as still as possible.

But most urgently, I need to know why on earth they don't do these sliding things all together, instead of one at a time. Then, it would be a proper race and take a couple of minutes instead of a few days, and it would be exciting. I'm sorry, I'm going to ask this again, because it seems so obviously a design fault: why don't they have races together, like running races or motor races? If the entire population of Fulham can slide down Switzerland during spring half-term, why can't eight blokes with buttocks like VWs do it in Utah? And, while I'm here, who decided that any activity that demands judges for artistic content could be called a sport and have records? I'm beginning to think a lot of this slow stuff was invented by recreational snowboarders as a huge practical joke to fill in two weeks' schedules, because for every other event, we're breathlessly told the bollard-limbed winner only started doing it a week ago.

So far, my favourite bit has been the perky commentators moaning that we Brits have yet again failed to qualify for some utterly pointless bit of falling over. Is it any surprise? Have you looked at the countries that have scored gold? All have one thing in common. Take a wild slalom of a guess: what do you think it is? It's snow.

We don't win any medals for the same reason that Ethiopia and Cuba don't win any medals: we don't have the meteorology. That and, of course, we're rubbish. Now, if they had a wet-weather Olympics, we'd piss the twenty-yard dash with a Sainsbury's bag on the head.

Snooker

I caught the end of some sort of snooker championship last Sunday. For someone who finds watching sport about as attractive as sitting in an inner-city casualty ward with a prolapsed colon, snooker is the twilight zone of the inexplicable. In fact, it's so far from being any form of human pleasure or purpose I understand that it's strangely compelling. Snooker looks like nothing so much as waiters trying to explain Newtonian physics: 'A tricky shot, this one. Can the lad from Cardiff prove that every action has an opposite and equal reaction?' If all sport is a metaphor or training for some facet of real life, then what on earth is snooker for? To train butlers and steakhouse busboys, perhaps?

This game clunked and clicked to its soporific climax. Climax, of course, is altogether the wrong word. We have to rely on the commentator to tell us when it's finished. 'Oh, and it's all over. The lad from Devizes has won the Ready-Rubbed World Championship.' How would you know? Certainly not by looking at either of the two YTS bellboys who have been playing. Covered in cold sores and snow-capped pimples, they have the surly, glazed look of lads who've been kept behind after school. Both excavated their nostrils with a devil-may-care insouciance, searching for the brown behind the green, perhaps. Presumably they're habituated by a short life spent poking things into holes.

Snooker has a raffish reputation for being the game of worldly ne'er-do-wells. Nothing could be further from the truth. It's a game of sheltered innocence. These young novitiates patently know nothing of the outside world; their lives are devoted to green baize and the endless cycle of reappearing balls, like telling an endless rosary. Snooker players chalk up a life of simple vows: intellectual poverty, chastity and Clearasil. The only people who look up to them are domino players and racing greyhounds. But one day they'll step out into the daylight and realise there is a whole world going on out here, and that there are more holes worth investigating that aren't string pockets or noses.

Robot Wars

Last year, at the Edinburgh Television Festival, I was asked what I thought a new channel should do to attract viewers. How about make good programmes that entertain, inform and educate? Didn't go down at all well. There was a lot of eye-rolling and sighs of 'Oh, how naïve'. The Tristrams wanted specifics, which is trickier. Buying in ready-made crowd-pullers such as *ER* or *Friends* is hideously expensive and the competition fierce. A soap opera, of course, is the holy grail of programming. But soaps take years to grow, and the mortality rate is high. What I finally suggested made the Tristrams' eyes roll in opposing directions: I would devote a sizeable proportion of my income to inventing a new sport. 'Ugh, how idiotic, how absurd, how typically, stupidly Gill.'

Actually, I still think it's a first-class idea, and I offer it to any passing channel gratis. Though in general I loathe sport, I can see that, combined with the box, it's a match made on the Elysian Fields. Sport and TV are after exactly the same things. Sport reduces plot and drama to its constituent parts and delivers them up in an infinite variety of ways that are always different while comfortingly the same. Most of it can be understood by invertebrates with brains the size of peas, but it can also be deconstructed in a way that makes Kierkegaard sound like Aesop. It has numerous collateral advantages. It grows outside its ordained slot with leagues and competitions, it produces heroes and stars and it sells merchandise. Sport is the one programme you can try at home (not so easy with *Pride and Prejudice* or *Panorama*). And if you did invent a new game, it would be under copyright, there'd be none of that hysterical bidding; you could lease the concept to foreign channels and have internationals.

But television has always been content to be a passive fan and pay the ticket price. There is a general belief that games have a Darwinian gestation; that they aren't invented, they just evolve. It's not true, of course: almost all sports are nineteenth-century, and many, such as downhill skiing or basketball, have been invented from scratch very recently. Television nearly got a made-to-measure game with *Gladiators*. But there was a design fault (if only they'd asked me): the competition was three-sided, not directly between contestants but between contestants and professionals, so it never generated the necessary excitement of feeling involved. The box has just produced another made-to-measure game, and it's the most unlikely success on television: *Robot Wars*. The contest is between teams of the most frighteningly dermatologically unstable drip-dry nylon nerds, who build psychopathic sewing machines in their bedrooms and then fight them by remote control.

If you've never seen it, I know this sounds awfully like a bad wind-up computer game. But let me tell you, that's nothing like as titanically ghastly as having to watch it. But it's been a great success. Television has turned the most unlikely pastimes into quasi-games – painting the spare room and gardening. Tristrams should really go for a brand-new sport. Actually, I've just realised that what I'm talking about isn't new at all, it's ... whisper the name with dread ... *It's a Knockout*.

Summer Olympics

No sooner is *Big Brother* over than the BBC starts up with a group of competitive strangers marooned on a distant island doing absurd things for our amusement – the Olympics. The real bane of the Olympics is that they are on late at night. Just as you're turning in, you do a final flick through the channels to see if there are post-watershed breasts or lap-dancing transsexuals, and there's this extraordinary malformed youngster doing something to music that is so unpleasantly uncomfortable you cannot imagine attempting it twice, let alone devoting your most socially and sexually active years to remorselessly practising it.

But once we start watching, we can't stop. It's like the shopping channel. There's a hypnotic rhythm to the Olympics. Before you know it, it's 4.30 a.m. and you have spent half a working day staring at the heats of the 10,000-metre tango, or something equally absurd. This year the real excitement is the kit. Sportswear being probably the biggest consumer business in the world, it comes as no surprise that the Olympics is now a fortnight-long trade fair for the spandex fashion industry.

I was particularly taken by the new swimming kit. Australia's Ian Thorpe looks like nothing so much as a seal. If I were him, I would stay away from Canadian competitors bearing baseball bats. We're told he has size 17 feet. Well, I'm sorry, size 17 feet aren't feet, they're flippers, and they're cheating. What is the point of drug-testing when someone can turn up with Orca extremities and be waved to the podium? Drugs are nothing compared to genetics. Have no doubt: by the end of the century there will be competitors with dorsal fins who train on a diet of plankton. By far and away my favourite push-me-pull-you event was one that involved swimming, cycling and running great distances. Why those three? Why not hurdling, diving and dressage? Or gymnastics, weightlifting and skeet shooting? Anyway, the best thing about all this was that a lot of very butch men did it in bras and panties. I'm not making this up. I'm not even exaggerating. They were wearing the Agent Provocateur sporty honeymoon combo. Presumably this happens because sportsmen don't think about anything else except their ridiculous games. So they end up in this kit, blissfully unaware that the rest of the world thinks they look like clubbing trannies on E.

Try standing back a moment and looking at the Olympics as if you'd never seen or heard of them before. Try to imagine them as one long episode of *The X-Files*. They're pretty weird, pretty bizarre. To begin with, there's the brain-boggling consumption of time, energy and resources. The Olympics is the largest single withdrawal on the world's physical, mental and economic resources, and it produces nothing but two weeks of television, a lot of pulled muscles, a swimming pool of tears, and thousands of medallions that should only be worn by Sicilian disco dancers. Yet I've never heard anyone question whether or not they're a worthwhile, or even moral, expenditure.

Why do we watch it, what is the fascination? I can understand the World Cup: lots of people follow football, know the players, understand the rules. But whoever follows 2,000-metre medley swimming, who has posters of airgun target-shooters in their bedrooms? It isn't the sport we watch, it's the repeated small nursery-rhyme dramas of winning and losing that we plug into; the small adrenal doses of disappointment and excitement, the soft-centre satisfaction of tears and flags and national anthems that sound like *The Phantom of the Opera* played backwards. We see it in terms of jingoistic drama, but the performers don't belong to a country, they belong to a specific sport. They physically grow into their disciplines: their first allegiance is to a pair of spiked shoes or a baton or a bike, not a place.

Still, despite my best efforts and intentions, it gets to me. Blearily I look up and realise it's 3.30 a.m. and I've spent four hours watching small blank-faced Eastern European girls covered in chalk jumping over furniture. If someone said, 'Come to the Albert Hall and watch permanently prepubescent acrobats from Romania', I'd ask how much they were going to pay me. But once every four years, along with the rest of the world, I become riveted by springboard divers and tandem races.

Records come and go, but one has remained unbroken for sixty years. Leni Riefenstahl set the standard for filming the event in 1936. Say what you like about the Nazis, they knew how to throw a decent sports day. An awful lot of how sport is filmed and presented is a homage to Riefenstahl. Sport, by its very nature, is fascist. Forget all that guff about young people coming together in a spirit of healthy, frenzied competitiveness. It's sport that's war by other means. The BBC's opening title sequence captures the sense of all this exceedingly well. It's a bit of Riefenstahl and erotic neoclassicism, cut in with a bit of *Gone with the Wind*, Jesse Owens and Martin Luther King, plus a snippet of car ad and *LA Law*. It's very post-modern and slick, a cultural gumbo of received ideas and images, and it wins the irony medal by a length.

A Game of Two Halves (1)

Which dingbat was it who first called it the beautiful game and what was he on and had he ever seen Venice? 'Yes, I've seen Venice and I still think football's beautiful.' Right, here are Monet's late water lilies and here's Motherwell playing Arbroath. Want to change your mind? 'No, no, the football's still beautiful.'

I caught a moment of some match and heard a commentator say in that preorgasmic voice they manage to keep up for ninety minutes: 'Oh, it's men against boys – no, it's gods against boys!' How can anyone say that sort of thing to an open mike? What shamelessness frees a grown-up from a lifetime's carefully laid-down social embarrassment to allow them to say, 'It's gods against boys'? I prayed there would be a puff of smoke in the commentary box and that Kali, the Hindu goddess of destruction, would appear, six arms flailing, necklace of skulls, blood dripping off her bosoms, and shout: 'You dumb prat. I'm a god; they're a bunch of Brazilian peasants – got it?' 'Here, Brian, did you see that?' 'Aye, big lass that Kali. Great goalkeeper. Of course, Indian gods aren't playing in the final. Mind, they had a useful winger with an elephant's head, deadly in the box, but they were knocked out by Tibetan Buddhists in endless extra time. The bald lads in saffron kept reincarnating.'

Television this week has been entirely about football. Football tournaments are like black holes: even if you don't watch them, you know something's afootie, because everything else is distorted by its gravitational pull. This is when television gives up and gets out its bumper book of stereotypes, and assumes that every human with a penis is holding it with one hand while stabbing the other at the screen shouting, 'Rooney-Rooney!' They also assume that there are some sadly penisless women (whose principal career ambition is to appear on *Big Brother*) who will also be pointing at the screen shouting: 'Beckham-Beckham!' And that the only people not yearning for a surfeit of football are rural spinsters who fancy Leslie Phillips without irony.

In the fallout of a football event, the rest of television puts on women's movies, repeats and documentaries of an unwatchable yet worthy tedium. Football is pretty much critic-proof. The television is simply a means of imparting information for gain. I could point out that football commentary is a string of rushed truisms interrupting an endlessly repeated list of names, like the roll-call at a school for hyperactive children. Then there's the ritual of the pre-, mid- and post-match studio dissection, but there's no point in being snotty about it, sniggering at the clichés or the strangled syntax. It would be like criticising a church service or pantomime for being predictable and corny. It is what it is, a ritual that is precious because it's always the same. The form is comforting. And if you're watching from ten rows back in a pub on a wide screen with the intensity of a night-light, you know you're not missing much if you can't hear anything. The point of football on television is that you're there, and so is everyone else.

A lot of guff is spoken about television as the electric hearth of the nation and what a cohesive thing it was back when Dad's Army hadn't had children yet. Now the audience is a scattered babble, and only for footballing events do we all join together round the glass box and shout 'Rooney-Rooney!' This is a thing that doesn't bear aesthetic examination. It's not football's or television's or the audience's fault, it's an aesthetic problem. The best way to appreciate football on television is to walk down a city street when a big game is on and listen to the synchronised roars coming out of the buildings over the empty pavement. It gives you a very strong sense of alienation, of not being invited, of being alone.

And for a moment, you know what it must be like to be Piers Morgan.

A Game of Two Halves (2)

'Culture is not a democratic process, Brian.' 'Indeed, it's not, Desmond, it's not indeed. But you must concede that a crowd adds something to an occasion, that the audience in a very real way adds a patina of gravitas to performance.' 'Absolutely, Brian, patina was just on the tip of my tongue. The audience has a non-participatory yet strangely proactive role in any cultural event. It is after all, put simplistically, their culture. The performer is merely a focus. It could be said that the performance per se only exists as a conceptualisation of the collective will of the audience, that all culture is validated by the emotion and acceptance, the very commitment of the crowd. Who stand on the touchline of performance, omniscient, omnipresent, essentially godlike ...' 'I'm sorry, Desmond, I'm going to have to cut you off there, you're breaking up.' 'The great sadness for me, Brian, was that Britain didn't have a tenor in the World Cup.'

I yearned for a studio discussion with the lyric tenor John McCormack in a boxy suit and Gap shirt saying: 'I don't know what's the matter with English singing at the moment, Trevor. Maybe we don't have enough competitive oratorios in schools or the lads sing too much during the home season. I fancied Harry Secombe for the qualifying round, but when you see these Latin boys you realise he's not in the same class.' I rather fancied Carreras for the final. Small, fast, lovely turn of phrase, good in the cadenza. The favourite was, of course, Pavarotti. There was some question over his fitness but the boy came good on the night. He may have been past his best, not quite so deft on the top notes, imprecise in his phrasing, but there was still magic there. The old one-two of 'Nessun Dorma' had them in the aisles. It was the stuff of memories. The match itself was pretty predictable, a lot of midfield arias and Italian syrup interspersed with the inevitable Hollywood medley which lacked vowel control. I've always thought 'Moon River' an irritating stupid song, but sung operatically in a second language it becomes bonkers beyond anything. What on earth is a Huckleberry friend? Or Oucleberry frien'?

At half-time the score was still nil, nil, nil, and some Desmond back in the studio said blissfully that it was a concert of two halves. Halfway through the second, Domingo came from nowhere and headed in the winner with Pagliacci. It was pure poetry ... set to music. On the subs bench, Frank Sinatra and Gene Kelly sat rheumy-eyed and confused, apparently advertising Astroturf. How opera and football have got entwined in the world culture is completely beyond me. It's just a joyously mad sandwich – sardines and peanut butter. My favourite bits of the whole month have been the little compilations of dramatic moments cut to music. They were wonderful. You realise all football needs to make it tolerable is good editing, and Puccini.

News

Breaking the News

What's an Alvar Liddell? Quite obviously, a grand tourer with leather straps holding down the bonnet and a flapper in the jump seat. I would be surprised if there were more than a handful of you who actually know who Liddell was. Even I am too young to know. But he had one of the best voices ever to broadcast, a clipped, sharply enunciated delivery, once known as BBC English but now entirely extinct. Liddell was a wartime newsreader, on wireless, of course: he was one of the men who read the messages for resistance fighters in occupied Europe after the tum-tum-te-tum of the morse V-for-Victory sign. 'Uncle Vanya has a sick tomato. Uncle Vanya has a sick tomato. The gander's accordion sleeps in the meadow. The gander's accordion sleeps in the meadow.'

These dadaesque haikus were broadcast with an appropriate solemnity, and still whenever you hear them they send a chill down the spine, make you turn down the sound and check the curtains. These beautiful, dreadful stanzas were the weird high point of the great truth of broadcast news. It was mentioned in a throwaway line of the BBC's new four-part series, *Breaking the News*.

The news, particularly television news, makes news as much as it reports news. In the crassest terms, the presence or promise of a camera incites people to do things. Without television, both the IRA and Band Aid would have no power. But also, in a wider, more insidious sense, the news makes news.

In the forty years since television really got a grip on daily bulletins, it has created an unquenchable thirst in the public for current information. There is no end to the things you want to know and the people you want to know about. The power of television is equally in what it doesn't show you as in what it does. Deciding what is broadcast, and therefore elevated to news is a terrible responsibility. Over the years, the net has spread wider and wider, until on any one night the news seems to be almost capricious, a chance bran-barrel of events and people who a generation ago would have gone by in obscurity. I don't think it is too portentous to say that this has changed the way we look at our own lives. A lot of it for the good, some of it not. But today the likelihood is that in the course of a three-score-and-ten existence, all of you will at some point come up against the bright eye of the camera – and that is the hugest difference between our times and our grandparents'.

News editors have one of the most testing and precarious jobs in broadcasting. They have to make minute-by-minute decisions of real life-and-death importance, not just for the people directly involved, but to the audience and, most importantly, to concepts such as democracy, freedom of speech and morality. They do it against not only the pressure of time and resources, but despite the bullying and pleading of pressure groups and politicians, who all imagine the news would be better if it was slanted in their favour. It is always astonishing how the people who shout loudest about freedom of speech are invariably the ones who are willing to go to the most Machiavellian lengths to get the greatest slice of that freedom to shout it.

It is a style that is born out of our adversarial judicial and parliamentary system. And politicians get their own studio and the lion's share of the time. I would wager that if the customer had a say in the agenda, politics would be relegated to the 'and finally' slot. But the relationship between news editors and politicians can be unhealthily symbiotic. Press officers slide into becoming journalists, journalists pupate into political advisers. Between them they decide what is important. Network news is up for grabs, it belongs to the quick and the dead.

Breaking the News had wonderful news across the board – the stalwarts of the old *Tonight* show, Ed Murrow's wartime reports, that kind of thing. It was the sort of programme that is tailor made to appeal to people who watch television for a living. We could all watch Alasdair Milne talking about internal boardroom politics with our jaws hanging open for hours. But I am not sure how riveting the rest of you find it. I think most viewers are not particularly fascinated by the practice of television. They would rather have the performance.

Deadline (C4), a six-part series of behind-the-scenes looks at *Calendar*, the local Yorkshire news magazine, was parochial in the best sense; by which I mean it was a good look at the sort of news that is of some use to people, local news. Reporters and editors rarely ask what the point of news is. So much international news is simply Peeping Tom *schadenfreude*. Local news is useful and manageable. *Calendar* had a good mix: a missing child, football hooligans, a new cheese and Poison Ivy from the Street. I warmed to the editor who waved a cassette and said: 'I've got a fire for you,' and then added despondently, 'not many flames though.' It was a neat encapsulation of all the problems in television news: plenty of heat, precious little light.

Newsreaders are like giant pandas: there are very few of them, they are picky and bad-tempered, they move very slowly and nobody has seen them mating. Basically, the reason there's so few of them is because they rarely fancy each other. Kirsty Young has been matched with some poor Autocue sap, who looked terrified. I don't hold out much hope. She ignored him and instead talked to a racing driver called Jenson Button. 'You can't do it with a racing driver,' we all shouted at the screen. They're a different species, albeit just as difficult to mate. Newsreaders are always complaining that they're not taken seriously as journalists; that all we, their print cousins, do is look at their legs and hairdos and snigger at their ties. They complain vociferously from the pages of *Hello!* and *OK!*, from the couches of daytime chat shows and in between celebrity guest slots on comedy programmes, quiz shows and lingerie shop openings. I think they mean it.

Television likes a celebrity death. It's a denouement, a plot device, a commercial break. Television can put on its serious face, and newsreaders know they are the voice of history, not just of current affairs. Correspondents can go purple – and they certainly rolled out the papal purple for the passing of the Pope. There was a steep curve in hagiography as the rolling news stations outbid each other to write the application for beatification: he started off as a good man, then a good pope, then a great pope, pope of the century, one of the greatest popes ever and ended up on Fox News as the greatest human being in the history of human beings and an über-pontiff for all mankind. You could almost hear the Hollywood producers saying 'Hey, do you think there's a movie in this Pope guy? See what Bruce Willis's availability is. Maybe Mel will direct.' Television news pretends it deals in facts and vérité, but really its currency and first joy is emotion. It wants death, court cases and weddings.

War (1)

Last Sunday was tough. The time for discussion and prevarication was over; a hard decision had to be made. It was down to me and my conscience: Iraq or the Oscars. I pushed the button. It all went off. 'Live from the Kodak Theatre in Hollywood, we present the 75th Oscar ceremony, joined by a billion people from around the globe.' All of whom had had to make the same tricky choice. Six degrees of separation, they say, is all that parts us from everyone else on the planet. On Sunday, there was barely one degree between the 101st Airborne and the Oscars. For those of us watching in bed to those of us watching under the kitchen table, it was just one click down the remote. Both events were real-time, both live (if they were lucky). The Oscars wore black, the 101st wore camouflage, the Iraqis wore brick dust and I was wearing nothing at all.

Imagine watching the Oscars in Baghdad: 'Oh, I do hope that musical about a pair of murderers who get away with it wins. I could really do with a feelgood movie.' Back in Kuwait City, the nominations were Saddam's palace, a party headquarters, the ministry of information and a barracks. And the winner is ... all of them. I don't mean to blame the Oscars for being irredeemably Oscarish, or to sneer at actors for being actors, it's just that all this was so profoundly, uncomfortably weird. These two events, My Big Fat War and the slimmed-down Oscars, elided into each other.

The rolling war coverage is compulsive; it always is. Veterans of other television wars call me up and say: 'Hey buddy, how are you coping?' I'm fine, I'm embedded in bed, it's four in the morning and those damn sirens keep waking me up, and I've been looking at a picture of green blobs for half an hour and it's beginning to resemble those ink spots Freudians use to ascertain lunacy. The big difference between this war and the last war and the war before that is technology. The whole nature of conflict has changed: much more precise, more clinical. This time, I've got satellite guidance and a smart laser remote and another dozen choices.

When you find yourself watching Abu Dhabi TV first thing in the morning, it really is time to question your war aims. I like to think of the different news channels as a virtual coalition: they vary in style and emphasis, but they're essentially all on the same side. They all want the same thing: they want this war to go on for as long as possible, and to be really exciting. Rolling tragedy is what soap-opera news channels were invented for. This is what they do, and they can barely keep the effervescent joy out of their voices. No madcap paratrooper dreams of glory half as heartily as a young reporter with a video link.

But the fact is, there are so few facts about. Most of what we're offered is television reporters finding ever more baroque ways of telling us they don't know anything. Every titbit of information is passed from mouth to mouth. There are equipment nerds who just want to be next to bangs, and empathists who want to tell you how they feel about how they suppose other people they can't see feel. There are gossip strategists and sound-bite Hemingways. There are the curators of cliché. There is also real courage and sincere journalistic commitment, but there isn't much journalism. Most of these Waugh-like Boots are reduced simply to constructing off-the-cuff picture captions for shots of something that may happen in a minute or did happen an hour ago. It's like a very expensive version of *Badger Watch*.

All the news is narcissistically self-referential and the dressing up in bits of military kit has grown ridiculous. Nobody comes out of this well, and that includes us, the conscript audience. Why are we watching? Do we really want to know, or are we just slack-jawed, fascinated, by the outward-bound Oscars?

War (2)

In these gloomy times, we must snatch what shards of mirth are offered and be thankful. A couple of weeks ago, when I thought the Western world might never laugh again, I came across a joyous sight: John Simpson in drag. Why the sight of John Simpson in drag should be so windingly funny when, say, the sight of Lily Savage isn't is one of Dame Humour's small mysteries. Our man/woman Simpson bravely donned the Afghan burka to be smuggled across the Pakistani border. The report he filed was laden with an absence of news: 'Behind me, you can see an Afghan village that seems to be deserted, in these hills perfect for guerrilla fighting,' etc., etc. You know the sort of thing. The image that stuck was of a six-foot-plus serious Englishman imitating a female tent in pursuit of not very much news.

It's not that Simpson is innately pompous, it's that, over the years, he's attracted a sort of ponderous gravitas. He is the pope of news, perambulating around the needy offering the succour of insight and holier-than-thou experience. Simpson makes programmes called things like *Simpson's World*, as if he were disaster's landlord and the huddled masses were merely his tenants. I don't mean to scorn his bravery or diligence, but as so often with bravery and diligence, there is more than a faint whiff of the ridiculous. I watched the report, and it struck me that we could have been in the Cairngorms. And then I thought how do I know it's Simpson under the duvet? Perhaps it's John Cleese, or indeed a very tall Afghan lady with a Rolex?

This brings me to a point I want to make about the news we've been seeing, and all the stuff we will undoubtedly see over the next few months. How can we tell that it's what it says it is? Take, for instance, that film of Palestinians celebrating the terrorist attack. I've been told this footage came via the Israeli military. Of course, it may not have done. This itself may be disinformation. And that much-repeated Taliban training film of masked men firing guns: how do we know it's what it says it is?

We accept news film on face value because we inherently trust our news-gatherers, and generally they're very reliable. But in the dash for news, and particularly for pictures, when there is pressure to fill vast expanses of time and simultaneously react very fast, there is always the opportunity for misinformation. In the past, news organisations have bought film that has come via some pretty circuitous routes; and at the moment there are a lot of ingenious and shadowy agencies desperately competing to manipulate the news. You must remember that most of the world is still waiting for proof that Osama Bin Laden is responsible for the bombing. We in Britain and America seem to agree that this is already a fact. It was assumed in the West that worldwide satellite news would spread freedom and information; in truth, most of the world, living in countries with highly censored media, believes very little of what it sees from over here, assuming it to be lies and propaganda. In the West, on the other hand, having lived under a free media, we tend to assume that everything we're told is true.

The truth, as always, is probably buried somewhere in the middle. Film is not always self-evident; it isn't always what it says it is. And what would be useful now is for news-gatherers to acknowledge on screen the provenance of their images and, just as importantly, the date when they were shot. Sometimes they do this, mostly they don't. But film can be made by anyone with a video recorder; it's passed from broadcaster to broadcaster in a matter of moments, its origins lost in the electric tangle. We should be more sceptical. The one thing you can have no doubt about is that, at the moment, public opinion is of paramount importance. Living in a free country makes us particularly gullible. We instinctively think free information is synonymous with true information, and that belief has been, is and will be exploited.

Why do all reporters feel the need to imitate Dr Foster and stand up to their waist in the waters of Gloucester? 'As you can see, Tracey, I'm up to my waist.' I've seen umpteen 'casters standing in the deluge, being watched by locals from terra firma. Do they think it is somehow more real? Is it part of the new clean transparent broadcasting policy? Or are they just pillocks in awful Millet's windcheaters?

Dunblane

I'm writing this in a hotel room on the back of a menu. It's scene-of-the-crime reporting. I'm not much of a reporter, so reporters tell me, but I'm witnessing something really very upsetting, very shocking: CNN's rolling news from Dunblane. Another reporter is stopping people in the street and asking them to please, please tell him what they think about the intrusion of the press into the community. They tell him, with weary good manners, and it's back to the studio for reaction to the reaction of the news victims' reaction to the news. This is all done without the slightest, merest ghost of a scintilla of irony. It might be a scene from *Drop the Dead Donkey*, but it isn't funny.

Like most of you, I really only ever catch CNN in hotel rooms. You watch it with that strange, anonymous, slightly vulnerable sense that comes from being away from home in a place with a different language and joke money. CNN is both weird and familiar. We surf through the Boutros Boutros-Ghali indigenous game shows, studio chats and dubbed *Little House on the Prairie*, and come to this bright but dim, shiny but dull creature called Flick or Chip or Biff introducing us to corpses. CNN reminds me of the ferris wheel scene in *The Third Man*. Orson Welles looks down and asks, if one of those dots ceased to exist, would you care? And Joseph Cotten, if he'd been a CNN reporter, would have said: 'No, I wouldn't care but I'd interview his neighbours.' The slaughter of the innocents in Dunblane has had a lot of commentators casting around for something to blame, and a number have picked callous, sensational television. No line-up of possible culprits is complete without television commentators wagging fingers. By the age of twelve, we're told, the average child has seen 12,000 murders, or maybe it's 120,000, and as many rapes and acts of violence: surely, surely the box must shoulder some responsibility. In a neat bit of synchronicity, this week brought news of the V-chip, a gismo that will censor your television and finally allow parents to abrogate all responsibility for their children's education. The continuing bubbling row about the responsibility of culture for the otherwise inexplicable evil in society seems to me always to put the cart before the horse.

Surely the eternal quandary isn't 'Does bad culture make us bad?' but 'Why on earth doesn't good culture make us good?' I'm writing this in a place that begs that question louder than anywhere else on earth, a place where, regularly, one third of the population died of plague, where murder and assassination were endemic and made downtown Harlem look like Moreton-in-Marsh, a place that had so many prostitutes that it arranged them in leagues, a place that gave the world one of the most unpleasant words ever coined: ghetto, a place that was built on exploitation, despotism, greed and war. It is, of course, Venice, arguably the most transcendentally beautiful, cultured and civilised couple of square miles man has ever created. I've just walked round a room that sported vast graphic depictions of a woman nailing her lover's head to the floor with a tent peg, and a whore holding up the severed head of a blameless man who refused to sleep with her, and a man bound and slowly shot to death with arrows. But the most distressing image I've seen all day is a CNN reporter talking to a pensioner outside the church. Explain that in five hundred meaty words.

Civilisation is weird stuff. It isn't simple and it doesn't work with empirical cause-and-effect clarity. Without doubt, it's powerful, but how the power electrifies is a divine mystery beyond explanation or censure. Bad art doesn't infect us, but, far more worryingly, good art doesn't inoculate us. Spitting the accusation of liberal elitism at people who stand against censorship doesn't alter the fact that being brought the head of Michael Grade on a satellite dish or inserting a V-chip isn't going to make anyone any nicer unless, of course, they insert them in our cerebellums. Nothing that should be simple ever is.

What is it with the new left? Why do they all have to look like such Dave Spart caricatures? And why does the right wing always get the best tailoring? Socialism has the best music, the best books, poetry, plays, dancing, slogans, jokes, arguments and sex. The right got architecture and dry-cleaning. Yo, brothers and sisters, let's get a grip: get a decent shirt. It's time to reclaim personal grooming for the people. Take Rod Liddle. Take him and shampoo him. Liddle slouched on to our screens for his first high-profile TV gig this week, *Seven Ways to Topple Saddam* (BBC2). Oooh, as Ben Elton used to say, a bit of satire there. Yes, but only a very itsy-bitsy Liddle bit. The intellectual content was Liddle sneering and dabbing on spots of sarcasm at the end of each item. But, mostly, it was in the way he looked. The university hair he should have grown out of, a shirt hanging out (of course) to cover the grotesque 'I sink pints and watch footie' gut, the general slouch and bolshie grubbiness – the whole experience was a bit like being moaned at by a fat Irish water spaniel.

New Orleans

The coverage of the New Orleans flood has been very strange. It is as if none of the news teams knows how to treat what is in essence a Third World disaster in a First World country. News grows to be a formula in much the same way as all other genres grow to be formulas – it has its reusable and repetitive shorthand. Wars grow to look the same, demonstrations are cut from a loop of video, and natural disasters have their stock shots, their reverential tone and their lexicon of clichés. But the news never really agreed what this story was. Was it the disaster, or was it America having a disaster? Usually, the name of the country is just a tag, because natural bad stuff most often dumps on Third World people whose addresses are only really of importance to themselves.

It turned out that CNN was the most all-at-sea. It likes to think of itself as a stateless, pan-global news purveyor. It doesn't have foreign correspondents because nowhere's foreign to it. But it utterly lost the plot, and any sense of dispassion or distance, over this story. The emotional range of the reporters grew operatic as they tried to outdo each other in mawkish empathy. I watched with surprised disgust as reporters repeatedly broke into manly tears.

The low point was passed on to me by another viewer, who said she had seen CNN follow a woman who had been rescued but whose child had been washed away. They found the child and set up a classic Esther Rantzen-style 'You thought he was dead, but in fact ...' sentiment sting. They waited a few hours so they could get the moment on camera. It was adding a little reality TV to reality. How many seconds of thinking your kid is dead do you reckon is worth a news award? It all got very *Broadcast News*. The tearful reporters, the set-up sympathy. It was a reminder, if we needed any more reminders, that there is no such thing as disinterested news, and that you must always question not just what's in front of the camera, but who's behind it.

GMTV

Now, I must admit that I haven't ever seen *GMTV*. I once saw ten minutes of *The Big Breakfast* and it was quite enough to convince me that television in the morning was like drinking in the morning: only real addicts could possibly do it without throwing up.

First thing in the morning is a delicate, softly lilac time. The day needs to be slipped into gingerly, not screamed at by a childish prat with a clipboard and an overworked pituitary gland. But still, with great expectations I crept downstairs to the room where the television sleeps at six o'clock in the morning. That's 6 a.m. real time. Not an hour for grown-ups. I sank on to the sofa, yawned the yawn of the nearly dead, and thought, 'You're a professional. You're being paid for this. Get a grip.' With trepidation, I pushed the button and went over the top into no man's land.

The first thing was Sally, the newsreader, for whom the process of imparting information about world events was obviously entirely novel. She stared at the autocue like a five-year-old watching *The Jungle Book* for the first time. The plot was beyond her, she just liked the colour and movement. When she finished, she smiled brightly and said: 'That's the news at six minutes past five,' but the little clock in the corner said five minutes past six. God, next week she should just stick to 'the big hand's on the six and the little wee hand's on the one'.

Then we had a weather Sloane. Well, frankly, she didn't know whether it was six o'clock or the last trump. She waved a limp hand over the map of Britain – it might just as well have been the Canaries – like a demonstrator trying to flit you with scent in Boots. She was dressed in the sort of hideous suit Harvey Nichols reduced to clear the week after Ascot last year. And for all she knew or cared, it could rain frogs and brimstone all day, because she was going to have a massage.

But these two were mere softening-up for the true ghastliness to follow. This being Bank Holiday Monday, *GMTV* had decided to take the day off. Instead of putting on a really exciting lounge-style cabaret of wit and information, they just did a compilation programme of all their best bits from the last year. They showed a bowel-curdling hour's compilation of family videos. 'We've had some really famous people on this banquette,' said the interlocutor lady, whose name I have scrubbed from my memory. This was the C-list party from hell.

It was like being forced to eat Max Clifford's address book. The lively 'now' people who had sat and plugged their new book, film, TV series, pop song, herbal remedy, comprised Cilla Black, Jim Davidson, Kate Moss with her agent-come-translator, Linda Thorson, the girl from *The Avengers* nobody can remember, Howard Keel. Good grief, Howard Keel. He was the Kaiser's favourite baritone, a sad old has-been even when he was in *Dallas*. Now he's older than God's belly button, but he's still a happening guy for *GMTV*. And, wait for it, Zsa Zsa Gabor's less attractive sister, Eva. How do you think you'd have felt if you'd been woken up at 6 a.m. and found yourself alone in a room with that lot?

And not just that lot, but a him-and-her pair of perky, Celticly lilted morning people who had all the sweet charm of a syrup colonic. It's the same old story. If there's a really dirty job to be done, the English still send in the Scots and the Irish.

Well, that's it for me. Never again. At 7 a.m. I crawled back to bed a broken man. My wife turned over and said: 'Where have you been?' I could just mumble: 'The horror, the horror ...' It was the longest day, and it hadn't even begun.

Aids

Hasn't Aids been fun, hasn't it been jolly? Just think of all the pleasure Aids has brought to the world, all the bottles popped, all the party frocks expectantly tried on, all the flashing, grinning premières, the performances, paintings, poems, plays, pop songs, all that glitter, energy, fizz and bonhomie. Aids has been a happy catalyst for so much creativity and conviviality, and more than that, oh much more than that, it's been a password to friendship and social elevation. It's been bonding and cohesive, an easy-to-grasp catch-all moral philosophy. The little red ribbon worn with such supercilious pride is like a medal in the war for liberty. It's a mason's handshake that says: 'I share your politics, your concerns, your outlook. We agree on so much; racism, sexism, funding for the arts, polenta and I want to come to your party.'

It's quite right and proper that BBC2 should follow in the caring, sharing, dare-to-be-joyous path hacked out by Channel 4 with its sex weeks, homely violence weeks and gay Christmases, to bring for our deep, safe, mutually satisfying, consenting-adult pleasure and prophylactic entertainment, World Aids Day awareness week. BBC2 would never bore you with Dysentery Week, where you'd have to wear lavatory-paper ribbons. Oh no, no, heaven forfend. Or disgust you with Colonic Cancer Week, perish the rubber thought, or challenge you with Kuru Week (kuru, a disease rather like BSE, associated with cannibalism. It has been suggested that it may be rampant among Tristrams, where it's called Mad Toady Disease). For Aids is far more than an illness. 'You mean it's an illness as well as a photo opportunity. Well, I never.'

Not all that long ago, Aids awareness was virtually unknown. It seemed only to affect a few men in the close-knit underground world of doctors. It spread through the habit of going to foreign hotels with strangers for conferences. From this secret seminar society it moved to freelance journalists, artists and bohemians, and then exploded into the world. The tell-tale red ribbons, the first sign of Aids awareness, started to emerge at smart dinner parties and rapidly tore through a community that was all too susceptible to promiscuous charity. Some experts predict that there won't be a family in the country unaffected by Aids awareness by the end of the century. I don't want to frighten you, but remember: every ten seconds, somewhere in the world someone is planning an Aids benefit.

The main event of BBC2's lamentable, lip-smacking celebrating of Aids was *Fine Cut: The End of Innocence*, purportedly a programme about the impact of Aids over the past two decades. It turned out to be nothing of the sort. The true joy of Aids has been that it's a one-size-fits-all plague. It can be used to back up anyone's agenda. Not since the Church got hold of the Black Death has a disease been so cynically manipulated. The fundamental right have claimed it's a gay plague. Politicians have used it to prove they care and are doing something. Actors and singers have used it to resuscitate flagging careers. Shy women have used it to say no. Society hostesses have used it for a bit of fun.

Television has used Aids remorselessly as a means of showing erotica that, in any other context, would have been unacceptable. *The End of Innocence* was an angry paean for homosexuals to be given their disease back. There was no such thing as heterosexual Aids, we were unreliably informed. Aids is ours, Aids is gay. We want the sorrow and the pity, the concern, the indignation and the money and the power of it all for ourselves. Aids belongs to the gay community, whether or not there is any such thing as a gay community any more than there is a cohesive heterosexual community, was the unspoken hole in the middle of this programme. What was truly sad and honestly pitiful about this documentary was that homosexuality was solely defined by susceptibility to Aids. Just consider how awful it is to have your sexuality, your love and your desires defined by a disease. Aids doesn't happen to the gay community because there is no gay community. It is a horrible pestilence among many horrible unfair pestilences, and it strikes individuals: friends, lovers, the great, the good, the dull, the talentless, the ugly and the bonny. Having it doesn't make you political or moral or part of a crusade; it makes you a victim and then it makes you a corpse. And any portion of society that will use a disease and its victims for special pleading and self-aggrandisement or entertainment is quite simply beyond cynicism. This was dull television and indefensible immorality.

Actually, if you wanted to see the absolute nadir of shameless bandwagon-jumping cynicism, then there was always *Red Hot and Country*, a tacky compilation of good old boys and girls singing along for Aids. Country music: the sound of the fundamental, ignorant, redneck, queer-bashing, poor, wife-beating white heterosexual. It was like getting the Luftwaffe band to play at the Cenotaph, only the music was worse.

Class

Considering how much of it we watch, it's surprising that there aren't more of what the art critic might call 'culturally load-bearing totemic icons' in television: moments that are pinned to the collective noticeboard, those things we have all seen and remember in common.

Film has dozens of them. Louis and Rick walking across the slick Tarmac, Gary Cooper going for his lunch meeting, Britt Ekland gyrating her sweaty naked body while Edward Woodward tosses in his jimjams (perhaps you don't know that last one: *The Wicker Man* is a favourite of mine). Yet there are remarkably few culturally cohesive television moments. Television, like newspapers, is transitory. It all mulches down to a sort of flickering papier mâché. There are one or two nationally retinised scenes. 'They think it's all over. It is now.' The dead parrot, Morecambe and Wise dancing off, and the class sketch from *The Frost Report*. You remember John Cleese and the two Ronnies standing in descending order. John Cleese: 'I'm upper class and I look down on him.' Ronnie Barker: 'I'm middle class. I look up to him and down on him.' Ronnie Corbett, in cloth cap: 'I know my place.'

Well, it's funny when you see it.

While television doesn't have many bright gems that transcend the off-switch, it does have abiding themes and plots that it works over and over like fairy tales. One of them is class. The upper-middle-lower sketch was more about the world of television than it was about the real world outside. Class is an issue only on the small box. At the time Cleese and Co. were looking up and down at each other, television was uncomfortably aware that it was principally made by middle-class people to impress upper-class people and was watched by lower-class people. There was an embarrassing need to get more real lower-class faces, voices and perceptions into the nation's drawing rooms. Fast forward twenty years, and a lot of provincial grammar-school lads and lasses later, and we can unveil the state-of-the-art Tony Parsons. Tony Parsons is just what television was looking for: the classless interlocutor; a vision of the new post-Thatcher, post-modern, post-haste medium, a bloke who knows the difference between a sound bite and a condom.

Tony Parsons isn't classless. He's the wrong amalgamation of all the classes. He's got a working-class voice, middle-class pretensions and upper-class arrogance. He has the sort of face that appears to have been made during feature rationing. There are only hints of the familiar topographical points of interest. And the voice. It isn't just gratingly class-bound, it has an impediment. I have some sympathy with this as I have a class-bound voice with an impediment, too. I sound like Bertie Wooster's homosexual friend who can't pronounce his 'r's. And here he is in a three-part series *Parsons on Class* (BBC2), which started this week with uppers on their uppers.

Parsons made it to your living room via pop journalism, and for all his self-regarding, ironic, three-piece pinstriped suit, which he uses as gravitas ballast, he's still just Gary Rhodes with a library ticket. For all the cor-blimey vowels, it was his petit-bourgeois soul that showed us round the Gordon-Duff-Penningtons' Cumbrian castle. Tony was smitten, well and truly. He could have added a barrel to his own name and become Pooter-Parsons. Ooh, the upper classes, their self-confidence, their lightness of touch, their manners, their breeding, their taste, their stoicism. It was sick-bag embarrassing. It wasn't that I disagreed with much of what he said; it was his dribbling agog assumption that a nice family was nice because of their class, not because they are decent individuals.

'They've been here for a thousand years,' Pooter-P sighed again and again. A thousand years. Would you believe it? How long did he imagine the rest of us had been here? Perhaps we were cobbled together in Stevenage in the 1930s. The ancient family is the dumbest of all class myths. Let me say this clearly just once: all families are exactly the same age. We all go back precisely the same number of generations. Simply because someone has been writing down names makes absolutely no difference, and having stayed in one place for a thousand years might be looked upon as being a touch unadventurous, agoraphobic even.

The arguments about class have been dead and buried in the real world for a generation. Only a handful of irrelevant Burkes and television still bang on about it. Tony left us with a passionate forelock tug, insisting that the state picks up the £2 million tab for the Gordon-Duff-Pennington home improvements. This was a kindly charitable thought but I would have been more sympathetic if he'd added that everyone ought to have a new roof and central heating on the social.

Before anyone starts singing 'The Red Flag', let's be clear this is not a class issue, it's a fiscal one. Money, not breeding, is what the real-time world cares about. Money is capitalism's token of work and luck, not class. Television likes class because it's a shorthand for character. We all know what to expect from Terry-and-June-middle or Brookside-working or Brideshead-upper. Giving a drama the trappings of class makes audiences do the scriptwriting. It's why we've got so much Jane bleedin' Austen. It's the same with region. Northern people are all the same. Rural people are all the same. People with triple-barrelled names who have been here a thousand years are all the same.

And it's all nonsense. The truth is that only the self-consciously classless late-night talking heads are actually all the same. Television is fascinated with class, race, gender and region because it is produced by the insecure, deferential middle classes. Culture of all types is a middle-class aspiration. Writing, journalism, painting, film, theatre; it doesn't matter where you started. If this is where you choose to end up, you are middle class, matey. Leave your forelock and chip with the commissionaire.

Reality TV

Fame

In the course of a normal, happy life, a chap could expect not to have to consider Ann Widdecombe's breasts. They are something that it's best to draw a veil over. A veil, and perhaps a tarpaulin. Sadly, distressingly, Widdecombe's dugs have fallen into my life and there's no way round them.

I thought that perhaps I could watch *Celebrity Fit Club* (ITV), a title that's obviously misappropriated a vowel, and just pretend they weren't there. But then the honourable member started to jog. Oh, my God, it was like watching the last shot of *The Prisoner* with Tommy from *Ground Force* being Patrick McGoohan trying to escape a pair of huge spacehoppers. *Celebrity Fit Club* is the latest in the 'what can we do with celebrity leftovers?' format.

Forget barrels and the sound of scraping: this was celebrity archaeology. These were people who had been dug up from so deep in the midden of collective unconscious that even their parents would not have remembered them.

Now, admittedly, it must have been a thankless task being the celebrity booker on this show. How many people do you know who would agree to go on television purely because they're obese, and give up six months to being humiliated by an American marine sergeant and chased around country-hotel gardens by Ann Widdecombe's knockers? What can have induced one of the Nolan sisters, for instance, or the fat boy who came nowhere in *Pop Idol*, or Ian McCaskill, a man who used to read the weather, or other grotesque panto Bunters to say, 'My agent's just offered me this great opportunity, I'm going to be ugly on the telly'?

The first episode's humiliation quotient was satisfyingly high. Bulging victims were graded from merely grossly fat to morbidly obese. They were then forced to wear hideous trailer-trash romper suits and made to stand on scales, where they discovered that they weighed more than dray horses, and indeed probably more than the dray. We were lovingly shown their attempts at push-ups, and listened to their pitiful excuses.

The self-delusion of fat people is, I suppose, understandable, but no less pathetic for that. The only things that are more unattractive than grossly, marmoreally corpulent flesh are the jocular explanations and Blitz-spirit quips the obese make to maintain their morale and explain away their bodies. Though this formless, lazy show couldn't make up its mind whether it was self-help or sniggering Teletubbies, it inadvertently shed some of the received wisdom about fatness. These were not, for instance, jolly, jokey, life-and-soul characters, they were miserable, desperate, short-tempered whingers for whom avoiding personal responsibility seemed to be a life goal. Widdecombe herself furiously blocked any attempt: 'Talk, talk, talk. Actions are all that matter.' This from a woman who devoted her life to talking incessantly over everyone else in a talking shop.

Obesity is not a mere lifestyle solipsism, it's not a cruel by-product of the fashion industry or a cynical ploy of fast-food manufacturers. It's not unfairly having a sturdy frame or being cuddly, and it's not a comfortable place to lay Dickensian euphemisms. I think it's a symptom of misery, self-loathing, weakness and, above all, fear and anger. Inside every fat person, I reckon there's a furious fat apologist, and inside this programme, there were eight fat people apparently desperate to be loved for what they plainly weren't – attractive.

At the other end of the scales, we were offered *Model Behaviour* (C4), the second series of a show that sets out to find pre-eminently beautiful mannequins. It was impossible not to see these two programmes as opposite ends of the same conveyor belt: a sort of industrial celebrity factory. *Model Behaviour* is an equally nasty idea. It's nasty for those same cynical reasons that most we'll-make-you-a-star reality shows are. Kids from grey cities queued for ten hours in the hope that someone luckier than them would see in their faces that something that would lift them out of boredom, drudgery and a lifetime of predictable sameness. Unlike the *Pop Idol* programme this revised formula plagiarises, there was no subjective talent for the passed-over to hide behind. This was simply, nakedly, about how they looked. And for an unemployed urban teenager, how you look is pretty much all you have. So the rejection was an uncompromising slap in the face.

The fascist nature of the selection was particularly vile. None of the cranked-up levity or phoney soul-searching could mitigate the casual brutishness of the process. We were just invited to stare at kids who were being teased with success and the future, and then thrown back. I'm utterly convinced that television is not just wrong but morally bereft to use its tantalising power publicly to abuse people's lives like this, particularly young people, who are especially vulnerable. It is no good saying that they volunteer enthusiastically, or that they understand it's just a bit of fun, because it plainly isn't, neither to watch nor, I'm sure, to take part in. *Model Behaviour* is the middle-aged cynically trading on and manipulating the dreams we all have at the beginning of adult life, to glean some sort of smirking, murky, jealous pleasure.

After you reach a certain age, all youth looks beautiful. It also looks extraordinarily blank. Almost worse than the disappointment on the faces of the losers was the sudden coquettish acquisitiveness that played across the winners' faces. This was the theatre of cruelty from Tristrams who would hold their hands up in horror at the very suggestion that they might broadcast a Miss World contest or a seaside beauty pageant.

Britain's Got Talent (ITV) may or may not have come with a question mark: Simon Cowell's latest impression of Hughie Green, with Amanda Holden as the reincarnation of that strange cockney girl who also appeared on *Opportunity Knocks*. What was her name? Ah, how nebulous is national celebrity. The series is supposed to prove variety isn't quite dead, but it should see it off. The only pleasure is watching the skin-crawling Piers Morgan, Gore-Tex man, impervious to any emotion or sensitivity. He seems to have learned human as a second language, possibly from Derren Brown. He is by far and away the weirdest act in the room. His descent (ascent?) from editor of the *Mirror* to ventriloquist's invigilator is, it must be said, one of the most comforting comeuppances of contemporary celebrity. He kept asking awful kiddie-party turns if they thought they were the sort of thing the Queen wanted to see, when you knew the one person the Queen would abdicate rather than sit next to was asking the question. If HM is to be the ultimate arbiter of modern popular entertainment, then the massed bands of the Brigade of Guards are a shoo-in, and I suspect she rather likes Lenny Henry – so restful. I've always thought the whole point of the Royal Variety Performance was two hours of torture for royalty and royalists put on by arty republicans.

Trading Races

I'm a woman, and I'm proud – proud and empowered. Proud, empowered, and my feet are killing me. In a brave, mould-breaking, agenda-rewriting experiment, the *Sunday Times* has decided its writers should dress up to find out what it's like to be someone else. Bryan Appleyard is pretending to be an Icelandic cod fisherman with an ear infection, Michael Winner is Ronald McDonald, and Jeremy Clarkson's a jockey. I'm told editorial conference looks like Harry Potter-meets-*La Cage aux folles.* I myself am sitting here in a bias-cut Joseph frock, fishnet hold-ups and this season's must-have stiletto fetish boots from Patrick Cox. A little light foundation, a touch of mascara and the merest smear of matt Kosovo Corpse on the lips – I don't want to look like Lily Savage, this is serious. I need to know what it's like to be a woman, and drag is plainly the way to find out. I expect the more sensitive of you have already noticed an inclusive, less judgemental, lyrical tone creeping into my writing. Truth to tell, this wasn't an original idea: we got it from the BBC, which has made a great song and dance (perhaps that's not quite the right expression) about blacking up a white guy and greying up a black one to put a little chiaroscuro into the racism debate, in *Trading Races* (BBC2).

Now, I know there will be many of you who say this is the most cringingly embarrassing, insulting concept it is possible to conceive, but frankly, that's because you are not seeing it through Lancôme all-day, tear-free, thick-lash mascara. You may well imagine this was *The Black and White Minstrel Show* colliding with a makeover programme, but you'd be wrong. My new, feminine side tells me it's a brave and daring attempt to bridge gaps, shine light on misunderstanding and gently massage the shoulders of prejudice; an attempt to bring a little of the *Guardian* into your guilt-ridden, bigoted homes. It was also, unintentionally, honkingly funny. For a start, the two chaps were both whingeing liberals, desperate to see all sides of every coin, have their glasses half-full while being even-handedly aware that they were still half-empty. The white guy simply needed make-up to look like an Iraqi janitor. The black bloke, for reasons we weren't told, because I suspect we might have construed them to be racist, needed a rubber mask. It was at this point I started sobbing with mirth. He looked like an extra at Bilbo Baggins's birthday party.

And it got better, mostly because the programme kept up such a maniacally high-minded mien. It simply wouldn't admit that this was deeply comic or even smirkable. So when the white bloke's wife burst into tears at the sight of him as a homey, we weren't told whether this was through fear that he might burst into 'Camptown Races' or through joy that the weekends suddenly promised to look up. His son mentioned in passing that he preferred having a black dad. Well, if the choice is between a guilt-racked children's book illustrator from the 'burbs or a funky black dude with a gold tooth, what would any self-respecting five-year-old choose?

At some utterly risible, imitation-white black dinner party, where our liberal Othello laid out his self-lacerating guilt, a large Rastafarian asked how he'd feel if his daughter came home with a black man. Oh, how we yearned for him to reply: about the same as you'd feel if your daughter came home with Andy Williams's *Greatest Hits*. The black chap in a fright mask didn't do much better. When he admitted to being black, the surprised man he'd been having dinner with said, 'Bless my soul, and I thought you were Jewish,' opening up a hysterical line of questions that the programme-makers obviously felt was better left unanswered. We got our touchy-feely moral at the end, and the credits rolled over a general feeling of rosy warmth, leaving me astonished that even Christians could have thought this programme worth making. I tell a lie: I wasn't astonished in the slightest. The idea that black or white sensibility is a question of slap and latex is chronically but typically remedial. The fact that two perfectly nice men are still perfectly nice with make-up on is so, so … oh God, I suppose it's so what passes for prime-time, mainstream investigative TV these days. As a woman, of course, I just want to mention how disappointed I was that they chose two men.

Ideally, *Castaway 2000* (BBC1) should have been a cross between *The Archers* and *Survivors* (you do remember *Survivors*?). Actually, it's a mix of *Charlie's Garden Army* and watching peat dry. Rural life is very boring. Rural life with bickering is desperately boring. Which is why most of us live in cities. The audience is left with a sense of damp gloom where there ought to be vicarious pioneering excitement. The fault isn't the castaways', though they do seem to have been plucked from a Posy Simmonds cartoon about a Surrey allotment collective. It's the format and the place – there's just too much chore tedium to get through. 'Steve and Nicola can't agree on who should dry out the casserole,' says the funereal voice-over. 'Tom tries to fix the plumbing without much success.' This is *Sesame Street*, or perhaps *Sesame Bog*, for grown-ups.

Popstars

There's a type of woman who can look across a room at a type of man and say with absolute certainty: 'The thing about him is he hates women.' The type of man is invariably a chap whose entire life has been devoted to attracting women's attention: flirting with them, flattering them, chasing them, bedding them. In fact, a bloke who'd tell you with a hand on his heart that his one absolute lifelong truth was that he adored women. The classic example of a man who loves women because he hates them is James Bond. There are, so the received feminine wisdom goes, two sorts of misogynist: the passive and the aggressive. Passive avoids women, joins a gents' club, does hobbies in a shed, becomes a priest. The active courts them, charms them, serially marries them so he can humiliate and dump them, in the manner of a big-game hunter stalking trophies.

I am beginning to think television has the same deal going with teenagers, given that teendom stretches from legal consent to somewhere in the mid-twenties. Television professes to love these kids, says it'll do anything for them, will go to any lengths to spend time in their company, wants to kiss them all over. But I suspect the box secretly only wants to make them cry.

I haven't reviewed *Popstars* (ITV) because, frankly, what is there to say? You deconstruct something like that and it falls apart in your hands; you're just left holding butterfly wings, feeling guilty. If it's what you like, then you'll like it. What makes me mention it now is that so many of you obviously do, and it is currently the subject of innumerable water-cooler conversations. If you don't know what we're talking about, *Popstars* is a talent show that started with a lot of kids who wanted to be pop singers more than life itself and then, week by week, whittled them down to a lucky bland five. The Juilliard School it wasn't. The purported purpose of this was to make dreams come true (and isn't that television's only desire these days?).

Actually, truthfully, it was so you could see a lot of young people who weren't grown up enough to deal with it getting publicly rejected – sometimes brutally, sometimes with a cloying senti-mentality. In the Antipodes, where this show originated, I'm told they call it 'train-wreck television', and it does have the shaming compulsiveness of rubbernecking an accident. What's more, it has become a whole genre: *Big Brother*, assorted *Castaways*, Ibiza-and-all-those-other-bonking-holiday-shows-unzipped. And the auntie of them all? The failing *Blind Date*. All these programmes rely on teenagers' emotions for their entertainment delectation. And it's easy to see why one of the defining characteristics of being an adult is the ability to mask your feelings appropriately. That's bad TV. Teenagers are close enough to being children to cry for the cameras with a little prodding. This hormone-rich, grown-up stuff is all new to them. Now, ask yourself a grown-up question: is watching young people lose their fragile self-esteem a nice way to spend an evening in?

The more I think about it, the more I'm convinced that this is actually why teenagers were invented. They arrived in the late 1950s and were a construct, like Sloane Rangers, yuppies or Essex girls. Immediately the media and business had created them and identified them, they started making them unhappy and insecure. From James Dean onwards, teenagers have been adored and viciously punished for being teenagers, and we vicariously peep at them through the one-way mirror of television, dribbling over their sex lives, their drugs, their music, their ambition and their bodies. And when they get pregnant, overdose, grow fat, throw up and weep, we smile and say: 'I told you so.' Tristrams will tell you they're making TV for the teenagers, but they're not. They're making programmes for thwarted, bitter old people like you and me, and they have invented an endless audition of disposable dreamy entertainers who come cheap on the promise of stardom and fame.

Popstars, like *Big Brother* and the rest, has all the ingredients of Greek tragedy: hubris before nemesis, with a handful of unlovable flabby executives acting as Olympians. It's all deeply unpleasant and unedifying, but what the hell if it keeps some of us amused? Anyway, they're young, they've got their whole lives ahead of them to get over it, which is rather the point of this teenage-hating – most of us haven't.

The Apprentice with Alan Sugar – a small, frenetic, stubbly haemorrhoid, who comes over as a plutocratic Abanazar shouting at a covey of gelled and power-suited young Aladdins who imagine they are taking part in a head-hunting contest for a great job when in fact they are cheap victims for a reality TV game show. Which doesn't say much for their nous right from the start. In fact, they all appear to have been grabbed from the staff room of PC World.

Celebrities

I'm not making this up. Of course, I never make anything up, I simply steal things other people make up. This was made up and sent to me by a man who signed himself a 'senior producer' at the BBC. It starts: 'Dear Mr Gill/AA, Sometimes the god of television hands out dream shows to produce, and today he has dealt me the card of celebrity boxing.'

Now, let's just push the pause button there and consider for a moment. Leave aside the fact that a producer, a senior producer who has access to considerable amounts of your licence fee, believes there is a god whose ethereal remit is not only scheduling and content, but also being a croupier. Just savour celebrity boxing. How much do you want to see that? On a scale of 1–10? It's a lot, isn't it? 10+. He goes on: 'We are going to get a series of dream duels on BBC2, including, probably, Julian Clary v. Paul O'Grady and Jeremy Vine v. Jeremy Paxman. It will entail real training in real gyms under real trainers [in your real dreams].' Paxman v. Vine: that would be worth the licence fee all on its own. Could the winners fight each other? Paxman v. O'Grady I'd buy a new television for.

He continues: 'Do you fancy it?' Fancy it? I could rip the jock-strap off it. Here and now. But that's not what he meant. Did I fancy doing it? And he mentioned a man who is at least ten years younger than me, six inches taller, who runs marathons. Are you mad? Have you just gone ten rounds with a revolving door? Why would anyone sane want to get trained by real trainers in real gyms, then get really punched? Worse, wearing shorts on television? He must have me mixed up with someone else. A celebrity, perhaps.

Much as celebrity boxing is to be yearned for, it's a symptom of a sad current problem. Fame – there's too much of it about. An oversupply. Celebrity is prone to market forces in just the same way as Porsches and cottages in Somerset. For the past two decades, we've had a free-for-all, a bull market in celebrities. It's made dotcom and telecommunications look like whelk stalls. We have manufactured thousands and thousands of famous people, from household names to garden-shed names, from the instantly recognisable to the barely remembered. And they're all just hanging about, waiting for something to do. We've got a glut. I suppose we could make jam out of them, or get them to do celebrity boxing. Or send them to the rain forest.

Let me tell you, you're going to see a lot more programmes like this until the celebrity economy picks up. I have to disagree with most reviewers on *I'm a Celebrity: Get Me Out of Here*. I'm finding it utterly compelling. What I thought was dispiriting and faintly disgusting about *Big Brother* and *Castaway* was the bribery of, let's face it, special-needs adults with celebrity in exchange for looking ridiculous and pathetic. In the case of *I'm a Celebrity*, that doesn't apply. In fact, the effect is quite the opposite. Instead of taking nobodies and pretending they're somebodies, here we have somebodies who are slowly reverting to being anybodies. Have you noticed that they seem to have lost one, a blonde girl? She was a model or something. I think the others must have eaten her. Now there's an idea: celebrity cannibalism. It's a Swiftian thought. Fine dining with the stars. *Get Me Out of Here – I'm a Takeaway*. You've seen the show, now eat the cast.

As the job description 'writer' vanishes from the placement of television, as if it were some arcane heritage discipline, like engraver or postilion, so it is being replaced by new, shiny callings performed by new, shiny people. I'm particularly keen to meet a reality producer. They're everywhere. I can while away quite a lot of traffic-jam time imagining the complex and delicate life of a reality producer. Sometimes, I hold imaginary job interviews for them. 'When did you first become interested in reality? And what made you think of television? How does reality compare with unreality, and how can you tell? Where do you think you'll be in ten years' time?'

I like to imagine them all arguing in the green room – a symposium of *Monty Python* philosophers. 'Call that reality, you neo-Kantian empiricist twit? That's just a random collection of dystopian occurrences. Get real.' Or perhaps they're like an ecumenical conclave of outré deities. Gods do move in eccentrically mysterious ways. Take Jesus, for instance. He's about as likely to return as a carpenter as he is a writer. I expect 'reality producer' might be just up his Via Dolorosa.

Big Brother

What do I hate most about *Big Brother*? Oh, how shall we count the ways? It isn't the cynicism of its casting, nor the cretinous, knowing, sly gullibility of its contestants, nor the limbo of low expectations the audience must have of entertainment to watch it. It isn't even the torturous boredom.

What I hate most is being told by Soho Tristrams and media rubbernecks that not liking *Big Brother* (C4) is simply my snobbery, a posh distaste for the culture of the masses; that it's my fault. Not to applaud it is to prove I'm out of touch with the vitality of the young, who understand that free-form texting the gossipy interactivity gives them editorial control over celebrity and their own entertainment. And, anyway, they say, all hip people watch it through the magic spectacles of irony. That's what I hate about *Big Brother*: rationalising the exploitation of the audience and the sad, incarcerated victims.

Big Brother contestants are an artificially made Aunt Sally for the nation's prejudices. Perhaps this is part of their attraction – we can hate them with a deep and irrational loathing while feeling no shame or guilt. I'm surprised nobody has thought of doing *Big Brother* in an illegal immigrants' holding centre: the winner would get a work permit. The inherent problem with reality TV is that it has to continue to crank up the volume. Each outing must be more vivid than the last, and therefore less real.

Each incarnation of this programme has to up the loony quotient, seeking out ever more damaged, psychiatrically challenged exhibitionists with low self-esteem. This time, within the first week, they've got one they claim is on suicide watch. How entertaining is that? Happily, I can sense that the concept is grinding to a turgid standstill under the weight of its own irony. There has never been a golden goose the cynical Tristrams haven't worked to an early death.

Actors complain that the genre is putting them out of work.

They're quite wrong, of course. It's actually just producing more performers who do extempore slapstick. The contestants have to be chosen with more and more extreme emotional and behavioural abilities; there is now a payment to the first couple who prove that *Big Brother* contestants are easy. I predict that before long there will be courses at drama school for kids who want to succeed at reality television: 'For my audition piece, I'm going to do Tara hearing she's lost *I'm a Celebrity: Get Me Out of Here.'* They've all already got agents, and egos, and can do air-kissing. An Equity card's the easy bit. Reality television is just too important to ratings and advertisers to be left to amateurs; I promise you that within five years there'll be tearful acceptance speeches at the Baftas for best comedy performance on a reality show.

The Great British Village Show (BBC1) came to rest in Highgrove: the fête worse than death meeting the hereditary principal. This series has regularly scored full marks on the Trevor McDonald scale of TV: so desperate, you can't drag your eyes away. It finished up with the Prince of Wales and the Duchess of Cornwall. Charles's vocal cords are plainly trying to strangle him. He may well become the first monarch to lose his head from the inside out. He simply loved the community spirit of village fêtes, he gasped. It's not a community, your stratospheric highness – it's a lot of set-aside peasants on your lawn. It's *Big Brother*, with marrows.

42 Up

I rarely invite you to kick yourself hard for missing something on the box. Generally, there'll be something similar along in a day or so. But this week I'm afraid you've got to bend over; and when you've finished, I want you to limp to the busiest road you can find and pin a notice to the seat of your pants saying: 'I failed to watch *42 Up*. Please kick generously.' Perhaps that will remind you to be on the sofa in seven years' time, when *49 Up* comes around. Because there is nothing, nothing else on television remotely like this extraordinary odyssey.

If I was asked – and, oddly enough, I often am – to name the handful of programmes that would justify television as the pre-eminent medium of culture this century, then *7 Up* and its ensuing episodes, the latest of which, *42 Up*, was screened last week (BBC1), are in my first five. This is some of the best television ever made, and you missed it.

It's a very simple idea: take a group of seven-year-olds, ask them what they expect from life, and then go back and find out how it's going every seven years. The children are now middle-aged, and perhaps my enthusiasm for this series is in part because I vividly remember seeing the first programme when I was nine and because the subjects are my contemporaries. Theirs is the story of my generation, and I've watched every one since, quietly measuring my own life against theirs. Twenty-one and twenty-eight were a bit rough; actually, thirty-five was pretty depressing, too; and now here I am at forty-four just bumping along the bottom. Here we are in the hair loss and thickening girth of middle age. The juxtaposition of lives half-run with the black-and-white enthusiasm of seven-year-olds was poignant to the point of tears. The thwarted hopes, the failed marriages, the lined faces, the sickness and poverty and loneliness and the accommodation that are all part of growing up were in their way actually as splendid and deeply humane as the happy marriages and successful careers.

This series ought to be depressing, but it isn't. It's the most hopeful and tender thing on the box, because the time scale shows that the true measure of success is not in ambition and goals achieved but in how you make the journey. There are children here who have done exactly what they said they'd do when they were seven, and those who have done precisely what they said they wouldn't do. It is the march of Everyman, of the post-war generation.

Michael Apted, whose magnum opus this is, went on to Hollywood to make films, but this is his masterwork, and he returns every seven years to update it. The subjects now call him Michael when they're being interviewed because they've known him most of their lives; his camera in turn treats them with a respect and humility that's virtually extinct on television. We never forget that these are real people with real lives, and they're precious. There are no punch-lines and no easy morals. It's also interesting to see how far we've travelled as a nation in these thirty-five years. The original programme was heavily aware of class: the voices were branded with accents that could have come from two distinct countries, and the commentary talked of the shop stewards and the executives of the year 2000, implying that these positions were ordained by God and birth. Now the accents have elided into one homogeneous English. The cut-glass teeth and aching vowels of the toff, and the cor-blimey Eliza Doolittle consonants of the working class have vanished. And do shop stewards still exist? *7 Up* was made before modern feminism, so the young girls' aspirations do not stretch much higher than the counter at Woolworth's and a bit of a good time before settling down to marriage and kids. Their concerns were not whether, just when. That would be very different today. And there is only one black boy and no Asians; all this was before this country's great human lottery win of the East African exodus.

I finished watching the second programme with a soaring sense of having been party to a really classy achievement, an idea that could only have found light on television. No other medium has the breadth to take it on, and *7 Up* so perfectly exploited television's strengths. It was intelligently conceived and made with great integrity and vision. It was not just the small triumph of a boy we last saw as a deeply depressed tramp in the north of Scotland who is now a Liberal Democrat councillor in Hackney that made this joyous, but because it was a microcosm of the country. We have all come such a long way, and it seems almost all in the right direction. It's not the goals we've set for employment or productivity or health or education that are the measure of us; it's, like these children, how we've managed to get through the years. I find it all very heartening, and moving.

Cookery

Cooks

Food is one of those subjects that television keeps going back to for seconds but can rarely get to rise quite right, like Crown Green bowls, how to paint watercolours and Michael Aspel. Only animals eat naturally on television. People on television never swallow anything. Very occasionally a Stanislavsky-trained thesp will push a forkful of something into his mouth and then pouch it like a provident hamster. Actors sit down to endless meals and never eat anything. Remember the eternal Kellogg's interruptus of the *Dallas* breakfast? Tables were laid more often than Lucy Ewing, but nothing ever got eaten. Then there's the cornucopia teacup of plenty. All actors worth their RADA certificate can get at least a couple of pints out of an empty teacup. I fondly remember one edition of the sorely missed *Strathblair* where Ian Carmichael managed to drain the same thimble-sized coffee-cup six times. And then there's the *Coronation Street* beer – some potato-faced Lancastrian moseys into the Rovers and says: 'By 'eck, my throat's as parched as Wigan pier at low tide, give us a pint, love.' Then he'll just sniff it as if it were a renal-ward potty.

Even in commercials where the whole point is the food, the models will go to extraordinary sleights of mouth to avoid chewing. I especially enjoy the girls with the plaster of Paris teeth, snogging apples to the sound of crumpled cellophane. And can anyone tell me what happened to the sugar on the cornflakes? You and I know that cornflakes without sugar taste like week-old scabs, but on the TV nobody uses it any more. How come actors can ride horses, shoot guns, punch each other in the throat, have sex without using their hands, but they still can't perform with meat and two veg? It's one of the great mysteries of the magic box, like why are all suitcases empty? Why don't taxi drivers ever give change? And why don't TV women mind sleeping with men who never take their underpants off?

Ah well, television is essentially the mutual and willing suspension of belief. I've had my belief suspended so high that it is now eligible for air miles. I resisted the impulse to review the first episode of *Rhodes Around Britain* (BBC2) because I thought the second course in Norfolk might redeem the starter. (All chefs can have off-days.) It didn't. If you're thinking of losing a few pounds, forget the complicated diet books and the repetitive steamed vegetables; just watch Gary Rhodes three times a day in between meals, you'll shed pounds. I ate three cushions and a handkerchief in sheer naked sweaty embarrassment: that's less than 50 calories.

With all the charity I can muster, I assume Rhodes has fallen into bad company. Some slick producer girlie (all television producers are girlies, whatever their gender) has decided that he's just too sexy for words, the Nigel Kennedy of the grinder, and has encouraged him to be all flirty and cocky. The horror that turned up in Lancashire and Norfolk was out of new bloke and beyond new lad, the cringing personification of new geezer. If you didn't catch it, here's just a little appetiser of *Rhodes in Lancashire*. Gazza the Geezer stripped off to kick a football about with Manchester United. Well, in chef's togs he looked pretty wallyish, but in shorts, with that naff Bay City Roller haircut, he looked like a Bernard Matthews reject with rickets.

Patronising real people is the stock-in-trade of television cooks. Gazza Geezer did it with all the matey sincerity of an oleaginous pop star visiting a geriatric ward for *Stars on Sunday*: 'Come on, love, give us a kiss.' He even patronised inanimate objects: 'An' 'ere we 'ave good old Worcester sauce, one of the great old English seasonings.' Please. All of these TV cooks stick in my craw because they manage to take raw ingredients that are naturally good, wholesome and entertaining, and turn them into snobbery and platforms for their own aggrandisement and half-baked books. The hottest dish on Gazza the Geezer's menu is his own ego. It made you yearn for the Galloping Gourmet. I doubt that anyone learned a single useful recipe or tip but then, that's no longer the point of food on the box. It's now all lifestyle, soft porn and pouty personality.

The programme ended with a scene of such awe-inspiring embarrassment that I'm sure Denis Norden will be showing it every Christmas until the millennium. Gazza the Geezer was dragged off to a fish-and-chip shop by the Nolan Sisters. Honest to God, the Nolan Sisters. They sang 'You're Simply the Best', a cappella, in a crowded restaurant, apropos of nothing, to a smirking, nodding Gazza and a thankfully dead rock salmon. I would have happily changed places with that fish: it wasn't half as battered as I was.

Raymond Blanc – to the Manoir Born, the man who brought us the joy of baby vegetables tied up with parsley stalks, is now fronting *The Restaurant* (BBC2), the hospitality version of *The Apprentice*. He looks and sounds like Peter Sellers crossed with a small carrot, and speaks the sort of effortless accented bollocks you generally find in the mission statements of overpriced menus in country restaurants.

Fat Ladies

Clarissa Dixon Wright and Jennifer Paterson ... I must be careful what I say about Jennifer and Clarissa. I know them both through my day job as a food writer. The first time I met Jennifer was at a demonstration of filleting skills given by Anton Mosimann, a hygienically bow-tied, precise gent. We both sat in the front row. She kept up a whisperd commentary. Now, Jennifer's whisper could be used to guide supertankers through fog. She has simply no volume control. Come to think of it, neither does Clarissa. 'Look at him, he's going to wash his hands again. I've never seen someone wash so often. Look, he's doing it again! Do you think he's a gynaecologist? Or perhaps it's because he's Swiss. Does he think he's Pontius Pilate? He certainly crucified that fish.' I was rendered helpless with laughter.

When I started writing about food, Clarissa was a godsend. She knows more about ingredients, recipes, manners and bad behaviour than anyone I've ever met, and she was always garrulously hospitable with her expertise. So when their cookery programme, *Two Fat*

Ladies (BBC2), came on, I was rather worried. Actually, I'm rather frightened of both of them. What if it was dreadful? What if I had to send it back? But after two minutes I breathed a huge sigh of relief. I adored it, every mouthful. The camera has managed to capture their singularity without diminishing or patronising them. This week they were cooking fish in Cornwall. Hardy salts backed away down quays as the brace of cooks bellowed like ravenous sea cows: 'We've come for your scallops.' Men were taking to the ebb tide without waiting for a boat. One quivering chap was caught and made to decapitate an angler or monkfish. 'Oh, isn't he a hideous thing?' lowed Jennifer, and we were forced to consider the terrible accident that might occur if either of them fell over near a daydreaming fish-filleter.

The actual cooking bit is no-nonsense sensible dinner, without garnish or placement cards. It's wholesome and enjoyable eating, but that's not really the point. The joy of *Two Fat Ladies* is that it brings two huge characters to the screen. Even though a thousand thousand personalities ripple across the glassy surface of the box every day, there are precious few original, unscripted natural characters. Clarissa and Jennifer are rare spices.

Christmas

I was asked last week to take a slice from the rich fruit cake of my seasonally moist wit to mull over the punchbowl of my spiced cynicism and come up with a parody of the Christmas Day schedules on BBC1. Auntie is still the electric Lapland of Christmas: we turn her on through ancient tribal memory, hoping to see the ghost of a Morecambe and Wise past.

This is what I came up with. *God's Surprise*, live from the parish church of St Nicholas, Newbury. Surprise! I'm pregnant, and God's the father. I thought that St Nicholas was a nice touch. The *Queen's Christmas Message* – no surprises here – then straight into *Rolf's Merry Christmas*: Rolf Harris and Gaby Roslin surprise individuals in need of a Christmas treat. Ooh, it's all surprises this yule. Imagine you're alone and miserable, and you think the festive period couldn't possibly get any worse – but there's a knock at the door. Who can it be? Aaah, Rolf and Gaby, the dark riders of hysterical bonhomie, Joseph and Mary from the dark side. All of a sudden, the rule of thumb by which you measure diabolical awfulness comes up short by a couple of yards. You are in a bottomless Corryvreckan of pain and horror. Screaming, you stumble on into the Mordor of *Terry Wogan's Dazzling Bloomers* and emerge gabbling and gasping, only to find yourself outside The Vic – it's Christmas *EastEnders*, where somebody with Aids marries somebody who's pregnant, but the baby's father is no angel. And on and on to Alistair McGowan imitating *EastEnders*, and just when you think it's all over, it's *EastEnders* again, with the subheading Events Take a Turn for the Worse. Then it's David Jason – either swimming with dolphins or the cast of *Only Fools and Horses*, whichever is the more animated and can do the most hilarious pratfalls. And then there's right-on *Battersea to Bethlehem*, a funky new look at the nativity story quite unlike all the other funky new looks we get every year. And finally, just to show that the spirit of Christmas is really repeats, Louis Theroux meets the Hamiltons yet again.

The editor who commissioned this thought it all terribly funny – 'One of the best pastiches you've ever done,' she said kindly. 'Can you imagine if Christmas telly really were this dire?' And then I had to tell her (you're way ahead of me, aren't you?): these really are the schedules. You see, they are beyond parody: nothing you could make up is as darkly shiversome as Rolf Harris and Gaby Roslin bothering a hospital.

The one programme you really don't want to get lumbered with making at Christmas is the one in the kitchen. Worse than *Wogan's Bloomers* or *Celebrity Who Wants to Be a Millionaire* is having to do the cooking at Christmas. There's absolutely nothing to be said about Christmas food, and this year, Nigella Lawson has drawn the short cheese straw, in *Nigella Bites* (C4). Personally, I'm a great fan of Nigella – she's one of the few TV cooks who actually seems to understand that the point of food is eating, as opposed to medicine or showing off. But, most important, she looks like the evocation of endless bounty and harvest festivals, one part Jessica Rabbit, two parts Willendorf Venus. She's a great post-modern fertility symbol – I'm sorry, am I dribbling into your lap? Her phenomenal popularity, and the priapic adoration of every swaying curve and pouting purr, plugs into some ancient pre-Christian folkloric fertility deal. I wouldn't be at all surprised to hear that druids were camping out in her bedroom, waiting for the first rays of Michaelmas sun to strike her breast, or that barren couples walked round her seven times withershins. I expect that, as we speak, morris men are making up a Nigella dance, and wicker Nigellas stuffed full of farmyard animals and Edward Woodward are being burned on rural hills to guard against foot and mouth, BSE and the common agricultural policy. Those of you who carp at Nigella simply don't understand or don't want to face her ancient, pagan, sensual linking of fleshly indulgences. The chopping board and the carnal mattress are both household utensils, and each a metaphor for the other.

On a more prosaic note, I would also point out that she is the only television cook who can talk eloquently about food. Not an easy thing, English being a language that is famously bereft of gastronomic adjectives, as I know only too well. She does have the advantage of being a journalist first and a pre-Christian goddess second.

Jamie Oliver

Frankly, food on television is a vile disgrace. How can we expect our children to grow up to be, well, grown-ups and responsible viewers of *Panorama* if we stuff their heads with processed rubbish like *Ready Steady Cook*, with its genetically modified presenters and battery-farmed format? Most breakfast and lunchtime offerings are fast food, sickeningly clogged with sweet clichés and fatty truisms. What we need is a Jamie Oliver to reorganise the schedules into healthy, organic watching, to get rid of the junk snacks and the quick-fix recipes. We are producing a generation of kids who think dinner is something you have to do against the clock for money. Then there's Gordon Ramsay, who makes cooking look like a cross between *The Sweeney* and *Tiswas*, and the dozens of sadistic slimming reality shows, sadistic healthy-eating makeovers, and that awful woman who resembles an oven-ready guinea-fowl and who humiliatingly confronts fat underclass epsilons with their own faeces as an unsubtle analogy of what she thinks their lives are worth.

Food has become cynically and commercially re-engineered into yet another ingredient in the self-obsessive, navel-gazing, dysfunctional and unfulfilled lives of consumers. From being a metaphor for happiness and conviviality, it has been made the har-binger of lovelessness, disease and premature, lonely death. Jamie Oliver's school-meals campaign was one of the few bright, right and sensible food programmes on offer. It was watchable, popular and important, and it encapsulated all that was most Reithian in sustainable programmes. Last week, he revisited the subject in *Jamie's Return to School Dinners* (C4), a programme that had the unavoidable smell of reheated leftovers. Little had changed, less had been paid for. But, with his Sisyphean enthusiasm, Jamie continued to try to get something wholesome into kids. By the time he was reduced to dressing up as a pixie and jumping about on a bouncy castle to catch the attention of Lincolnshire parents and get them to care a jot or tittle for their children's wellbeing, I thought, enough's enough. There must be a point where you stand back and say: 'Actually, it's time you took responsibility for your life and your kids' health.'

There is a limit to the help you can force down people's throats despite themselves. Ultimately, what you shove into your mouth is a personal liberty. And now there's been the Oliver backlash: fat mothers lurking outside schools, pushing saturated, processed junk through the railings to kids for money so they won't have to eat that low-fat, healthy rubbish in the canteen. They look like drug dealers, and there is a Hogarthian dark humour in this that is such an English joy. Soon we'll need a fast-food offenders' list. Jamie is already asking the government to post snack-searchers at school gates. There'll be janitors asking you if you packed your rucksack yourself, and whether you were given any packages by strangers. Fat is the new civil liberties. Your BMI will be an indication of your status, education, wealth, employment and marriage prospects. You want to do well at school? Forget the exams. Eat the vegetables, stay thin.

The added bonus of Jamie's programme was that Alan Johnson and Tony Blair took part, attracted by the propinquity of celebrity. So we could compare and contrast the old faker with the young pretender. Johnson is a non-starter: hopelessly awkward, insubstantial, lost and slippery when confronted by the camera and Oliver's relentless celebrity. Blair, though, was ephemerally brilliant. He so plainly loves this. He thinks he is the Jamie Oliver of international statesmanship. You can tell he's always felt that politics ought to be more like a reality TV show. He adores the little pause before delivering the happy ending. He likes the lump in the throat, the gasp of surprise. They should resurrect *That's Life!* for him. He is Esther, with less teeth and hair.

I wonder whether the people who made *Kill It, Cook It, Eat It* (BBC3) thought about rolling out their format to other countries. I would dearly like to see viewers in Nigeria, Tunisia or Cambodia shouting: 'Put that chicken down and come and watch this fantastically politically sensitive, monumentally patronising programme that is going to introduce us to the truth that meat comes from animals that have to be killed quite dead and emptied out and cut into pieces before we can put them in our mouths.'

The presenter had the exaggerated, exclamatory delivery of a junior-school teacher at a parents' evening. The presumption of certain Tristrams that the audience is by and large a collection of barely functioning imbeciles, who know less than nothing, but lie on sofas having vague feelings, is breathtaking. The truth is that eating freshly killed meat is rather nasty, and the most likely result of this series, apart from bored incomprehension, will be to encourage some people to take up slaughtering as a hobby, but to put most off cooking altogether. Next it will be *Shear It, Weave It, Wear It*, with Shaun the Sheep, or perhaps Lay It, Coddle It, Suck It, for grandmothers.

Fanny and Delia

I lost track of how many times Fanny Cradock got hitched. Apparently, she did it serially, without bothering to divorce in between. I suppose she just turned up with one she made earlier. In fact, for most of her career the only person she didn't marry was that half-full piping bag Johnny, he of the apocryphal 'Now all your doughnuts can look like Fanny's'. Fanny Cradock's life was fork-droppingly riveting. My dear, I had no idea. *The Real ... Fanny Cradock* (C4) was a wonderful documentary. I mean, even as a child I knew that Fanny Cradock was deeply weird. But never quite how appallingly sociopathical, snobbishly bizarre she was.

Last week, by chance, the Huw Wheldon lecture touched on the subject of television reinventing itself as a sort of national therapy for the nation. What wasn't mentioned was that ever since its inception, television has acted as an outpatient psychiatric playpen for some of the most twisted, socially malformed, self-deluded people, who found solace for their demons in becoming presenters and stars. Without the constant therapy and fantasy of their television lives, I genuinely believe that a lot of game-show hosts, special-interest presenters and newsreaders would have ended up in prison or straitjackets. I've mentioned before that the lens takes certain character traits that would in a normal life be crippling flaws and turns them into something terribly watchable. Fanny Cradock is a prime example. When boring old Tristrams talk nostalgically about a golden age of television, just say Fanny Cradock. To the young and impressionable, she was very, very frightening.

Cradock didn't quite invent TV cookery; what she did invent was hostile hospitality. Food to put the neighbours down with. Ego canapés. Only someone as deeply insecure as she could find the snobbery in an egg. The things she did with food were disgusting, they don't bear thinking about. She was the person who took the word 'garnish' and made it the most feared expletive on television. She was a Serbian stormtrooper of garnish. She'd grab naked ingredients, abuse them and then bury her crime under garnish. Dinner looked like a mass grave with floral tributes. She's still capable of giving me nightmares.

If you want one good reason why television is streets better than it was, you only have to look at Cradock's natural successor, Delia. The undisputed kitchen doyenne, as homely as a Teasmade, as irreproachably fresh as Fairy Liquid, as wholesome as a split bloomer slathered with lemon curd, Delia has devoted an unimpeachable life to undoing the satanic work of Fanny. They are the darkness and light, the yin and yang of the kitchen. The Wicked Witch of the West and Dorothy. The evil queen and Snow White.

Last week, Delia started her new series on basic cooking, *Delia's How to Cook* (BBC2). She began with eggs. This is an egg, she said. Not for her is an egg a devilled, pink-piped social landmine; for Delia, eggs are blameless and white and perfect metaphors of holy oneness. She showed us sinners how to tell if an egg was without sin, but you just knew that all Delia's eggs were always fresh-laid by hens who sang psalms and wiped their bums with Wet Ones first. You knew that none of Delia's eggs ever had an embarrassing red bit in it. And you can rest assured that when she cracks omelettes, she doesn't do Hermann Goering impressions. Her series is laudable and a wee bit worthy. Her manner, even after all this time, a touch awkward, as if she understands that television isn't a medium made for simple good souls like herself. And, indeed, I wonder if she isn't, despite all the good intentions, like Lot's wife, turning back for one last look at an audience irredeemably mired in Sodom and takeaway chicken tikka pizza. You don't want to be saved for cookery and perfect eggs: you want Ainsley Harriott. As at the moment I'm toying with the mysteries of reincarnation after my sojourn out east, I am becoming convinced that Ainsley Harriott is the rebirth of Fanny Cradock. After her monstrously pretentious life, it would be wonderfully fitting for Krishna with a wry sense of humour to bring her back as a six-foot two-inch black man. Listen to that laugh. Look carefully into the eyes. Fanny's in there.

Philosophy

Philosophy (1)

Philosophy gets a raw deal from television – in fact, philosophy gets a raw deal from all of us – and personally I feel guilty, in a philosophical way, about it. It ought to be a subject I'm interested in, and God knows I've tried. I've picked up the books and concentrated, but you know, I read the same sentence twenty-seven times and feel the synapses close down. I get my philosophy from T-shirts.

So I was particularly looking forward to *Human, All Too Human*, three programmes on the twentieth century's greatest thinkers, Jean-Paul Sartre, Nietzsche and Heidegger. These worthy, sensible, belt-and-braces shows did indeed offer a great truth, or, rather, asked a great question: viz., if you're so damned clever, then why are you so pathetically miserable? Apparently the one thing philosophers can't do is smile. When looking for a philosophy to get about in, it's important to know the cut of the philosopher's jib. Like buying a used car, you want to kick the wheels, see what's under the old bonnet. In all other scientific disciplines, what the genius was actually like doesn't really matter. It wouldn't matter, say, that Darwin wore his mother's corsets or that John Logie Baird had to turn round three times before answering the phone: their subjects are external. But a philosopher's raw material is in his head, so it's germane – or, more precisely, German – to ask what sort of person he was.

Now, would you buy a used philosophy off a man who was a solitary syphilitic, who signed himself 'the crucified one' and spent the last ten years of his life as a frothing carpet-chewer? Probably not. But they're not the weirdest things about Nietzsche. The weirdest thing was that he had a rabbit up his nose. I'm sorry, but I can't listen to you go on about Superman because you've got a bunny up your nose. How did he eat with that thing? What was it like when he got a cold? No wonder the only girl he ever loved went off with his marginally less hirsute best mate. Sleeping with a German philosopher would be unpleasant; sleeping with a German philosopher with a rabbit up his nose would be quite unthinkable.

And look at Sartre – look at him because he couldn't look at you: his eyes pointed in different directions. He was appallingly hideous, a frog frog, and it bothered him; in fact, he only became an existentialist to appear interesting so he could chat up Juliette Gréco. For a brilliant man, Sartre said and did some of the dumbest things this century. And finally there's Heidegger, another truly hideous Kraut and the greatest of them all in the thinking department, the Mercedes of philosophers. Fine, well, we'll take a second-hand philosophy off him, then. Ah, there's just one small design fault – he was a Nazi, not just a sympathiser but a rabid, card-carrying, inform-on-your-mates Nazi. He was so smart, he went on being a Nazi even after Hitler had given it up as a bad idea.

Have you noticed there are no women philosophers to speak of? Like hobbies, philosophy is a sad, smelly, lonely, anorak, male thing. Smart women are just too smart to be philosophers. When you think about it, which I'm sure you do all the time, it's extraordinary how little effect philosophy has had on sentient life. From Plato to Russell, you'd barely have noticed they ever existed. This century, Gandhi, Freud and Bob Dylan have been more influential on the way we actually think and live than Sartre, Heidegger and Nietzsche and his rabbit. If you missed the programmes, here's the T-shirt version: Nietzsche killed God because he wanted to be God; Sartre killed God so he wouldn't feel guilty sticking his hand up Juliette Gréco's skirt; and Heidegger killed God because he thought Hitler could do a better job. God, meanwhile, who is blessed (one of the perks of the job is being permanently blessed) with an omnipotent sense of humour, just laughed. And when they died, He crept up behind them and went boo, giving them the fright of their ex lives, ruining their philosophies and teaching them a jolly lesson in hubris.

Philosophy (2)

There are two sorts of philosophy. There's the Wittgenstein sort and the Terry Wogan sort, as in asking Miss World what her philosophy of life is. Alain De Botton, having read the former, has realised that this dotcom-frenzied, galloping-consumerist, stressed-out, etc., etc., society has a market for turning that into the latter. His new television series does what those trendy vicars who ride motorbikes and have glove puppets in the pulpit do. It's a bit like saying: 'Look, you've always wanted to run a marathon, but don't want to do the training. Well, if you walk around your living room in a pair of shorts, you'll grasp the essentials.'

The first programme in his new series, *Philosophy – A Guide to Happiness*, tried to sell us armchair Seneca. Seneca's great claim to fame was that he taught Nero everything he knew, which you and I might have thought was grounds for an ethical red card. But then, what do we know? De Botton tried to explain Seneca by tying a small terrier to the back of his bicycle. I didn't have a clue what this was about, but I liked it. And I hope by the end of the series he has a whole zoo of anthropomorphic philosophers tied to his saddle: Plato's goat, Schopenhauer's slug, Nietzsche's rhino, Voltaire's poodle. I look forward to him peddling across Kensington Gardens chased by Disney-animated philosophers, all barking (of course), 'We're not here and we can prove it.'

It turned out that Seneca was a miserable old Scottie dog whose brilliant idea was that if you expect the worst, you won't be disappointed. When the time came for him to kill himself (not a moment too soon, by the way), he turned to his acolytes with a smug smile as if to say, 'I told you so' – thereby guaranteeing himself eternal pole position on all syllabuses.

Put like this, it was as plain as the nose on your face. He was a Yorkshireman. He was Michael Parkinson trapped in the body of a bald Roman. De Botton's problem, and I expect to see that set as an exam question, is knowing when philosophy becomes run-of-the-John Stuart Mill common sense, because philosophers are rare, but common sense is free and ubiquitous; and common sense might tell the audience that, on the whole, they'd be better off watching something else.

Music

I have this terrible feeling I've been invited to the most sensational party and have gone to the wrong address. As we come to the end of the century, it's pretty safe to say this has been the most culturally pyrotechnic one hundred years ever. I've lived through almost half of it, and most of it I don't understand. It's like being the Elizabethan who got to heaven and was asked what it was like to go to the first production of *Hamlet*. He replied: 'Oh, that Shakespeare – bit modern for me, all that anguish and metaphysical stuff. No, no, the missus and I like a nice miracle play, a good musical and a lavish production.' And then a bloke from Florence chips in: 'I know what you mean, all this modern art stuff, this Renaissance business ... Rubbish, isn't it? Give me a medieval icon, every time. Chiaroscuro – I ask you, it's just an excuse for bad drawing. It'll never catch on.' And then an ancient Egyptian says: 'You should see what they put up in a lovely bit of unspoilt desert. Brutalist skyscrapers, completely out of keeping. Give me mud bricks and a rustic papyrus roof every time. And have you seen what they've done to Athens?'

The truth is that the vast majority of people who are alive in culturally interesting times actually live in the previous century. It's a worry. The twentieth-century room I feel most embarrassingly lost in is serious music. I drift in and out, picking up bits and pieces, absurdly thankful when I can appreciate something. Ah yes, Mahler, Sibelius, Stravinsky, jolly bracing. Then a couple of mathematical Frenchmen and a touch of Philip Glass, and that's my lot. But I'm uncomfortably aware that what I cling to are the bits that remind me of nineteenth-century music. I strain for a comforting tune or a rising scale and a regular beat. Occasionally I appreciate something utterly modern and come down with the most chillingly uncomfortable sensation known to a critic: liking something and not knowing why. Simon Rattle has arrived not a syncopated beat too soon. *Leaving Home* (C4) is a guide to the music of the twentieth century. I nearly said a beginner's guide. But it manages to be complex, high-minded and erudite. Rattle looks and sounds like a 1970s *Play School* presenter with his free-form atonal hair and trust-me-you'll-like-this grin. You don't get the feeling he's talking down to you. He probably is; probably he's lying in the intellectual basement with his head down a hole. But he's quite high-minded enough for me, and his straight-to-camera lectures with piano are a harmonious mix of the technical and the philosophic. 'Through the round window we have Tristan and Isolde. This is where it began, with this chord; this is where we break with harmony for ever. It should have sounded like this: plunk plunk plink. But instead Wagner did this: plunk plunk plonk.' It was very exciting, really, an apple-on-the-head moment of enlightenment.

Rattle went on to explain that the breaking of the bonds of harmony and the tonic scale were symbolic of doing away with class structure and hierarchy and top hats and empires and visiting cards. The twentieth-century modernists were the sound of democracy. Well, up to a point; I'm with you in principle. But if 'plunk plunk plonk' is the sound of democracy, why do so few people listen to it? The answer comes back in an echo of kettle drums. They don't listen to it now, but in a hundred years Webern and Berg will be on CDs of *These You Have Loved* tunes from telly commercials. If the history of culture tells us one thing over and over, it's that today's inexplicable cacophony is tomorrow's lift music. To live through a renaissance and not be part of it, not even understand it, to dismiss it with precious ignorance and trite second-hand aphorisms – 'I've never heard Stockhausen but I think I've trodden in it' – would be a shocking waste of a life. In the first programme, Rattle pointed out that turn-of-the-century Vienna was at the centre of a volcanic modern movement in art, music, politics and psychoanalysis, but the Viennese themselves were possibly the most conservative, narrow-minded, reactionary society on earth, full of people eating chocolate cake, listening to Strauss waltzes and reading

Schiller. I had a horrible sense of déjà vu: I think he was talking about me.

Art

How Art Made the World

You've probably noticed that there seems to be an all-purpose big-series co-production script that gets passed around presenters who want to do broad-brush overviews of coffee-table subjects. They always start out something like this: 'From the moment we are born, we're surrounded by (family, soft furnishings, music, farts, whatever). They inform and change our lives, yet we never ask how (water, bathroom scales, philosophy, infectious diseases, men who want to put their hands on your knee, whatever) came to be so central to the existence of Homo sapiens. To find out, we must travel back in time to (Egypt, China, Siberia, Slough, a cupboard under the stairs, wherever). And here (presenter trudging through desert, waving hands), we can see the beginnings of the very first (dinner party, fugue, horse, breast implant, whatever).' Camera elevates on crane, then helicopter; orchestra rips clothes off; presenter appears to be small dot surrounded by (sand, Tupperware, tuna fish, whatever). You can write the rest yourself.

You know the territory we're in: short, dramatic statement of cosmic importance, punctuated by overwhelming music and lashings of visuals. *How Art Made the World* (BBC2) has been trailed for weeks as being the story of – well, I suppose – how art made the world. It's one of those fill-in-the-blank titles: *How Mud Made the World*, *How Hunger Made the World*, *How Bovis Made the World*. *How the World Made Art* would have been closer to a defendable truth, but not such a punchy headline for whichever American TV station with an education budget to waste put the co-production money into this. It was portentous nonsense, a parody of all those Robert Winston, Alan Titchmarsh, Howard Goodall shows that are themselves already *Reader's Digest* versions of *The Ascent of Man* or *Life on Earth*.

Our presenter on this was one Nigel Spivey, and what he told us was that from the moment we are born, we are surrounded by bodies. But to discover why, we had to travel back to prehistoric Austria and find some bird with a fat arse and a pinecone for a head: the Willendorf Venus, a Stone Age fertility symbol, which Nigel said looks like it does because we humans have an innate need to exaggerate. To prove it, he showed us herring-gull chicks. I'm not making this up. The herring gulls pecked at lolly sticks with red stripes on them. This was supposed to be the oh-my-golly-gosh moment where you made a connection that would change the way you saw naked bodies and everything for ever. It made me think that what we really, really need is editorial peer review before people are allowed to go on television and say the first thing that comes into their heads, to crashing music and a helicopter shot, pretending it's a fact, or even half a fact.

The idea that all art, culture and aesthetics is based on some neural imperative to deform the buttocks of Austrian women is really beyond humour. Nigel didn't even begin to try to explain why a brain would develop a need to exaggerate things. Why would Greek sculptors need to see bodies with big chests and little willies, whereas West African ones had no chest but huge willies? What does your herring gull have to say about that? There is, though, in all this bilge, an important, salient truth: anyone can make any educational programme they want if they have the money (and television is the place most people get most of their information). Before you know it, we'll be having a natural history series that proves the truth of intelligent creation and disproves Darwin, and one that points out that global warming is a communist plot to undermine the motor industry. At the moment, anyone can get away with saying anything they like on TV, as long as they don't fall foul of Ofcom. You can put facts on television in the name of education that you wouldn't be allowed to tell a class of eight-year-olds.

Imagine did *A Short History of Tall Buildings* (BBC1). It could have been *A Short Man's History of Tall Buildings*, and it could have started: 'From the moment we're born, we're surrounded by things that are taller than we are – to find out why, we need to travel back to ancient Egypt.' Thankfully, it didn't. It was little Alan Yentob taking a characteristically sideways squint at a subject that's absolutely of the moment. Post-9/11, tall buildings are all the rage, in every sense. Now every thrusting city thinks size matters.

Skyscrapers began with Mr Otis and his fail-safe lift. Once you've got the up and down worked out, you can go on building higher than any ordinary man wants to climb to discover he's forgotten the tin of anchovies and the lavatory paper. The oh-my-gosh fact from this programme was that the pyramids were the tallest man-made building for 4,000 years, only beaten in the nineteenth century. Since then, I doubt if any building has been the world's tallest for more than a generation.

Has any human record lasted that long? Man's seemingly timeless desire to be on the up-and-up may simply be because he mistakenly thinks God lives there, or because he likes the view. Or maybe he's hard-wired to live on a cliff, like the herring gull that's already chosen all his pictures.

Rolf Harris

It must be said of Rolf Harris that he's a difficult man to hate, though that doesn't mean we shouldn't try. He was born nerdily embarrassing. Time and exposure have not awarded him a scintilla of gravitas, sagacity or dress sense. All his long life, Rolf has walked into rooms in the sure and certain knowledge that, on every level, he will be the least fashionable person there. His great and unnerving quality is the reverse Midas effect: everything he touches turns to dross. Aim his panting enthusiasm at a subject, however culturally impregnable, and his grunting, mewing excitement will reduce it to a car-boot sale. Harris is the neutron bomb of kitsch.

And now, in an act of cultural philistinism matched in infamy only by the burning of the library at Alexandria, the Barbarians' rape of Rome and the sacking of the Forbidden City, some damn Tristram has dropped him on painting. Last week, in *Rolf on*

Art (BBC1), he did to Van Gogh what he'd already done to Led Zeppelin's 'Stairway to Heaven'.

Van Gogh is possibly the most complicated artist, both as a person and a painter. But not after Rolf Harris got to loving grips with him. We watched, properly dumbfounded. This was compulsively horrible. I think there may be something truly unholy about Harris. He is the great destroyer, the fifth rider of the apocalypse. Armageddon will come to the sound of Jake the Peg and Two Little Boys. We should understand that the devil will not be a fearsome thing, breathing fire and brimstone. He'll be a grinning, nerdy painter and desecrator, turning all to ashes and gall while making noises like a donkey humping a plastic bucket. We have seen pure evil. Rolf Harris is the great Lucifer.

Sister Wendy Beckett

Now there are a few things I want to know about Sister Wendy and there are many more things I don't want to know. I don't want to know what she thinks about the Lascaux caves, unless Huguenots are cementing up the door as she speaks. I don't want to know what this sister thinks about mummies' tombs, unless Boris Karloff is coming up to fulfil the curse from behind. I don't want to know what she thinks about ancient Greece, unless the bacchanal of centaurs, fauns and the great god Pan are panting in the green room to make her a bride of Zeus. What I do want to know is how come a nun who got a dispensation from a perfectly legitimate Pope to become a lifelong hermit ended up with a prime-time ten-part series on television. I understand Catholicism is a scented mystery, but this is truly bizarre. Perhaps television really is about as otherworldly as you can get. Perhaps the little box in the sitting room is the modern equivalent of St Jerome's cave. Perhaps the aerial is Simeon Stylites's pillar.

I also want to know why, if, for the past twenty years, all the nuns you've ever seen are dressed like dinner ladies in Terylene and Doc Martens, does Sister Wendy choose to look Hollywood-medieval? Why is she the last nun doing *The Sound of Music*? I expected to see a credit for 'Sister Wendy's Wardrobe by Ken Russell'. And furthermore, I want to know why her programme isn't made by that comedy company called Hat Trick Productions, as she is quite plainly Ben Elton wearing Dick Emery's teeth. She is a comedy turn. The whole point of Sister Wendy Beckett is that some sniggering Tristram can get shots of a professional virgin, dressed for the Dark Ages, next to a Renaissance Chippendale with his kit off.

Let's not kid ourselves, nothing she says about art is remotely original, useful, expert or enlightening. What they want, as they stuff their hankies into their mouths up in the directors' box, is for the grinning wimple to turn to some hung hunk and, with the stagey mannerisms of a precocious twelve-year-old ballerina, point at a marble penis and say: 'Notice the great thrust of the artist's vision, the delicate curl of pubic hair.' The word 'pubic' circumnavigated the dental disaster like a beery punch-line. Oh joy, oh heaven. She said it. She said it. It's pathetic. Sister Wendy, whatever her private motives and enthusiasms, is the sorry butt of a Tristram's ten-part, childishly smutty, practical joke. Well, I'm all for smutty childish jokes. If they were good enough for Boccaccio, it's fine by me, and if it's sacrilegious, well, God can look after himself. What I do mind is that it demeans art, which can't. What we are given are pictures made ridiculous by this freakish vision in front of them. Some people should be hermits for their own good and some should be hermits for ours. Sister Wendy falls into both categories.

David Dimbleby has a perverse TV manner, best described as a curate's smiling irritation. He's very bonhomous and smirkish, in the manner of a vicar visiting a borstal. You just get occasional flashes of a boiling distaste. He is, I guess, a man who has a public demeanour and a private attitude, and rarely do the twain meet. He plainly sees his new series *How We Built Britain* as a latter-day, colloquial and provincial *Civilisation*, and himself as a more relaxed and accessible, wattle-and-daub Kenneth Clark, a laudable but foolish ambition. Clark knew what he was talking about; Dimbleby doesn't. He tries to make up for the lack of academic or even intuitive intelligence with more vicarish enthusiasm – 'Well, golly gosh, will you just look at that.' He has a 1960s public-school boy's grasp of history, even less of architecture, and the aesthetics of a Surrey publican. But, leaving all that aside, his shortcomings as a presenter and scriptwriter are as naught compared with the hellish grandiosity of the production values, principally the music and the relentlessly hovering helicopter. The combination of soaring ersatz Russian ballet music and a swooping merchant banker's chopper was supposed to evoke elegiac, lachrymose, Churchillian jingoism for a timeless Albion. In fact, it felt much like being given a cream-tea enema.

Surrealism

There are cultural sheep and there are cultural goats. You come to identify them through experience, over time. Such as: people who don't like or understand literature read science fiction. People who don't like or understand music listen to brass bands. People who don't like or understand theatre go to *Riverdance*. People who don't like or understand opera listen to *The Three Tenors*. People who don't like or understand poetry have the Desiderata framed in their bathroom. And people who don't like or understand art simply worship surrealism.

Surrealism is the easy-on-the-eye, access-all-areas idiot's guide to subconscious metaphysical truth. In fact, it's the simple juxtaposition of disparate images, objects or words, offering a false impression of profundity. Surrealism is art for the imaginatively bereft and those with the sensitivity of blue cabbages. As a movement, surrealism was a very short, unprepossessing dead end. Anyone associated with it who had a modicum of talent or inquisitiveness, such as Buñuel or Duchamp, made their excuses and left. They left behind Magritte – a Belgian trying to work out his own suburban demons, who even David Sylvester, the man responsible for his catalogue résumé, ended up agreeing was a second-rate bore – and Salvador Dali, the Pamela Anderson of fine art. A painter who makes Russell Flint look intellectually rigorous,

Dali is an artist beloved of wigged-out heavy-metal rock guitarists and bald men with ponytails who customise the petrol tanks of Harley-Davidsons.

Jonathan Meades started his one-off exploration of surrealism, *tvSSFBM EHKL*, by trying to define what it meant, pointing out that it's a word that has slid into the language to become a sort of banal, thoughtless exclamation, and a synonym for 'weird'. No other art movement has lent its name to so much and so little. Disc jockeys don't say 'Ooh, Neue Sachlichkeit, man', or 'Very St Ives'.

Anything that can mean anything probably means nothing. Meades settled on surrealism meaning 'bizarre', which I'm not sure is any more erudite than 'weird', except that 'bizarre' is one of the very few words we have borrowed from Basque (along with basque), where it originally means a beard, and – if you're in the market for this sort of thing – that could be seen as being a bit surreal. From the definition on, this programme wasn't just a mess, it was a hirsute Pyrenean beard of a mess.

I can see how it happened. I can trace the thought processes that arrived at them, saying: 'Hey, if we're making a programme about surrealism, why don't we make it, you know, sort of surreal?' It's an almost inevitably attractive idea for a Tristram, who can visualise wobbly watches, naked nuns and Meades with an apple for a head. Attractive, but wrong. They should have knocked it on the apple right there and then, because, frankly, you wouldn't make a programme about Impressionists and shoot it all out of focus, and you wouldn't make a documentary about opera with a commentary that was entirely recitative. And you really shouldn't make a surreal programme about surrealism. The two positives make a negative.

What you get, if you try to do surreal on the very mundane reality of TV, is pastiche *Monty Python* – which is, indeed, what most of this looked like. (Interestingly, 'Pythonesque' has entered the language as a synonym for 'surreal'.) The thread that meandered through this stream of unconsciousness was *Alice in Wonderland*. Meades claimed Lewis Carroll was a great surrealist, which he simply wasn't. Lots of artists lay claim to the past in order to bolster their theories. Picasso grabbed West African animist masks for cubism, but that didn't make every Congolese witch doctor a cubist. Dodgson wasn't a surrealist; he wrote children's books and fancied children. What we ended up with was a programme that was funny, partly by intent and partly by accidental association, which inadvertently pointed out a lateral truth. What 'surreal' has really come to mean is not 'funny weird', but 'funny ha-ha'. It wasn't meant to be like this, it was supposed to be angry and anarchistic and revolutionary and dangerously sexual, but, in fact, it's just funny. In the end, I'm sorry, it's only bad *Monty Python*.

I'm sorry, because anyone who likes and understands TV loves Meades. He is one of its finest practitioners and someone I admire without bounds. He is also a fellow food critic and, I hope, still a friend, so this hasn't been easy to write. But I think, in mitigation, I could offer it that most faintly wan compliment: very brave. It was very brave.

Presenting

'Here's some advice,' said the presenter of the first television programme I appeared on as a pundit. 'Go for it, attack the camera, get right in its face, be assertive, think of presenting like doing that All Blacks rugby thing.' The haka? 'That's it: presenting on TV is doing the haka. Okay, camera, sound, off you go.' When I finished my thirty seconds on some fey and tentative watercolours, there was that moment of silence dreaded by all Tristrams. Television folk know that hell will be dead air. The director coughed and said: 'Good, good. Could we just run through it again, lose the arm-waving, try to keep your feet in one position, and perhaps no tongue at the end? Just be yourself, be natural.'

'Be yourself and be natural' should be engraved in the lobby of Broadcasting House in place of 'Nation shall speak peace unto nation'. It's what every guest on local news or late-night chat shows hears, whispered by a fat girl in black leggings carrying a clipboard as she shoves them into the limelight. Everyone has a moment of blind panic where they think: 'This is about as abnormal and uneasy as anything that's ever happened in my life.' It's like asking a ballet dancer to act normally, or trying to be yourself in a train crash.

Television is pretend reality: it pretends it's not happening, which is a bit like pretending the tiger in the corner isn't there. Why some people are good at it and most of us aren't is a mystery. There are any number of failed weather presenters and *Look North* autocue-readers who run cottage industries teaching wannabes and politicians how to give good camera, but if you have to teach naturalism, then it ain't natural, stupid. Virtually every television professional I've met has a spare personality they keep for broadcasting, a cartoon version of themselves. Occasionally, they're completely different, a user-friendly Mr Hyde. Directors prefer it if they don't move in front of a camera, so this means they're reduced to putting everything into their face and voice. It has to be big and simple and quick.

Which brings us to the British Empire, which was big and complex and very slow. The new series *Empire* (C4) produced yet another dilemma: do you get it fronted by a professional presenter who will do a glib job but won't know what he's talking about, or do you get a historian who comes across like an academic chatting up a tiger? The perfect presenter is, of course, David Attenborough, who's both, and really can chat up tigers. Or you can go the Simon Schama route: he's just the windward side of hopeless on TV, but this adds veracity. It's sort of how we want clever blokes to be.

The presenter and writer of *Empire* is Niall Ferguson, a respected right-wing monetary historian who has been populist in the press and academic between hard covers. His problem is that he plainly wants to be good on television, he wants to be asked back, he's aching to be admired for himself and not his subject, which is fatal. Because nobody knows what makes a good TV presenter, presenters themselves tend to copy each other, and Ferguson has made this understandable mistake.

He's a varsity punt who wants to sound like an aircraft carrier, so he's gone and contracted a terminal dose of the Clarksons. In fact, he sounds like a cross between Jeremy and Fife Robertson.

Clarkson is, of course, incredibly good at television. He got his delivery direct from the Moses of presenters, Alan Whicker, the best there has ever been. An enormous amount of contemporary television owes its foundation garments to Whicker, but Clarkson is like 'The Birdie Song': once you've got him in your head, he won't come out. His trademark is the syncopated semicolon. It turns up; (pause) everywhere. As in: 'This is the biggest big end; (pause) in the world,' delivered with a dying fall. Ferguson does it remorselessly, usually as 'Blah, blah, blah; (pause) the world had ever seen'. He's not helped by being an old man caught up in a young man's body, which is the wrong way round on TV. Far better to be the other Attenborough, Dickie, who's quite plainly a twelve-year-old playing Abraham.

The history itself was a gadabout gallimaufry of *Daily Mail* headlines. Just the title alone, *How Britain Made the Modern World*, is plainly daft. It's all very well wanting to start an argument, but it's got to be one that's worth having. If some bloke at the end of the bar shouts, 'The world's flat, and I'll fight anyone who disagrees,' most reasonable folk just say, 'Fine, whatever.' Ferguson's history is a series of bellicose Churchillian assertions that leave you thinking: 'Actually, why bother?' It's an odd thing that almost all television history is of the Sellar and Yeatman type, an idealised Edwardian public-school syllabus, as if Strachey had never written *Eminent Victorians*; as if none of the twentieth-century historical revisions had ever happened. It's as if all the presenters are modelling themselves on cuddly old Macaulay.

Trinny and Susannah apply the balm of their gushing encouragement and enthusiasm like Barbara Woodhouse patronising a special-needs mongrel. Now you and I might think the whole point of shopping is that it's harmless recreational fun, and the universal selling point of makeover shows is empathy and aspiration. But this one looks like an invitation to find a cure for a self-inflicted terminal illness: 'If you ever wear a roll-neck again, you'll die, do you understand?'

I have a tender spot for Brian Sewell. He is a man whose life has been devoted to pissing elegantly into any and every wind. He manages to be both biblical and whimsical simultaneously. What's interesting about Sewell is not his arch views on culture, but the view of him as a strange folly: he is an edifice of tense contradictions, a man who wants to be on stage and off it at the same time. It's an awkward way to go about making television.

Stars in their Eyes started its umpteenth series this week, and the big question is: who does Matthew Kelly think he's doing? Having spent a decade introducing dental nurses who want to be Gloria Gaynor, he seems to have lost even the remotest grasp of who he actually is. His voice is a Linguaphone advert of accents that slide across continents and oceans, pausing to pick up a consonant here and a diphthong there. His body language, of which there is an entire orthopaedic textbook, bears no relevance to what he's actually saying. Kelly has watched so many people be someone else, he's nobody. It's like watching a cheap hologram do human.

Melvyn is twenty-five this week. I know, I know, he doesn't look a day over fifteen, but he has been carrying the nation's middlebrow on his head for a quarter of a century now. *The South Bank Show* took time off to pat itself on the back, to go 'mwa mwa' and say to itself 'Darling, you look absolutely ravishing, you've been utterly extraordinary, nobody could do the arts like you do'. And nobody does. But the arts weren't the real joy of this show. That was the trip down memory lane in Melvyn's wardrobe. My, here's a man who knows how to walk into a gents' outfitters anywhere in Worthing and say, 'I'll take that jacket, that's very me, that's very me on TV.' I think all of you who saw the show will agree that the high point was a very fetching knitted tank top circa the early 1980s, worn with the trademark tie, which always reminds me of a badly reefed spinnaker.

Have you ever seen Parky and Melvyn in the same room at the same time? I think not. And I know why: they've pooled the barnet. When Parky gets to wear it, Melvyn has to stay home in a darkened room, as bald as an egg. It is the most extraordinary hair. It reclines like a lascivious odalisque. It's provocative, come-up-and-part-me-some-time kind of hair. You know that Barry Norman took a photograph of it into the special effects department and said: Make me one just like this. As Parky gets older, his face gets baggier, but his hair is forever bosky and luxuriant, albeit touched with Frost (Jack not David). Perhaps it's made a Faustian pact with Teazy Weazy: it may be grey, but it's Dorian Gray.

Carol Vorderman

Carol Vorderman. What's that? I hear you shout? More! More! More! You want to hear more about Carol Vorderman? Well, of course you do. We all do. We haven't heard anything like enough about Carol. Oh, dear me, no. I for one hunger for ever more information. There is no Vorderman titbit too small or foolish that I won't value higher than rubies. My hunger for Vordermanalia is bulimic. What's her waist size? How old is her hair? How many naff events has she been photographed at this week? How many times has she been on television today? How many inches of thigh can we see? Add them all together, divide by her IQ and you get the number on the board.

Vorderman's latest task is to front a live television show that indeed proves she is a greater physicist than Einstein (as if you needed convincing). She manages not just to bend time but to slow it down so it's barely moving. During *Find a Fortune* (ITV), I truly believed that my life would end before the credits. My set seemed to have lengthened until Vorderman stretched on and on over the curve of the Earth. Lobotomising boredom is the least of this programme's worries. When you get all aerated and you talk about the muck and immoral garbage on television, you usually mean a couple of Styrofoam stripper's tits on Channel 5 or a transvestite dickectomy on late-night Channel 4. But these are Reithian public-service broadcasts compared to *Find a Fortune*; light entertainment from an original idea by Uriah Heep.

This is a vile, venal programme; essentially probate and executors as fun. Carol hands out pathetically meagre amounts of money to a dutifully grateful studio pond life, from insurance policies and legacies they're too dim to remember. This is coupled with the greedy bits of *Antiques Roadshow*, where retired folk are told their memorabilia might be worth a grand at auction. Vorderman herself presents with the brain-dead, uncaring, patronising chirpiness of a rep on an OAP's coach tour. She presents so many of these bottom-scraping shows that she must lose track or interest. Only the intellectual capacity of the studio audience blankly lowing back at her remains constant.

Look at them: if you wired all their brains together they wouldn't illuminate an orphanage Christmas tree. And what does Oh Carol think she looks like? No, what does she want to look like when she gets up in the morning? What she actually looks like is mutton dressed as yak. The skirts that are an embarrassing innuendo, the come-and-get-me coiffure, the factor 97 make-up, with thickly sticky lips that look like she's been drinking warm chicken fat. The whole edifice is an embarrassing and desperate fanning of the dead embers of sensuality. There's a middle-aged woman who looks like this perched on the end of every wine bar in Cheshire. The moral of Vorderman is like your granny said: clever is as clever does.

> I've always enjoyed watching Michael Barrymore. He has always seemed to be a body invaded by demons that throw him round the box, talking in tongues; not so much a smooth performance as an incubus convention, or do I mean succubus? Anyway, if they ever wanted to make a farce version of *The Exorcist*, Barrymore would be the perfect green slime-chucker.

> John Peel's voice-over was music to the ears. He sounded like Eeyore intoning the succession of the Avignon popes.

Terry Wogan

Oh, now, where was I? What's he rambling on about, I hear you say? (As well you might.) All things considered (which they rarely are … if you ask me), it used to be so simple. The world was divided between and betwixt those who hated Terry Wogan with an allergic reaction and those who hated him with irony. There was talk, once upon a time, of an army of fundamentalist fans who lived only for his maundering circumlocution, but nobody any of us knows has ever met one.

Still, for more years than I care to remember, Terry Wogan has been the monkey wrench of British broadcasting. Any nutty

format, he'll do. Nothing is too ridiculous or grisly or rusty for
him not to be able to fit his jaws round it. He is now the king of
lost and lousy telly. That semi-anaesthetised, third-person ambling
stream of whimsy that is his verbal motif has all the infuriating
repeatability of a summer novelty single. Once you start thinking
in Woganish, you can't stop dropping everything into parentheses
and inverted commas. They say (and who, pray, are the 'they' that
are forever saying this, and how can we get them to shut up?) ... they
say that women, buildings and politicians all become respectable
with age. Well, something similar happens to light-entertainment
broadcasters. If they can just hang on in the old cathode grey tube
for long enough they wear down the hard edge of your repugnance
and you can't remember why it was you hated them in the first
place. So it is with Tel. It's pathetic, but I'm growing rather fond
of the old git. Mostly because he's so plainly given up caring, or
even concentrating. If you listen carefully to his self-deprecating
act (not something we'd recommend to the sensitive or the emotionally unstable, madam), you'll realise that it's all actually straight
carpet-slipper camp. Turn up the falsetto a little and take one of
the meanings out of the double entendres and you've got Graham
Norton. Though I expect neither Terry nor Graham would thank
me for pointing it out.

A week ago, I saw a gardening programme in which Diarmuid Thingy
– the Irish lad with the gone-to-seed head and laundry-basket looks
– was called the 'bad boy of gardening'. I'm sorry: bad boy of gardening? The herbaceous Uday Hussein? For a moment, I had a fantasy
about a film called *The Magnificent Seven Perennials*, about a collection of garden presenters who go to save an allotment for provincial
peasants from genetically engineered rape. Alan Titchmarsh as Yul
Brynner, Monty Don as Steve McQueen and Diarmuid as the little
bad boy whose name nobody can remember. Then again, that's the
plot of every gardening show anyway. Gardening has got completely
out of hand. Nobody warned us that this would be a consequence of
global warming – television muck-spreaders springing up like Russian
vines all over the schedules.

Louis Theroux

I'm slowly being worn down on Louis Theroux. 'Oh, you can't hate Louis Theroux,' nice girls say to me. 'No, we love Louis Theroux, he's a poppet and so funny – don't you think he's funny?' No, frankly, I think he's a conniving, phoney, insinuating Uriah Heep who has this routine of coming on all wan and floppy and unthreatening and then stitches up his victims later in the cutting room. I suspect that, in real life, Louis is foul to waiters, loses his temper at airline check-ins, sniffs his own armpits, sets fire to his digestive gases and says 'Do you know who I am?' in an American accent as a pick-up line. In short, I don't trust a word he says. Apart from that, I suppose, grudgingly, I'd admit he has a sort of relaxed presence, if you go for that sort of thing.

Actually, I like him a little better now that he's turned into Ruby Wax and is doing *Hello!* on the box. Last week, in *When Louis Met Paul and Debbie* (BBC2), he went in search of the perfectly formed Paul Daniels and his other half from the weather-vane house, Debbie McGee, in their beautiful Thames-side home. The great joy, of course, was simply seeing what a lot of money will get you by way of interior design, if entirely unencumbered by taste or style. And their outfits, oh my dear. There's a certain type of clothing, virtually tribal costume, that's unknown outside Surrey and parts of Cheshire. Where on earth do you go to get a Paul Daniels-style jacket or Debbie McGee lounging-around-the-breakfast-bar outfit? They're just too wonderful to be worn by us common folk.

Louis managed to do something I'd have sworn was impossible: he made me warm to Daniels, almost smile at him. Louis's whole illusion depends on his victim liking him, feeling sorry and protective of him. Well, Daniels knows a thing or two about illusions and telly. He was distant, bored and taciturn, and he made Louis beg, then plead, for some sign of chumminess. Consequently, you rather despised Louis-no-mates and admired Daniels, though admittedly this is all relative. If all three of them were hanging by a thread in a window-cleaner's cradle on the 38th floor, you'd wait until after coffee before calling the fire brigade. It was a lesson in interviewing technique: the camera can stand anything but lack of interest. I think appreciating Theroux is an age thing, and I'm on the wrong side. Those who imagine he's terrifically clever and amusing never saw Alan Whicker.

If you haven't seen Trevor McDonald's satirical *News Knight* (ITV), press the red button now, because it can be only a matter of days before someone pulls it off the screen. Sir Trevor is old, black and a newsreader – three things you're just not allowed to laugh at. Together, they are the most powerful anti-comic entity in the universe. Watching him deliver a monologue is like watching your mum lap-dance in school assembly, only more embarrassing. It's not just that he has no sense of comic timing; he has absolutely no idea which way round a gag goes. He reads the words with a rising tone of baffled incomprehension, like a madman reading the ingredients of his medication. And he does it in the company of three professional comedians, who stare at him with terror. They are like pallbearers at the funeral of their own careers. It's brilliant.

The Truth about Killer Dinosaurs (BBC1) was yet more reconstruction. This one desperately reduced palaeontology to *Robot Wars*, with yet more repetitive soulless Manga animation. It made you realise that the upside of extinction was not having to meet Bill Oddie, who looks and sounds ever more like a frantically irritated British Rail ticket collector. The more I see him, the more I'm convinced that both Bill Oddie's parents were Jim Henson. He is made entirely out of old socks and fly buttons and is an example of the truth that we all grow into our names.

If God has a thousand names, so must the devil. To that of Rolf Harris, we should also add Alan Titchmarsh. I know some of you think that at worst he's harmless, but wake up and smell the roses. Don't be fooled. He is the slug in the shrub. You must resist the cosy charm. It hides a soul of fungi. He has neat DDT in his veins. I can't stress too strongly that Titchmarsh has done more to desecrate England than the Luftwaffe. He is a one-man blitzkrieg, turning this soft rolling land into a decked-and-paved Belgian hotel forecourt sprouting emetic water features and Japanese grass. The man is the Leylandii of television presenters, his new series, *How to be a Gardener*, a Leni Riefenstahl epic of species-ism. Gardening has always been vegetable fascism and Titchmarsh is its Führer. You may think I'm overreacting, may think he's just a daytime bit of OAP totty, but beware: today it's disgusting eugenic experiments in a potting shed, tomorrow the front lawn, and the weediest of us will end up on the compost heap of history. Oh yes, he may make the euphorbia bloom on time, but he wants to build a straight herbaceous border from John o'Groats to Land's End, with crazy paving that will last a thousand years. We must resist. We must macadam, firebomb a garden centre. Today it's hanging baskets, tomorrow it will be the rest of us.

Paxman is playing up his role as the Hook of pantomime politics. The politicians rather love this. It's like going on some terrifying funfair ride, horrible at the time, but great to boast about afterwards. He got hold of the first Tory black candidate to win a seat. The poor chap had only been an MP for three minutes and he had Paxo all over him like the Spanish Inquisition with Ebola.

Ant and Dec, the ubiquitous Polish plumbers of presenting …

Do you know what to do with Ray Mears? These days, few people know the correct use of a Ray Mears. It's a skill we've sadly lost. If you were, say, caught at the end of a strange and foreign dining table next to Ray Mears, would you be able to make him interesting? Or would you just give up, go to sleep and wait for a merciful death? To those of you who haven't come across him before, Mears is a telly survivalist, always whittling and rubbing things together.

I must admit I find Mears strangely fascinating. He is quite plainly a really severe case of arrested development: the cub scout who never grew up; the little fat kid who built dens in the woods, played cowboys and Indians on his own and set fire to cats. Fire looms large in Mears's childish view of the world. He has about himself, at any one time, at least a dozen combustible elements, just in case. If you ever have the misfortune to find yourself on an aeroplane with Mears, quietly inform the stewardess and have him thoroughly cavity-searched.

Clive James is a man who's so multi-talented he can supply his own simultaneous laughter track; a man who looks like his eyes need cuff-links, a man who is an ambient polytechnic, but then again, a man who's living his life backwards. He started off at the end of a brilliant career, a fearsomely clever author and journalist whose TV criticism is a benchmark for those of us who slouch for a living. He wrote breathtakingly waspish contemporary satire in rhyming couplets in the manner of Pope. He used wit like a conductor's baton to arrange the orchestra of original thought. But today he has regressed to being just another TV comedy turn who beats time to his own one-man band of trite truism; here once there was insight, now there's just inflection.

Clive James – Postcard from Havana (ITV) walked a well-beaten track. Clive Anderson's been there, done that, so has Jools Holland and Jeremy Clarkson, and I'm sure Judith Chalmers has got the T-shirt. It all looked as familiar as Brighton. Clive now walks like an infant, or perhaps a man who's discovered too late that there's no paper. We all know that at some point he's going to dance badly, that he will be happily humiliated by giggling girls, and that his self-deprecation is merely the good manners of a chap who learned Japanese so that he could read Proust in translation. The truth is, James doesn't seem to care any more. He doesn't care if we're interested or informed or impressed; he doesn't want to know us, he's quite happy with his hands in his pockets, knowing himself.

Richard Whiteley

So, he for whom all conundrums are literal has prematurely taken one from the top. Farewell, then, Richard Whiteley, friend to the long-term unemployed and those in sheltered accommodation. He was the Mother Teresa of television, a person who tirelessly loved the unlovely and the marginal. Countdown was, as I'm sure you

know, the first programme to be shown on Channel 4, and probably still the cheapest. Whiteley had presented every single one for
twenty-three years, which is something, but not as much something
as having spent twenty-three years with Carol Vorderman, an act
of unbelievable and unimaginable endurance.

I met Richard once at a party conference in Blackpool. He was
Yorkshire TV's political correspondent – not many people outside
God's own county know that. We had a couple of drinks, and I
can confirm that he was possibly the nicest man who ever existed
in a cathode-ray tube. He was utterly without side or artifice; in
fact, disappointingly, Whiteley wasn't a conundrum at all. He was,
though, hopeless as a TV presenter: gauche, clumsy, slow, tongue-
tied, forgetful, dull and disengaged. He was a walking dictionary
of traits, any one of which should have barred him from appearing
in front of a camera twice.

Not only did he not miss a day for twenty-three years, he didn't
get one iota better. To stoically remain that utterly useless at what
you do, but continue doggedly doing it, and with eternal sunny
optimism, is actually quite inspirational. So, there we are, that's
Richard Whiteley: part Mother Teresa, part Candide. I do hope
they play the *Countdown* tune as he goes through the curtain to
the crem.

Gordon Ramsay is the most sought-after presenter on television at
the moment. There isn't a genre that doesn't think it will be improved
by being rubbed up the wrong way against him. And, indeed, he has
done little wrong. He's watchable, pantomime-rude and has that most
valuable telly comestible, boundless salty enthusiasm. I can see the
future of post-watershed terrestrial television being Gordon Ramsay
and Jonathan Ross sharing half the licence fee each, endlessly telling
each other to f*** off in a joshing, laddie sort of way while learning to
foxtrot for ever and ever.

I'm more than a little worried about Methuselah Harvey-Jones, who's
reprising his hit show of last century, *Troubleshooter* (BBC2), going
around telling square peg manufacturers that their threads turn the

wrong way. Given that promotion is a vital part of business, what does he think he looks like? If Harvey-Jones walked into your kitchen and told you it was an archaic, nineteenth-century shop floor that needed radical reorganisation and that your shepherd's pie was hopelessly outdated, you'd say: 'There's the mirror, Mr Pot, take a look at yourself. You look like an escaped bit of slow motion from *Ape-Man.*' I mean, would you buy a second-hand cannonball factory off the bloke?

It's not just the hair, which for years has been a horrible example of long-term neglect and mismanagement. I'm deeply concerned that he's lost all his teeth. As far as one can tell, and I grant you it's not altogether easy, he's missing an entire upper set. 'Troubleshooter gets his gums into British Industry.' Methuselah losing his teeth is as poignant a symbol for the state of British industry as a BMS salesman could hope for. Sad to say that Harvey-Jones has finally become the unacceptable face of capitalism.

Joan Bakewell

A couple of weeks ago, I bumped into Joan Bakewell on the stairs of the Reform Club – as unlikely as coming across Michael Winner in the queue for an Ibiza beach-rave Portaloo. The club doorman, by the way, had just made a girl take off her skirt because denim wasn't allowed, presumably on the assumption that a young lady freezing in a thong was less disturbing to the sensibilities of the dribbling old gits than calf-length indigo cotton. 'Rules is rules, I'm afraid, madam. We can offer you a club tie.' Not for the first time I wondered what it was the Reform imagines it's reforming – twelfth-century Switzerland, perhaps. But then, reform is one of those words, like thank you, charming and excuse me, that, placed in the mouth of a certain sort of Englishman, has a completely inverted meaning.

Reform could be Joan's middle name. She gave a little sigh and told me she was drained, wrung out, scrotum-eyed with watching pornography on the web. Now, just the thought of Joan surfing the dirty bits is enough to get gents of a certain age rearranging the gristly cruet set. It certainly does it for me. 'It's all for research, for my new television series on taboos.' Of course it is, Joan, of course it is.

The real joy of this programme wasn't the nudes – of which there were plenty, carefully neutered of eroticism – but Joan, whose sensible, politely modulated, studiedly untitillatable middle-class common sense couldn't quite hide the fact that she has a racy past. After all, this is the chick who was the original thinking man's crumpet, the girl who twined her miniskirted legs on the *Late Night Line-Up* sofa and smoked Gitanes provocatively while giving interviews, an act that, in today's absurd, morally whimsical climate, would be far more shocking than appearing naked.

In the Reform, she told me that the denouement of her show was a man with an erection. She would point at this piece of simple hydraulic engineering and tell us it was the one thing we'd never been allowed to see on television before. The Tristrams at the BBC were jolly excited. 'Jolly good,' they said, 'jolly brave of old Joan.' But, of course, it would have to be pixillated, like a criminal, thus missing the entire point. And so it was. We were shown a man with a weirdly op-art phallus that, due to the technicalities of censorship, looked far larger and more exciting than was feasible. Joan regarded him like an exhibit in the Saatchi Gallery. Indeed, the look on her face was the most revealing and human thing in the whole programme. A sort of restrained, flirtatious pride. Cats and cream came to mind. A fleeting smile that said: 'I did that, I can still raise the beast.'

It was damn impressive. How many other TV presenters would dare get in front of a camera to elicit a stiffy and say: 'Here's one I made earlier?' Vanessa? Esther? I don't think so. Clarkson, perhaps.

That's the thing about Joan Bakewell. She may be the last bluestocking on television, but we know, and she knows we know, they're held up with rubber suspenders.

I never believed Barry Norman really liked film, had ever enjoyed the warm sense of togetherness, the pounding excitement that you only get in the dark in the back row of the cinema when the Pearl & Dean trailer goes 'Pa-Pa-Pa-Pa-Pa-Pa-Pa-Pa-Pa-Pa' and your best girl reaches over for the popcorn when you didn't buy any. I never believed Barry ever bought a ticket for a cinema. He's permanently underwhelmed by movies, directors and stars, by the whole glittery business. If he happened upon something he quite liked then the closest he came to enthusiasm was to muster the look of a basset hound being given a eucalyptus suppository.

Was there ever a man who has been so comprehensively overlooked by Father Time as Peter Snow? He's the least cutting-edge person. Put him in a velvet dressing gown and he is an eighteenth-century quack about to discover the recipe for eternal youth using a phoenix egg.

One of the things that fascinates me about car programmes is that when all is said and done, cars are just another disposable lump of consumer stuff. Why don't they make programmes like this called, say, *The Hoover's the Star* or *Classic Food Mixers*? Scene: Quentin standing on gravel path of Surrey mansion, with Kenwoods lined up behind him. He speaks to camera: 'In 1964, Tommy Girder, Kenwood's inspired but erratic design supremo, unveiled the Malibu Cordon Bleu. The mythology has it that the shop floor broke into spontaneous applause and grown men wept. It was the beginning of a legend. The mixer was dead – long live the mixer. With its sassy curves and etiolated chrome, its 5-amp transversely mounted electric motor with six speeds and pulse function, it was simply the most beautiful thing in the kitchen. The bread-kneading attachment alone was revolutionary. This was the shape of soup to come. The Malibu had the body of Brigitte Bardot and the head of Mrs Bridges. That year Kenwood entered it in the gruelling five-day Ideal Home Exhibition and the rest, as they say, was dinner-party history. The legend in its own lunchtime was born.'

John Motson

Very occasionally, our European brothers and sisters show us the way forward on television. Just once in a while among the piles of Eurodross of German pornography, French philosophy discussions and Spanish beachfront talent shows, there is a gleam of pure gold. I'm thinking, of course, of *The Singing Ringing Tree*, *Jeux Sans Frontières* and that German detective series called something like *Dork* that had third-degree moustaches. Very rarely there's a ray of genius from across the Channel, and there was one last week.

I didn't see it; I wouldn't have understood it if I had. But I've been told an Italian television station has galvanised the nation by importing a single Viagra pill. Only the Italians could see the wider possibilities of Viagra. Live on television, it was presented to some hulking footballer on the understanding that he would return and give a blow-by-blow debrief. The nation was riveted. In the immortal words of Puccini, no one slept. Certainly not the footballer. The next day, from Milan to Syracuse, the streets were empty. The nation was glued to its sets. The hulk, bowed and breathless, looked deep into the camera lens and said words to the effect of: 'Eet was like a Ferrari. I was a performance machine. But, the poetry, eet was gone.' Aah, it was a moment of pure opera.

You see, Viagra inflates flaccid ratings. One pill can add ten million viewers to a performance. Think what it could do for *Blind Date*. I was considering all this while watching *The Full Motty* (BBC1), an evening with John Motson. In all the annals of pathetic, sad, cold, wet little England's television, this must claim the victor ludorum. A pandemically dull little man being grinned over by a celebrity audience that was just screaming for an earthquake. Here's a tip: if you ever walk into a brightly lit room full of vaguely familiar strangers and catch sight of Jimmy Tarbuck, and if he winks at you and says, 'The gang's all here, me and Lynchie,' you know the game's up. It's all over.

You may go on walking the earth for a few more years, but you have become one of the undead, a mere husk. Tarbie and Lynchie, along with Greavesie and Brucie, are the Four Putters of the Apocalypse from the clubroom of hell; the vampires of style, originality, vivacity and potency. When that cheeky-chirpy-scousy voice says, 'You are the guvnor. I've been watching you for years and you are a true professional. Lynchie will back me up on that,' that's the moment you're cast into the utter oblivion of a parallel Surrey universe of nafforama. Just to give you a taste of how bad *The Full Motty* was, they played a game that could have been pulled from *Crackerjack*. A gaggle of page-three lovelies were paraded wearing obscure football shirts. Motty had to identify the teams. 'Think you'll find that's Motherwell's away strip.' The girl then lifted up her shirt to reveal the club's name on her vest. Titters all round. I yearned, prayed, begged for the last girl to hike up her kit and reveal an absence of vest and shout 'Bristol City', and for Jimmy Hill to race across the stage, press a single Viagra into Motson's sweaty paw and say: 'Off you go, my son. England expects, on me 'ead. Give it the old one-two in the box and come back and tell us all about it tomorrow.'

Football, they think it's all over, but, oh God, it never is.

Un-facts

Tell me something: that's what you think when you switch on. Go on: show me something I didn't know. Widen my aperture, deepen my horizon, anecdote me up, Scotty. This is the information age, so inform me. That's what television does – it tells you stuff: facts, feelings, fantasies and football results.

Broadcasting is by far and away the biggest dispenser of information in the world. It makes the internet look like a provincial lending library. Now call me pre-modern, but I'm from a generation that believed information was a good thing – the more you had, the richer you were. Knowledge is power, and learning was the one thing in which moderation was not a virtue. You could never have too much. Cram as much as you can and the truth will set you free. But I'm beginning to have doubts. In fact, I'm beginning to think that perhaps there are limits and that, frankly, I'm running out of storage space. There are things that television is telling me I'd rather not lug about, not because they are distressing, just remedially ugly and useless. I have a nagging sense that television is laying cuckoo eggs in my head, and they are hatching and evicting weaker, more elegant things. For instance, I'm sure I used to have an opinion on late-Byzantine glass: I know I did, but now I can't find it. Every time I search, I come up with the nation's favourite pop song. And the Thirty Years War – I can do the first twenty-seven, but the last three have gone missing. In their place, I've got the first episode of *24*, which is annoying, because I don't care how *24* ends, but I'd really like to know what happened in the Thirty Years War. Television has managed to do something that should be metaphysically impossible.

Here's a conundrum: what do you call a box that, the more you put in it, the emptier it gets? A television. Television makes less of more. Take last week's offering, *The Nation's Favourite Food: Comfort* (BBC2). I now know what the nation's top ten favourite comfort foods are, and I wish I didn't, because it has eradicated the names of ten rare English butterflies. The nation's favourite comfort food is an un-fact. It has been mechanically created where there was no fact before. Nobody outside a television has ever asked what the nation's favourite comfort food is – in descending order. They have never asked because there is no need to know. Knowing what the nation's favourite comfort food is adds precisely nothing to the sum of life. It doesn't alter your own comfort or the comfort of strangers. It's an un-fact that squats in your head like a stupid tumour, and I don't see why I should suffer it alone. So, for those of you who had better things to do than watch it, like carding your navel lint or making chess pieces out of the dog's earwax, here's just a taste: soup, toast, rice pudding, ice cream, chocolate. Have you had enough yet? Can you feel the rules of bezique dribbling away like sea water out of your ears?

The recipe for an un-fact is simple. First, you think of an un-question: say, which endangered species would play the best football, or a top ten of what food tastes best when you vomit? And then you get the researchers to stand outside shopping centres in Cardiff, Sheffield, Taunton and Gateshead, and you ask 1,000 single mothers and unemployed stevedores on Valium for an opinion – and voilà, turn an un-question into an un-statistic, which becomes an un-fact. To make it a television programme, just get half-a-dozen celebrity-style people who happen to be hanging around the larder (you may substitute barely recognisable nonentities if you are cooking on Five). Record them for an hour. Chop up the tape. Mix. Broadcast in the early evening for an hour. This is now what passes for documentaries – un-factual broadcasting. The only edible thing about *The Nation's Favourite Comfort Food* was the delicious Tara Palmer-Tomkinson doing a fabulous, unintentional impersonation of the mouthwatering Nigella Lawson. Now, how often have you thought: what wouldn't I give to see that Tara do that Nigella? Well, if we could get a couple of dozen truants and security guards to agree with you, we could make it an un-fact and make it happen.

Nature

David Attenborough

It's obvious, isn't it? David Attenborough is God.

Consider the evidence. He is omnipresent. There is no corner of rain forest or tundra where Attenborough is not. He is omnipotent. He says come, and the elements come. He says go, and yea, even the waters of the deep recede. All elements are as one to Attenborough. All creatures great and small do his bidding, pose and prance, mate and die. He is timeless. He has been the still, small voice of calm at the heart of your life cycle since before you can remember. He was here before JC – Judith Chalmers. He has followed the course of all true deities: once he was corporeal, he strode and lurked with the furry denizens of the world, but now he has ascended into the ether, and is just a voice of unutterable wisdom and love that resonates from horizon to horizon around the world, echoing from snowy peaks, whispering in the smallest burrow.

But most important of all, dearly beloved, you and I know that when Attenborough says something, it's the truth. In a world of hype and puff and spin, his is the voice of absolute veracity. Attenborough is the word, and the word is Attenborough. *The Blue Planet* (BBC1), it must be said, is among the greatest creations of a beneficent small-screen god. It didn't quite take seven days to make, but the modern equivalent, £7 million, which, all things considered – and all things watery are considered – is, frankly, a miracle. That's the same as a Sunday-night costume drama. It makes you realise what overrated creatures actors are when one small fish with a brain the size of an aspirin can fill you with more real, ragged emotion than the RSC.

The filming and editing and sound on this series is staggering. The awe of the visuals never lets up for a moment. Whether it's killer whales hunting grey whales, or the underwater smorgasbord that is a shoal of sardines, we are left on the edge of our seats, jaws hanging, simply stunned at the complex, sleek beauty of the world out there. I had no idea, we all say, that I shared this small, spinning, drenched globe with so much beauty and wonder.

And here, we come to my personal purveyance of dissent. Because we don't. This is not the real world. This is Unnatural History, life cut together with the niftiness of a Guinness commercial. This vast place only exists, Tardis-like, in the small glass box. The sea isn't like this. Nature isn't like this. *The Blue Planet* is like being in a vast baroque cathedral. It's an idealised, hyper-realistic lie told on behalf of a deeper truth. You must remember that all nature films are shot silent. All the deliciously *Star Wars* sound effects are added later, by a man with a bucket, a pair of rubber gloves and a synthesiser. But most unnaturally of all, Attenborough gives nature a narrative, a story, a series of short parables. This imposes a human linear order and design on the instinctual chaos of natural selection. He does what all religions try to do: make sense of the random.

Attenborough's view of the world is all-pervasive. There are at least four acolyte channels solely devoted to its propagation. We all know, absolutely know, the truth about hundreds of natural things that only exist in our small box in the living room. We have never experienced them, and nobody ever will. Well, it's fine if the greater good that this soundtracked, edited, masterfully filmed vision provokes is a greater awareness of the fragility and privilege of life. But I also happen to think it can lead to the heresy of a sort of self-hating, utopian intolerance. Nature films such as *The Blue Planet* may also provoke a dysfunctional and twisted misunderstanding of mankind that ends up in the wackier and more violent nihilism of the extreme alternative eco-green movement. The species we should really be in awe of is not the one in front of the camera, but the one behind it.

Holly Hunter is a film star who became famous for playing a piano in New Zealand, so naturally she's perfectly positioned to talk knowledgeably about predators in Africa. She came to *Cheetahs with Holly*

Hunter (ITV) with two points of mutual interest: bounding enthusiasm and a name that's a weak pun. She also, like the cheetah, missed the point four times out of five. Unfortunately, she had less in common with the viewer. To start with, she has the most annoying sibilant speech impediment, and she talks a sort of pidgin psychobabble that is comprehensible only in California. She loved cheetahs because of their life force and their focus and presumably for their ability to meditate, juggle a career and a family and still keep their sylph-like figures. We got a bucketload of that anthropomorphic blather that turns nature into a catwalk-cum-chat show.

Shot of Holly driving: 'I'm doing fifty in my jeep. If there were a cheetah here (there wasn't) it could outrun me by twenty miles an hour. It could just cruise along beside me.' Why a cheetah should want to cruise along beside a jeep containing an annoying starlet was left pending. Or perhaps she thinks they're spotty dolphins.

'Oh, I can't look,' she said, as game wardens cut the head off a cheetah kill, 'I don't want to have that in my memory log.' Your what? Now she thinks she's the ruddy Starship *Enterprise*. What on earth did she imagine cheetahs cruised at 70mph for? Perhaps it's primeval jogging. I was worried that nobody had told her that cheetahs wear real fur. It would have come as a terrible shock.

Survival

I have been considering the brink of extinction. Where exactly is it? Why are we never shown it? Is Michael Palin going to walk round it? Will Cilla send some foul couple for a dirty weekend there? 'Oh, you've won a weekend on the brink of extinction. Now promise to come back and tell us all about it, chuck.'

Last Sunday's *Survival Special* (ITV), on the habitat of the mountain gorilla, was possibly the most extraordinary programme we've seen so far from the brink. Gorillas are spectacularly un-attractive animals. No neck, hairy backs, huge chests, tiny willies. They utter a series of grunts and give off a smell of stale sweat from special glands in their armpits. They have lousy manners and treat lady gorillas as sex objects. Altogether, it's amazing that Sky Sport hasn't signed an exclusive deal with gorillas. The extraordinary thing about this programme was not the gorillas per se, but the reason their habitat is slipping over the edge. It has been invaded by refugees from the civil war in Rwanda. Neither the gorillas nor the refugees had anywhere else to go. What we were shown was *Alice in Wonderland* moral relativism stretched to breaking point. The civil war in Rwanda was one of the most intensely barbaric episodes this century, and there has been plenty of television to show us how pitiful is the lot of the victims. But here, in the same breath, as it were, a natural-history camera crew without any apparent sense of irony turns the sympathy knob to full volume on behalf of ... the gorillas.

In one of the most tasteless pieces of editorial comment I've seen for ages, a film of soldier ants that had had their nests ripped up by apes was juxtaposed with speeded-up film of human refugees streaming into the jungle carrying the pathetic remnants of their shattered lives. It was jaw-dropping. The analogy and the conclusion were inescapable. The gorillas were having their animal rights infringed. They were the true victims of senseless ignorant brutality. The apes all had human names to make them personable individuals, while the people were reduced to a genus and shown in anonymous groups. This is always the way that nature films have their cake and eat it. Critters are rounded individuals, man a singular plague. Nature films do not differentiate between men who invest in logging or mining and men who are forced to poach to feed their families or who happen to be refugees escaping catastrophe and need a little wood on which to cook. It is all very well complaining about women wearing fur when animals regularly wear our humanity. Anyone who can take a camera to a refugee area after genocide and then make a film about the misery of monkeys, blaming the refugees along the way, does not deserve another good night's sleep in this life.

Congo

'Maybe Africa was never meant to look like Surrey.' Just think about that sentence for a moment: wallow in it, luxuriate, enjoy. It's been squatting in the back of my head like a pop-song riff, or a dead rat in the wainscot, for the best part of the week. Out of all the lank-brained, hole-filling, pre-school drivel that comes my way, why this particular piece of imaginatively atrophied garbage should have stuck, I can't think. Maybe it's the maybe. 'Maybe Africa was never meant ...' It implies that somewhere along the line, in some other scriptwriter's feverish scrabbling to fill the unforgiving minute, maybe Africa was meant to look like Surrey.

It came from *Congo*, a nature film about the river. It made me very, very angry. It was glossier than a Ronsealed mink coat. It was nature porn at its most lavish. Furry critters just the way you like them: young, tender, anthropomorphic and not eating each other. All shot in that magic hour when the golden light bathes everything in a trippy, hyper-real sheen, like a gauzy fantasy. It had those neat, silhouetted sunset shots with gambolling dainty-toed Bambi things, and helicopter panoramas of the mighty river and its pristine, verdant greenery, like God's Ground Force makeover. And the script burbled along in a look-at-life, *Reader's Digest* style, skipping from one slimy cliché to the next. It had all the wow! and ah! you could hope for without actually getting up off the sofa.

It's one of my personal rules of criticism that I never have a go at programmes for what they don't contain. But rarely have I come so close to putting a boot through the screen and going out to stalk the men responsible. What was conspicuous by its absence here in *Congo* was evidence of Africans. The few who did edge into shot were as softly photogenic as the wildlife.

The Congo makes it way through some of the most complex and benighted countries in Central Africa, but only dead white explorers manage to get mentioned by name. It's as if the geography of the place were completely separate from life there. And this isn't just one programme. It's virtually every film about Africa that isn't news or current affairs. The utter absence of human life in Africa on television is truly morally obscene. This is racism by omission, apartheid achieved by looking the other way. How many more white vets and white loony single-species eco-campaigners can we be shown before someone in Bristol or Shepherd's Bush says: 'Hang on, this is embarrassing, and it's wrong'? When was the last time you heard an African nature programme narrated by an African? (*Congo*'s bilge was spoken in, of all things, an Irish accent.)

Now, you and the Bristol natural history department might say this is all going a bit far. It's only animals, and it's in a good cause. These programmes don't actually hurt anyone. Well, you'd be wrong. The unrelenting impression is that there are two Africas, one beautiful and perfect and fragile, full of endangered critters, the other filthy and miserable and full of inexplicably nasty people, and we'd rather see the one, not the other.

Consequently, there are charities here that have black-tie balls to raise money to buy automatic rifles so that African gamekeepers can kill African poachers without any of the armchair conservationists ever stopping to consider what desperation could drive a man to risk his life for a rhino horn or elephant tooth. It's largely because of television that we just assume that African animals are worth more, aesthetically and practically, than African people.

The Great Auk

The great auk was a stupid bird; or rather, it was clever at the wrong things, or not smart about the one really important thing, which, in the great auk's particular case, was running away when sailors came to hit it on the head with oars. Auks were boiled whole in great numbers for their oil, which was used for lamps and lubrication. After hitting and boiling all the auks they could find, sailors started complaining that the auk was extinct.

At this point, Victorian England became desperately excited about finding the last great auk, and hugely expensive expeditions were mounted to discover it. Institutions placed prices on the auk's head. Finally, after many months of exceedingly dangerous exploration, a team found the very last one and brought it back to great hurrahs and rejoicing. It was dead, of course. They had killed it instantly. The point was to have a stuffed great auk, which was worth an awful lot more than a living one.

Now consider that story as a television programme. It would be perfect right up to the pay-off, but the Victorians who killed the last auk weren't innately any more cruel than we are – indeed, they tended towards extreme sentimentality. They just had a very different view of nature. Nothing has changed the way we see the wild world more than television. The camera, I don't think it's too extreme to say, invented the green movement and all its attendant special interests. Environmentalists would still be beardy, homespun specialists in tepees without the box. Television's propaganda on behalf of nature has probably been the most successful piece of mass manipulation ever.

The BBC has created a series about the way it made nature programmes, *The Way We Went Wild* (BBC2). On one level, this is a smart idea; on another, it's an extremely dull one. We've already had programmes on the technicalities of nature filming, which were a bit nerdy. This time they're looking at the presenters, who are even more nerdy. The first programme showed us the careers of Johnny Morris and Bill Oddie. Well, as I've said before, Bill Oddie is beginning to resemble some fat, moulting, flightless parrot, with the most annoying call in all nature. He has the irritated let's-get-on-with-it scout leader's demeanour. Even the promise of seeing mermaids mate or otters being torn to death by eagles would not be worth spending an hour watching Oddie for, so let's leave him aside. Morris was another bucket of fish altogether.

Indeed, a bucket of fish was Morris's main prop. He was forever flinging herrings at things. *Animal Magic* was the way many of today's ecowarriors first came upon the natural world (hum the theme tune now and it will be in your head for a week). Around the junior nature table at school, there was an unbridgeable schism between *Animal Magic* enthusiasts and *Zoo Quest* acolytes: Morris or Attenborough. I was an Attenborough lad. I hated Morris. If you never actually saw him, he was a round-faced Welshman who did funny voices for animals while pretending to be a zookeeper.

Actually, it was one-and-a-half voices that were supposed to fit everything.

Even as a child, I knew there was something not quite right about Morris. There was something of the carrion-eater about him. Like so many television presenters, he was a strange misfit until the camera made him complete. He was famously one of the most difficult people on television. Jeremy Clarkson still harbours strong memories of him. When he was four, he toddled across Bristol Zoo to get an autograph. The great man looked at him and told him to bugger off. 'When I heard he'd died, I said "Good", much to my wife's surprise,' says Jeremy. But did he say bugger off as a sea lion or just a bad-tempered Welsh bloke? Clarkson can't remember.

Morris was disapproved of among the weird hobbity fraternity of naturalists for being an anthropomorphist. I don't mind anthropomorphism. It's quite fun in bed. What I minded was that Morris was so cloyingly parochial and suburban about it. When you think about it, all nature on television is anthropomorphic. The box imposes a plot, makes a drama for wildlife. This is no less imposing human emotions on animals than pretending a camel sounds like a dowager duchess.

I wish this programme had tackled the really interesting question of the ethics of natural history broadcasting – the species-ism, the natural assumption that man is outside nature's loop and always the bad guy – rather than dealing with the personalities of presenters, who are frankly less interesting than three-toed sloths. A stuffed great auk went for £9,000 at auction in 1971, a world record for taxidermy.

My favourite programme of the week was *Animal Passions* (C4), about American zoophiles – people who love their pets too much. This isn't the love that dare not speak its name, it's the one that daren't moo, neigh or bark its name but comes when you call it. It was a show beyond parody. Grown men French-kissing horses is funny, but not as funny as listening to a man describe reversing the normal role and playing mare to a randy miniature stallion. A horse that is cheating on his wife – the man's wife, not the horse's. And I like the old guy who wistfully said he'd like to have had kids with his pony – whether it be child, foal or centaur, he didn't seem to care. A lady sociologist posed us vanilla, single-species society members an uncomfortable question: if it's all right to breed animals with the sole purpose of killing them, why isn't it all right to keep them to have sex with? Make love, not leather. I know there's a good answer – I just can't think of it right now.

Cruel World

Some time ago, I wrote a piece about a spectacularly depressed and depressing part of Russia. To illustrate the story, my photographer, Pete Marlow, snapped a bear in the local zoo. It was a pretty scrofulous example of a bear, and it was living in a slum of a cave. The picture, as ever with Peter, was a perfect, symbolic illustration – the Russian bear living in a filthy concrete bunker – and it captured exactly the tone of the article, which was, on the whole, about forgotten and suffering people. The following Monday, the paper's switchboard was jammed, and the e-mail server gave up. Over the week, I received hundreds and hundreds of letters, a few congratulatory, most hectoring, many imploring the paper to do more, and asking how the correspondents could help and where they might send money. Guess what? Every single one of them, without exception, was about the damn bear. Not a single call, e-mail or letter inquired after the people.

And that wasn't the end of it. Concerned folk from charitable organisations, who devote their life to such things, took the trouble to fly out there to buy the mothy creature and wag accusing fingers at the Russians. God, how I wish someone had shot the thing and eaten it, turned its hide into baby blankets and ground up its bones for aphrodisiac. It's at times like this that I seriously wonder why I bother. Why not just go and work for *Hello!*? Or simply write a pet column?

Very little about this country contorts me into such paroxysms of embarrassment and shame as our overwhelming holier-than-absolutely-everyone-else attitude to animals. There is no limit to the saccharine smugness and profligate largesse a sizeable portion of the population can manufacture on behalf of fluffy stuff.

So you can imagine how much I was looking forward to *Cruel World* (C5), the heart-ossifying story of a mutt's rescue from the hell of ending up as a dog's dinner in Korea. You can see from the title that this was hardly going to be an even-handed examination of a foreign culture. It was a very English tale of tabloid, anthropomorphic racism. Have no doubt, there is no politically correct 'ism' that's as bogus, morally bankrupt and philosophically demeaning as species-ism at the expense of your own species.

It hardly needs to be pointed out that, ethically, eating dog is no worse than eating pig. And that the conditions these fidos were bred and kept in were a damn sight better than those suffered by most of the animals you consume on your knee while watching this sort of pernicious rubbish. Or that the rescued creature was vomitously called Hope, and will undoubtedly be fed on tinned animals that have been bred and slaughtered just as efficiently. What shouldn't be forgotten is that within a hundred miles of Seoul, the worst and most prolonged famine in the world is occurring. North Korea is starving to death by inches. That someone decided that eating dog was a more important and worthy subject than starving humans is, frankly, beyond comprehension or salvation.

Actually, this programme was so stridently fluffy that, by halfway through, my anger had turned into something altogether lighter. We were told in tones of salacious awe that the Koreans also drop moggies into pressure cookers to make the blissfully named 'cat juice' as a cure for arthritis. As Oscar Wilde might have put it: 'You'd have to have a heart of stone to watch it without laughing.' If this stuff moves you to anything more profound than a fit of the giggles, then I'm sorry: you need to get out and get a real human life. And if you're considering writing to me, I hope you're gnawed to death by hamsters first.

Natural World (BBC2), about dolphins, was a tediously thin and poorly made piece of sensational and gullible exploitation purporting to show

NATURE   215

that dolphins will go out of their way to protect endangered swim-
mers from naughty sharks. We were shown this with an endlessly
unilluminating reconstruction of an ugly family of New Zealanders
treading water and trying to look concerned. Various experts from
universities I've never heard of were brought on to explain that dolphins look after us because they have bigger brains than we do, and
are generally nicer. The zoomorphic lesson was that we should all live
to be more like dolphins ourselves, because, hey, no dolphin has ever
shot anyone or dropped litter; their carbon footprint is zero; dolphins
don't fart in bed or forget to phone you the next day; no dolphin has
ever been a hit-and-run driver, abused children or posed for *Playboy*.
Look, frankly, we'd be better off if dolphins ran social services and
utility helplines. There is, though, a heretical explanation for the odd
behaviour of a dolphin apparently swimming round and round people
when there are sharks about. They are actually the great white's
bitches, and are drawing attention to this tasty snack so the shark
can first chop it up into dolphin-mouth-sized chunks. There is another
truth about dolphins that is rarely mentioned on *Animal Planet* – that
they quite commonly creep up behind people in wetsuits and try to
rape them. Let me tell you, an aroused male dolphin can make your
eyes water.

Finally, more meerkats, the boy band of African wildlife. *Natural World:
Meerkats – Part of the Team* (BBC2) was made by Simon King, a
fabulously banal Tim Nice-but-Dim character who spent a nerdy year
trying to become a small furry creature. It was like a *Monty Python*
spoof of David Attenborough and the gorillas; the little creatures ran
all over him and he beamed goofily. Anthropomorphism is the prime
sin of nature films, but the zoomorphism here was worse. King ingra-
tiated himself with meerkats to see up close how they lived, not for
a moment questioning that a galumphing human carrying a camera
might alter, if not their behaviour, then the behaviour of everything
that might want to eat them. He talked to camera a lot, but didn't say
much more than 'ooh', 'aah' and 'cute'. It begged the question: who
was behind the other camera? Sure enough, on the credits, there
was an invisible camerawoman. Had she perhaps been stalking him

for a year, being unthreatening, trying to look like a coffee shop? I know a lot of you will have watched this with tears in your eyes and a sigh on your lips. Personally, I was ardently praying for rabies.

Politics

Ballot Box

Politicians get a very easy ride from television. The Queensberry Rules for how the box treats our elected officials were set down by Lord Reith and the BBC in the early 1950s. They took their template from the wireless, which had just finished fighting the war and had grown used to being part of the national propaganda machine. When the country was fighting for its life, there was rightly no question of the media standing back and taking a critical overview.

This attitude of being part of the Establishment, albeit a corduroy-and-cravat liberal part, leaked into peacetime. The child television never really broke out of the mould. Oh, it has had a few adolescent radical tantrums but essentially television is very soft on governments and opposition. The standard format of political inquiry is to ask politicos to explain themselves and then to balance the argument by inviting other politicos of a different hue to reply.

Telly leaves the opposition and the criticism to others. This is a particularly sterile form of investigation. Committed politicians have always been better at manipulating the camera than the interviewers have been at putting them on the spot. Producers naturally bridle at this interpretation of their role, and point to innovative programmes such as *Death on the Rock* which, quite frankly, in the overall picture of world politics was pretty tame stuff.

News and current affairs directors also smugly remind you that politicians from both parties always complain that the box is biased against them, thus proving what brave, even-handed souls they are. This has always seemed to me to be like a man beating a chained dog just to remind it who put the minced morsels of franchise and charter into his bowl. Television is content to be a passive observer, but as part of a free press and the place where most electors now glean their information and form their opinions, this is really not good enough.

If you are passive, politicians use you and bully you. The whole ridiculous debacle of Gerry Adams's voice was an embarrassing case in point. If the box hadn't been such a craven puppy, no government would have dared to tinker with its current affairs output. Can you imagine them trying to stop newspapers quoting Adams? If the fledgeling television had learned its early lessons from the print media, it would have grown up to be a very different animal. *Death on the Rock* is the sort of programme that newspapers run as inside features seven days a week. No newspaper would put up with the soft cosy interviewing of Frost or that other bloke on Sunday morning.

Debates such as *Question Time* would be rightly spiked by every features editor within ten miles of Fleet Street. There are far too many passive interviews and nothing like enough profiles. When television does take the gloves off, it is invariably to go for small-fry local councillors fiddling the planning permission, and crooked plumbers. Or dead people. Directors are fearless when it comes to digging up graves and giving a political corpse a good kicking.

The box suffers from even on-the-other-handism. It is terrified of being seen as having a bias, as if the BBC and ITV were self-appointed referees, instead of a rolling pot-pourri of different programmes. There should be space for far more committed political columns. I'd love to see *Anarchists' Half Hour* or *Fun With Fascists*. Without all that studio discussion balance nonsense.

There was a very clear view of what television might have been if it had taken a leaf out of the paper press on *From Walpole's Bottom to Major's Underpants* (ghastly title, BBC2). Eighteenth-century cartoons are exactly what television ought to be imitating and if the makers of *Spitting Image* think that's actually what they do then they should lay off the sauce. If you'd said to me last week: 'You'll watch a programme inspired by an idea from Kenneth Baker in which he appears in fancy dress and you'll love it,' I'd have taken your temperature. But this was an exceedingly entertaining, well-made, exactingly researched and informative programme. Even the computer manipulation of Baker into cartoons was used sparingly and appropriately.

Walpole's Bottom traced the beginning of the political cartoon from his inauguration as prime minister. This might have been a bit arbitrary, as there were critical political prints before then, but it was an excusable conceit to make the clear link between prime ministers and caricatures. The cumulative effect of vicious wit was shown to be hugely powerful. The unfortunate and loathed Earl of Bute was driven to resign by drawings. The eighteenth century was a turbulent time, when most of the electorate couldn't read, so cartoons informed a lot of popular political debate – how like television today. Nothing on *Spitting Image* is as precise as the *Guardian*'s Steve Bell drawing of Mr Major and his Y-fronts outside his trousers. It's a brilliant, undeniable image.

Speaking as somebody who has been horribly caricatured only once, I know it must smart worse than a thousand thundering editorials. I've never been convinced that a photograph is worth a thousand words. But a single cartoon can certainly cut the crap faster than a whole season of *World in Action*.

Budget

'The Chancellor suffered from the very high expectations of his audience,' said some human draught-excluder in a scrofulous suit on *Budget 95* (BBC2). Come again? Sorry? Have you lost your spaceship? Which planetary system do you come from? The high, no very high, expectations of his audience? When this century, pray, has anyone ever had high expectations of a chancellor? When was the last time you had even modestly gently-inclining expectations of any politician? High expectations of a chancellor, indeed. Now there's an idea. The Budget is one of those features of British television that are fixed immutable points, chunks of tradition that don't have to be explained or justified against entertainment value, audience figures or artistic merit; they just are. Like an afternoon of hats on Ladies' Day at Ascot or the Royal Variety Performance.

The Budget is actually rather like the Royal Variety Performance: it's an anachronism, it's boring, it's full of sad old acts and nobody enjoys it.

Why television, which to all intents and purposes is only forty years old, should have lumbered itself with so much tradition is a bit of a mystery. But then we're a country addicted to inventing instant tradition. You only have to walk across a field the same way twice and it becomes an Anglo-Saxon national heritage trail. The traditional Budget has very little to do with economics and an awful lot to do with the heritage baggage of television. The Budget programme was born when television wasn't even allowed into the palace of Westminster and there was a Reithian deference to politicians. Now you can watch parliament on its own cable channel (or not), and the only people who feel deferential to MPs are Arab businessmen. But still the BBC goes through the time-honoured motion of the Budget. The hereditary Dimbleby, the panel of blinking university economists and confused politicians. The one act on the Royal Variety Budget we all look forward to is Peter Snow, Mr Swingometer; he's a real trouper. I've often wondered if, in between elections and budgets, he does the northern club circuit. 'Order, order, that was Doreen and her erotic parakeets, now welcome back to an act that always gets a warm welcome, ladies and gentlemen, a big Treadlegritters and Loomwanglers welcome for old uncle Penny-on-a-Pint, Mr Peter "How-will-it-affect-me" Snow and his all-singing, all-dancing aids.'

This year he came up with a truly wonderful bit of computer-graphic Ziegfeld nonsense, a virtual-reality Budget Town inhabited by virtual-reality you-and-mes. Peter excitably showed us around like a chemically enhanced estate agent. 'And here, living in this little terraced house, are our pensioners on £7,000 a year, and, oh no, they'll be 74p a week worse off, that's the cigarettes. And over here in the suburbs we have our better-off couple in a nice detached house with pillars, they're on 35 grand and have a car, so they'll be £4 a week better off.' Budget Town was blissfully British, a sort of modern Ambridge, an inspired piece of Hyacinth Bucket social snobbery. It had a touch of *Brookside*, a whiff of *Hello!* and a smidgen of National Trust nosiness. Peter intimated just the merest hint of Pooterish moral censure at his pixel people. We sucked our teeth at the unemployed couple who smoked, with all those kids. We shared the sense of shame at the pensioners having their income broadcast to the nation and wondered if he'd finally put her into the virtual-reality home, now that their savings were protected. Budget Town has real possibilities. Next year the BBC should make the whole show a cartoon.

Michael Heseltine

Do you remember *The Man Who Never Was*? Brilliant film and a true story about dressing up a corpse as a naval officer and dumping him on the beach with secret information in his pocket to fool the Germans. Well, it all came flooding back while watching Michael Heseltine's political eulogy, *Heseltine – A Life in the Political Jungle* (ITV). Heseltine is the man who never was. He would periodically turn up on the beach at Blackpool or Brighton and fool the Tories into thinking that he was the real thing. Of course, he'd like us to think that he was the best prime minister we never had. Throughout my lifetime, there have been dozens of these nearly wases, from Reggie Maudling to George Brown and David Owen. After all of them, the electorate breathed a sigh of collective relief and thought: 'Phew, that was a close call.'

But even in a profession stuffed with tunnel-visioned, ambitious monomaniacs, Heseltine was in a class of his own. For the two decades of the Thatcher era, he fulfilled for the Tory Party the role that Tony Benn managed for Labour: an outdoors, windy phrase-maker who acted both as the pin-up and lightning conductor for the wing of the party that was out of favour. They were both licensed loose cannons who would invariably end up shooting their own feet. In Jonathan Dimbleby's rather well put-together two-part review of Heseltine's career, what was most surprising was how deeply unabided he still was by his own side. All compliments were grudging and usually implied some greater fault. Of course, his shiny self-belief was untarnished. The programme was above all a tallying of his professional triumphs. In hindsight, though they obviously still warmed Hezza's cockles, they did seem fantastically unimportant to us. Hardly worth a week in politics, let alone a lifetime.

So many of these faint pyrrhic victories look like ignominious defeats – like the clash with CND when he was Minister for Defence. 'I won game, set and match,' he puffed, but the Greenham women were there long after him, and their influence was far greater and more abiding than his own. And that early business with the mace? Heseltine pointed out that the real story was that Labour tellers had miscounted, but his hot-headed waving of the symbol of government made the story centre on him, thereby letting the government off the hook. And the same with Westland. Heseltine became the focus, rather than the helicopters. Although, truth to tell, it was sometimes difficult to tell them apart – all whirly-whirly on top, a lot of wind and noise, and fundamentally unstable.

Defence of the Realm: Top Brass (BBC1): one of those lush, big, soft series that the BBC always points to when people start asking awkward questions about the licence fee. Following its look at the Foreign Office and battleships, here is the Ministry of Defence. The first episode, *Top Brass*, was The Nicholas Soames Show. Soames is a television natural. He is wasted on politics. Anyone who can dress themselves is wasted on politics. It seems particularly appropriate that, as the forces get smaller and smaller, the minister gets bigger and bigger. 'I am the third generation of my family to hold this office,' he said, trundling down the flight deck of an aircraft carrier. The unspoken implication was that we haven't lost a war yet. It looked for a moment as if he might launch himself off the end like a vast, shiny barrage balloon.

In a dinner jacket, Soames just is the great seal of state. The comparison between him and Michael Portillo, the Defence minister, could not have been more telling. Soames swaggers and bellows, slaps back, meets eyes, is hyperbolic and sentimental. His strengths are loyalty and enthusiasm and the sort of dimness that doesn't know any better. Portillo shifts on casters and has a voice like breaking chicken bone. His smile is the opening of a morgue door. His eyes slide. His strength is others' weaknesses and sense of duty. You get the feeling he would sacrifice a regiment for the sake of a by-election.

Nicholas, in full bluster, said that the army is the finest, most efficient business in the country. If the City and industry were run by the army, we would all be bloody Japanese. Hang about, sir, wasn't that what we fought the last war to avoid? He is magnificent, but he certainly isn't war.

Election 1997

So it turned out to be high opera after all. There I was thinking that this month-long campaign without an interval was an esoteric play by Samuel Beckett. Two men in dustbins shouting. But the election turned out to be Verdi after all. A lot of unintelligible shouting for two acts and then a bloodbath as a finale. I really could have sworn the election night specials were set to be as hideously dull as the campaigning. A small majority for Labour and a lot of 'Bovis South, Con hold, what does that tell us, Peter?' But the whole thing took off, got a plot, got drama, got excitement.

What was so effective was the slow build to rout. In 1992 the election was a straightforward Jeffrey Archer plot, where the suspense leads you to believe one thing and then with a twist the opposite happens. This time it was like a huge Cinemascope war film – *The Longest Day*. You know who is going to win but you are awed by the sheer scale of it all. The plot was driven by vignettes, personal stories of triumph and disaster. I should have been channel-surfing, comparing and contrasting, but after the first half-hour we stuck with the BBC. The different channels work on slightly different times and, like badly dubbed foreign films, if you switch back and forth you hear the same thing again or get ahead of yourself. And doubtless when the viewing figures come in they will show that as usual when the nation clusters together, it clusters round Auntie.

The longest day on the box started quietly enough. There was the concentration of the largest collection of electronic effects ever known – ranks of multicoloured bar charts, pie charts, swingometers, virtual-reality Cabinet ministers, ex-ministers and any number of exploding bomb-run maps regimented in a secret computer somewhere in west London. Montgomery Snow and Eisenhower Dimbleby spent a long phoney hour in exhaustive training and testing the bright flashing weapons of Tory destruction. The first really telling result came from somewhere in the Midlands, where a safe bunker held by the Tories since 1922 spectacularly went to a young Labour woman who looked as if she was going to have to have her grin removed surgically. She was German and made her acceptance speech with a discernible accent. After a campaign characterised by lowbrow, embarrassing foreign-bashing – particularly the Krauts – this was a delicious irony; perhaps the Germans were going to win the election.

After that, results queued up to storm the beaches. I am sorry for the military analogy, it is inescapable. It is another small irony that in a democracy a system which is the antithesis of war is inevitably characterised in the bloodthirsty language of attrition. As the BBC's graphics grew ever more pyrotechnically exuberant they made the election look like a nuclear Final Solution. Peter Snow was not so much Montgomery bouncing around the studio as Dr Strangelove without his wheelchair. As the night wore on, the gadgetry got in the way. What was riveting were the people, the close-ups of restrained triumph or grim stoical defeat, always made more poignant by the amateur, monotone mantra of the returning officer. Who exactly are returning officers, why are they so bad at it and what do they do with the rest of their lives? They only work twice a decade. Perhaps a nationwide youth returning officer training scheme will be what Labour spends its windfall tax on. 'No, I am not actually unemployed, I am a resting returning officer.'

The repeating tableaux on town-hall stages never failed to grip. They were like Shakespearean histories distilled into two minutes, all the characters lined up on stage for their inevitable denouement. The drama came from knowing the unspoken – that for everyone we were watching this was the most important day of their lives. The moment when work and hope and struggle either crumbled into bitter gall or blossomed into a new career. Of course there was also a great deal of *schadenfreude* in the mighty being laid low by this stumbling, bechained functionary. All those smug media-trained glacial Cabinet ministers and arrogant backbenchers who have strutted our televisions for half a generation finally getting their comeuppance. This was one question they could not avoid or refuse to be drawn on.

The most delicious of these was Michael Portillo. Before being put to the electoral sword he had to stand for the ritual humiliation of having his full name read out. 'So how does it feel, Xavier?' The incredibly young man who beat him probably spent the next day flicking backwards and forwards watching himself over and over. He looked like Pike from *Dad's Army*. It is likely to be the last time he sees himself on the box for a good many years. He will always be the boy who shot the sheriff. Jeremy Paxman's post-defeat interview with Xavier was vicious. No defeated sportsman would have been treated to such a kicking. And it might have been distasteful if it had not been so nationally popular. In Tatton, the real loser was Mrs Captain Haddock Hamilton. The look on her face was pure Hutu. In all his years in war zones, Martin Bell has never been this close to having his vital organs ripped out. Neil Hamilton made a predictably graceless speech. Interviewed afterwards, Bell looked like a man who had just been told his house had burned down, his car had been stolen, his daughter had run off with Norman Lamont and he had got impetigo. What do you imagine it would take to make this man smile? Perhaps we should have a competition to try to make Bell happy. Perhaps it could be part of the millennium celebrations.

The most moving statesmanlike moment of the night belonged to John Major. Like Charles I, nothing so became him as his going. As the odds grew longer and defeat became ever more certain, he rose almost to grandeur. His off-the-cuff acceptance speech in Huntingdon was a model of quiet decency. He may not have represented everything that was best in government but on election night he showed all that is admirable in politics. By Friday, what had become apparent was the remarkable sophistication and political nous of the electorate. Having endured being talked about in the third person like slow children for a month, they voted with the accuracy and delicacy of a symphony orchestra. This was no kneejerk reaction for change; while rejecting the Tories nationally they re-elected a lot of them locally. Television must take much of the credit for a well-informed public. We all woke up feeling like death but also feeling how heady and exciting a change of government really is. The look of joyous expectation on the pundits' faces was barely disguised. This should not be mistaken as partisanship, it is just that most journalists have spent their professional lives reporting on one static trench system.

In the middle of Thursday night I had torn myself away from the telly to witness my own constituency's count and declaration. It came as a bit of a shock. Where were the bar charts, the swingometers, the bomb-run maps? Where were all the pundits, screens and swivel chairs? It all looked so fantastically parochial. The whole scene could not have been further from the television image and it reminds you what you are really doing – what democracy is really for. It is not about politicians or television; it happens despite them. It is really about all of us.

Tony Benn

Tony Benn is a politician who has seemed to grow through failure. The further he has been pushed from the engine room of power, the more he has taken on the mien of a statesman of gravitas. Now out of the house altogether, he is commanding the sorts of crowds that haven't been seen since Keir Hardie. Not only are voters turning up in their hundreds to listen to him, they are paying for the privilege. His career has defied gravity: he has plummeted upwards.

Last year, I interviewed Benn, and watching his stage performance in *Tony Benn: Free at Last* (BBC4) gave me a sense of déjà vu. Here was all the same patter, the same anecdotes and the same quotes, delivered with the same knowing, Uncle Remus twinkle. And I must say, I could have listened indefinitely. You can, if you allow yourself to, just glimpse the New Jerusalem forming from the clouds of warm, aromatic smoke that he blows at the ceiling. At his best, Benn is an extemporiser, a political Dickens, weaving the great wen of humanity into a compulsive, teeming story. But then again, he can also be to governance what Rolf Harris is to painting – a man who flashes and dribbles about, with a brush that's so broad it covers up a fundamental weakness in design and structure. Impressive though it is to watch, you really don't want to live with it. But that isn't to detract from his amazing ability to take Lego politics on the road and sell out theatres. What other living politician could do that? What other living politician could be bothered to try? Benn has tapped into a great appetite for the fundamentals of society, the comfort of the grand sweep and the armchair vision of some distant horizon glittering in some new dawn.

Cherie Blair

It's a nugget of counterintuitive wisdom that the smartest thing Denis Thatcher ever did was gently and silently to collude in the cartoon character given him by the media. It grew to be the accepted truth that he was a golf-club buffoon in search of a G&T, with his foot in his mouth and a look of incomprehension at the world of politics and pretty much everything that had happened outside of Surrey in the 1950s. It was a useful disguise for Thatcher, who could carry on his real life uninterrupted. Nobody had been the male spouse of a PM before, so it was as good a way as any of inventing a job.

The partners of politicians are a soft target, and it is one of the nasty corollaries of democracy that, though they are not elected and have no power, no staff, no income, no role, no voice, they are endlessly answerable to the rhetorical spleen of commentators and comedians. Mostly, they are simply scorned, like Mary Wilson with her poetry and Norma Major with her petit-bourgeois sensibilities. But with Cherie Blair, the mockery grew truly vicious. She was created as a monstrous figure of national loathing in what became sustained bullying. Even her final, mild exit line about not missing the press much was flung back in her face with gob-flecked baying.

You'd have thought that would have been that. But here, before the spittle has dried on her lapel, Cherie is back on television in her own tell-all reality documentary, *The Real Cherie Blair* (BBC1). Like some ridiculously wronged and embarrassed It girl who sells her story to the *News of the World* 'to put the record straight', she isn't selling anything, she's not got a book out, nobody's twisting her arm. She chose to go on TV all on her own. For a clever woman, she's wondrous stupid.

The first rule of bad press is if you want to put out a fire, stop pouring petrol on it. This look at Cherie's life shows her to be brittle, defensive, quick to take offence, unwilling to take blame and utterly, completely, totally bereft of charm. In short, not a particularly attractive or likeable woman. With a huge self-awareness blind spot, she told us she'd never bothered about clothes or make-up or appearance because she was the clever one. Her cleverness may well be voluminous, but it doesn't begin to cover her vain regard for her cleverness.

There were some bizarre moments, such as the staged meeting with her father. 'Has he been embarrassing me?' she asked the camera. Old Father Booth giggled and wriggled, and in that moment you saw their roles had completely reversed. He was the naughty child; she, the long-suffering parent. Even Tony Blair, the great communicator and empathiser, failed to rise to a convincing encomium for her, finally grinding to a wordless, grunting halt. Cherie, for all her charity finger buffets and cleverness, is not a winning or sympathetic character, but failing at niceness doesn't preclude bullying. Victims don't have to be lovable to be victims. Part of her awkward unlovability is down to her life as a victim of one sort or another, although she'd hate to think of herself as one. Any inner-city teacher will tell you about the complex and unmentionable syndrome of children who connive in their own bullying. Cherie Blair's decision to go on TV was a sad and weird act of complicity.

Mandelson

Let me offer you a small insight into the difference between a television commissioner and a television consumer. If you commission, then *Alastair Campbell Interviews Peter Mandelson* (Five) is a high-five moment, a slap-on-the-back, pop-a-cork, promotion-grabbing, priapic coup. But if you're a viewer, *Alastair Campbell Interviews Peter Mandelson* is a finger down the throat and in the ears, cold porridge, high colonic, electrodes on the wibbly bits, dash for the remote. This would only be destination TV for political wonkers and, of course, commissioning editors. But if you did manage to strap yourself into the chair for it, it was spookily, horrifyingly fascinating. Not so much like watching a car crash as them trying to dig the bodies out of a car crash.

It could have been called Mr Pot meets Miss Kettle. Mandelson, for all his supposed promotional and presentational wizardry, hasn't the slightest idea how to make himself look remotely sympathetic or attractive. What's truly bizarre is that he refers to himself in the third person, something Margaret Thatcher would do when she was at her most barkingly imperial. But worse than that, Mandy refers to himself as not one person, but three separate people. There's the third-person Peter, the third-person minister and a third third person called Bobby. Who or what Bobby is, or does, thankfully we weren't told. It was all a seriously delusional, multipersonality deal. It was as if he'd divorced himself from the odium, ridicule and loathing of his public life. It had all happened to these other people.

It was very sad. Mandelson looks and sounds like a badly abused boy, smiling with bitter anger, constantly claiming to feel no rancour, to apportion no blame, while everything in his demeanour screams the opposite. He makes Campbell look attractive – that's how bad it is. Campbell himself, of course, isn't anyone's favourite dolly mixture. He said Mandelson was one of his best friends and then treated him to a snide, humourless kicking. It's a ghastly game, politics. They don't have mates because none of them knows how to be mates. They'll all die alone and friendless.

It came to me last Sunday exactly where John Prescott comes from: he's a figment of Jeffrey Archer's imagination. Prescott's life, as revealed in the political profile *Two Jags* (C5), was precisely the thuddingly bad papier-mâché plot (is there another sort?) of an Archer novel. More than that, given the evident truth that everyone in politics is the Jekyll to someone else's Hyde, Prescott is the Labour version of Archer: both are permanently hobbled by foot-in-mouth and both are driven by an ambition fuelled not by brilliance of vision but by insecurity. Prescott, it must also be said, is like Ann Widdecombe playing Falstaff in a girls'-school production of *The Merry Wives of Windsor*. Prescott has ended up as the bloke Tony has stand next to him so he'll look handsome and clever. Labour's Quasimodo: a butch, ugly figure of fun who makes a lot of noise.

Satire

Like Beverley Hughes, the minister for child protection, I didn't see the *Brass Eye* programme on paedophilia; unlike Beverley Hughes, I just missed it. Miss Hughes hasn't seen it on purpose. She screwed up her eyes, stuck her fingers in her ears and hummed 'Things Can Only Get Better' very loudly, so that she wouldn't have to be polluted by any part of it. There was reason in Miss Hughes's self-imposed fatwa: she had to go on the wireless and talk about *Brass Eye*, so, naturally, not having seen it gave her an uncommonly clear view. I heard James Naughtie, on Monday's *Today* programme, ask in amazement how she could possibly speak about something she hadn't actually witnessed, and Miss Hughes reply, with all the injured and self-righteous incredulity that only New Labour junior ministers and teenage girls seem to be able to muster, that she'd been thoroughly briefed. Well, that's okay, then, as long as she's been truly, thoroughly briefed. But just try to imagine a politician claiming that about any other subject. 'I don't actually know where Bosnia is,' said the prime minister last night, 'but I know a man who does, and I'm assured the RAF has been thoroughly briefed. I'm told the NHS does exist, and I'm having extensive meetings with a man who's actually seen it.' He added that he hadn't actually sent any of his children to a bog-standard comprehensive, but education was at the top of his agenda. That last bit wasn't a joke.

Not all our ministers are as dilettante as Miss Hughes. David Blunkett was – and I quote his spokesman – 'pretty dismayed by the programme and did not find it remotely funny'. Now, I'm sorry, and there's no sensitive way of putting this, but last time I looked, David Blunkett was blind. He had the dog and the beard to prove it. I don't know how funny *Brass Eye* was, but it'll have to have been brilliant to have been half as hilarious as 'Blind Man Doesn't See Funny Side of Comedy Show'. Now all we need is Gordon Brown's statement: 'Man with Glass Eye Thinks It Was Funny in Parts'.

Do you remember, ages and ages ago, someone said that this was the government who could be trusted to look after the arts, these were the people who understood that culture didn't stop at horse-painting and the band of the Grenadier Guards playing Gilbert and Sullivan melodies? Now that really was funny. But silly me. Of course, the rules of artists' freedom of expression don't apply to television. Television's far too popular to be culture; television is a medium for propagating health warnings and consumer advice in a blandly entertaining manner, and for government ministers to make announcements.

I didn't see *Brass Eye*, but I have seen the news coverage, and I know a silly-season, dull-news-week, cranked-up-hysteria story when I see one. Channel 4-bashing is an easy way to fill a hot day when everyone's on holiday, and it's a no-brain, no-loss opportunity for the government to look tough in front of *Daily Mail* readers without actually having to do anything. The Shining Path socialists suffer huge humour failure when it comes to satire. They can bear anything but being laughed at. They are collective proof of Gill's fifth law of criticism, which states that anyone who starts a sentence, 'Of course I can take a joke along with the best of them', is lying and about to prove it. The people who tell you there are some subjects that are beyond humour really mean that all humour is beyond them. Gill's sixth law points out that satire begins where humour ends. There you are: *Brass Eye*, the first programme I've ever reviewed without having seen. And that, by the way, is wit.

Tony Blair

Michael Cockerell's characteristically smooth and thorough look at *Blair's Thousand Days* (BBC2), including an extended interview, was a masterly piece of understatement. Cockerell just handed out the rope and gave quiet encouragement in knot-tying. Blair did the rest. I haven't seen anything so utterly damning for ages, or done with such a sure touch. The archive film of pre-mission Tony was riveting. With all the clarity of hindsight, it's astonishing to see how any of us ever thought he could be anything but an oleaginous, duplicitous douchebag with the manner of a Californian plastic surgeon and the sincerity of a Cairo carpet salesman. What once looked like open, straight-talking, kitchen-table directness is now plainly the tired-out gurning of a confidence trickster who's fed up with the subterfuge and just wants to get on with honest-to-goodness mugging. All that shirtsleeve business is just a hackneyed old ruse. It doesn't make me think he's getting down to work on my behalf, it makes me think he doesn't want us to see all the special pleaders, time-servers and open-handed donations he's got stuffed in his pocket.

John Pilger

A couple of months ago, Jon Ronson, the Norman Wisdom of investigative journalism, presented an odd little series on conspiracy theorists. They were rather good. I'm mentioning them now because the various paranoiacs and loonies he filmed all came from what could loosely be called the right wing of gut politics. Indeed, seeing global conspiracies at the bottom of the garden naturally leads to a sort of trust-nobody individualism that is a symptom of the extreme right. But just when I was thinking that, yet again, life's conservatives had got all the good looney tunes, up pops John

Pilger to prove that anything paramilitary survivalists can conceive, the old laager lefties can conceive just as well.

Pilger has been a feature of miserable, shroud-tugging journalism for as long as I can remember. He is the grim remake of George Orwell, without the humanity or humour. Pilger manages to be profoundly enraged on behalf of the collective, without giving the impression he cares a jot for the individual. Which is, by the way, the defining trait of megalomania. He still practises the sort of journalism that everyone with a left-wing bent stopped doing in 1968. Call me shallow, but I can't watch him without wanting to tickle him. I can't imagine him ever having fun. He's the closest an Australian atheist can get to being Job. Pilger wears the cares of the world like boils, with the sombre vanity of a suffering right-eousness.

This week he was off again on a quixotic crusade, tilting at the secret rulers of the world – which, as far as I could gather, were the IMF, the World Bank and a pair of novelty Gap boxer shorts. As ever with Pilger, the message was blindingly obvious in his own head, but hopelessly confused when it emerged from his mouth. This was really four, or perhaps five, maybe half a dozen, separate strands knitted, or rather knotted, together by a Buchanesque conspiracy.

New Rulers of the World (ITV) started with the almost gleeful discovery of a Pilger constituency: the equally confused anti-globalisation travelling-circus rioters. Pilger embarrassed them like a middle-aged man who finally finds a teenagers' pop song he can actually understand. Then we were whisked off to Indonesia to the familiar hidden camera in a sweatshop, and then off again to President Suharto's military coup, and thence by a precarious route to the IMF, the World Bank and International debt.

The thing with all Pilger's theories is that they start with the philosophical assumption that if you're mugged, it's your own fault for having a wallet. His is a 'through the looking-glass' world. Horrible practices in Asian factories are not the fault of factory owners, they're the fault of consumers. Vile dictatorships are not the fault of vile dictators, but of perfectly nice people who don't stop them. Government corruption isn't the fault of corrupt governments: the blame rests with the banks who gave them the money. So the innocent are all as culpable. When Pilger gets to interview a spokesman for the World Bank or the IMF or business, they run rings round him. Because at the centre of his argument is an infuriated, eye-rolling, cheek-puffing, everybody-knows-that inarticulacy.

Pilger is a big, free-floating, angry conscience that's unattached to any corporeal body. He can't see that not being entirely right doesn't necessarily make you wholly wrong. He's a real liability for those who do want to change the world order, cancel debt and improve the lot of the oppressed, because his crass, monotone absolutism is just the obverse of the dictator's inflated coin. His sort of cold-war head-banging gives them currency, and it goes without saying he doesn't have any solutions ... I'm sorry, almost without saying. He did finish with a trite answer: 'Let's scrap the IMF, the World Bank and global economy and replace them with ... with ...' Yes, John? 'With some other institutions that aren't the World Bank, IMF and global economy.'

I bet that will have them cheering in the sweatshops of the East.

The Queen

Into every reign, a little life must fall. It's the Queen's eightieth year, the fifty-fourth of her reign over us. What was most obvious in the birthday-card documentary *The Queen at 80* (BBC1) was that she has enjoyed the meagrest drizzle of real life in an existence of duty. Even the poorest of her subjects is free to flick two fingers at the sort of men who belong to the Aston Martin Owners' Club. But Elizabeth's bizarrely self-imposed, self-denying definition of duty keeps her on her feet in the rain watching them for an hour-and-a-half. Hers is a world set about with cliché and small talk, shared with the dullest people in existence, or interesting people rendered stupid by the nature of their meeting.

Royal documentaries are now a sub-genre with its own conventions and traditions and an agreed tone of toadying insider gossip that invariably stresses the hard work and the value for money. They have both that courteous cringe and nerdy statistics that always remind me of Raymond Baxter doing air shows. The first royal documentary, made in 1969, was a huge international event. Now they seem to be just another fly-on-the-wall, slice-of-real-life TV fitted in between airlines and cruise ships.

For the eightieth-birthday grovel, the role of Gold-Microphone-in-Waiting – traditionally the hereditary job of members of the Dimbleby family – was given to Andrew Marr, who happily slipped into the hushed tones of reverence, with just that splash of supine familiarity that manages to make the monarch sound like a cross between a steam engine and a public park. That, coupled with the vox pops from politicians – who always have that particularly infant-school tone when talking about the Queen, as if she were some gallant little special-needs pupil – made me think, not for the first time, what a ridiculous and disingenuous excuse for a head of state the hereditary principle provides.

Royal television has made me a convinced republican, not because I yearn for a President Roy Hattersley or Bobby Charlton, but because, through no fault of its own, the royal family now represents everything that is tacky, obsolete, corrupt and servile in the country. It's a magnet for lickspittle special pleaders, nostalgia snobs and men who have ties that say secret things to other men. I think that what we do to the Queen and her family is inhumane. What other eighty-year-old woman would we force to do what Elizabeth Windsor does? We should stop being humiliated as a nation by the exploitation of this over-functioned family. We stopped chimpanzees having to perform tea parties in captivity years ago – why do we still expect it of these humans? Like Elsa, the Queen and her cubs should be set free. Why don't we just have nobody at all? If the ambassador from Tuvalu or the Aston Martin Owners' Club turns up, just tell them she's out, running wild in the heather.

Michael Jackson

What a dysfunctional, solipsistic, spooky, tongue-tied, bizarre-looking man. Why did Michael Jackson ever agree to talk to him?

Actually, I think I know why. It wasn't because Diana, Princess of Wales ran so many rings round him that he looked like a candy-floss stick. It was because Jackson's people said: 'Look, Mikey, we could do with some good publicity. This weird, certifiable, perma-childish deal is out of control and is so 1980s you're beginning to look like the remake of Donovan. What we need is an interview with someone who'll make you look like a regular guy with a few screws loose, not all the wheels off. We've scoured the world, watched months of tape, and we think we've found the patsy. Just take a look at this poppy-seed bagel. Isn't he wonderful? Isn't he out there? Just stand beside this guy, Mikey, and they'll think you're Nelson Mandela.'

And so it was that the greatest enigma of celebrity got to do a two-hour interview with Martin Bashir, *Living with Michael Jackson* (ITV). Two hours, two whole hours, every minute counted out like a miser's change purse. But still I watched on the edge of my seat, only breathing during the commercial breaks. Michael Jackson I had had enough of after fifteen minutes. It was Bashir who held a cobra-like fascination. It was like watching Ebola hit a journalism college.

Watching this as a hack – I have no alternative – was the most desperately embarrassing experience since the last episode of *The Office*. There can now be no doubt Bashir is head, shoulders and strap-on-battery the worst interviewer around. There is nobody to touch him.

Let me say, interviewing isn't easy. It looks easy, and that's what's difficult. I'll willingly hold up my hand and admit to being a truly remedial inquisitor, and take my hat off (with the other hand) to anyone who does it in front of seven million people they've never met, but might in the queue at Sainsbury's – except Bashir. To be this chronically grotty and not know it is a self-delusion on a par with Jackson's assertion that the only plastic surgery he has had was so he could breathe easier and hit higher notes. It was like watching fantasies collide. They weren't coming from the same place – and wherever it was they were coming from, you couldn't catch a bus to it.

Bashir's interview technique – I use the word 'technique' in the way Eddie the Eagle did – made David Frost look like Judge Jeffreys. He asks questions so sloppily that he interrupts the answer to re-phrase the question in a new and sloppier way, adding a confusing addendum. It was exquisitely painful to watch, but not as bad as his repetition of the answers. So surprised actually to get a response, he gasped: 'Let me get this right – what you're saying is ...' and then said it again. We were watching a man with an unbelievable nose questioned by a man who didn't believe his ears. Then he throws in the most lickspittle, craven ploy of question-couching. He does it as if simply passing on gossip – 'Some people might say', 'How do you respond to those who accuse you of ...?' Oh, for Christ's sake. Have the guts to do your job, man. Although this went on for two hours, each interview segment was barely longer than four or five minutes, so there was no momentum, no sense of a conversation going somewhere, and certainly no revelation.

In between, Bashir droned a sloppy, unfocused footnote nar-rative, presumably because he still couldn't believe what he had already said. The big finale was an announcement that they couldn't show us the big finale because of the lawyers. Oh please. We were left with questions that were never asked, considered or followed up that were as long as a weapons inspector's must-see list. I now know less about Jackson and his life than I did this time last week. Where is Ruby Wax when you need her?

History

Secrets of Leadership

Like most parents, I've been stumped by homework – the big questions, such as: 'Why do we have to learn Latin?' Answer: 'So that you can understand the trite, unfunny little bons mots in the *Spectator*.' 'What is the point of geography – the pilot always knows where we are going?' Answer: 'If you didn't know any geography, people would think you were an American, and you wouldn't be able to put them right because you wouldn't know where they live.' And, most tricky of all: 'What's history for, exactly?'

This is a tough one. When I was at school, the official answer was 'How can you know where you're going if you don't know where you've come from?', or 'Those who don't learn from history are forced to repeat it'. The problem with both those little aphorisms is that the first one sounds smart, but is actually rubbish. Loads and loads of people have no idea what happened a hundred years ago, but know precisely where they're going. Indeed, I haven't noticed that lack of history has any correlation with a lack of direction. As for history repeating itself, it does that whether you know about it or not. Standing in front of history shouting 'Oi, you! You're very similar to the Treaty of Utrecht and the Diet of Worms, now clear off!' makes not a jot or tittle of difference. It's just that the folk who don't know any history don't know what's going to happen next, so they can sleep at night.

Last week, Andrew Roberts – or the Pinstriped Piglet, to use his SOE codename – might have come up with an original, practical use for all that past lying around behind us: turn it into a business tool.

In *Secrets of Leadership* (BBC2), he offered us Hitler's tips for better management, practical lessons on how to get ahead in commerce the Führer way. You've got a sales conference in Paris:

what does the Hitler-savvy CEO do? Drive through Belgium to get there, of course. You've got the staff motivation weekend coming up. No problem: hold it in a Bierkeller and stab the middle management in the back with P45s. Christmas party ideas? How about a synchronised torchlight parade at your local leisure centre? This was the Third Reich way, and Roberts made it all sound very smooth and attractive.

In fact, he was this close to making the Institute of Directors' version of *Springtime for Hitler*. If you take death, destruction, misery and horror and codify it as profit and loss, human-resource management and acquisitions and mergers, then fascism could well be taught at Harvard Business School and Rotarians might wear jodhpurs and sing 'Tomorrow Belongs to Me'. I can just see the little Roberts selling this to the horrified Tristrams. 'No, no,' he thumps the table, 'ignore the camps, the bodies, the smoking ruins. See the bigger picture.'

Businessmen rather love historical models of themselves. They're forever quoting Machiavelli or that fortune-cookie Chinese general or Napoleon. But have you ever noticed that they never seem to use the nice people in history? No steely-eyed businessman has ever written *Close That Deal the Gandhi Way*, or *Forward Planning and Blue Sky Thinking with the Buddha*, or *The Buck Stops Here with Mother Teresa*, or *Start Local, Grow Global – St Francis of Assisi: The Inspiring Story of Monk Management*.

Of course, those of us who like history recognise that historians are the one lot of people who love to see it repeated. Roberts's programme is pretty much a repeat of the daytime output of the History Channel.

Douglas Hurd's *The Search for Peace* (BBC2). They probably took 'and quiet' off the original title.

D-Day

It suddenly struck me, on D-Day, that all those old men are going to leave me. Having heard 'They shall not grow old as we that are left grow old' for nigh on half a century without ever really listening, the truth of the matter finally dawned: they were all going to die, and quite soon. My dad's generation was going to leave me all alone, undefended. I suppose I ought to apologise for being quite so monumentally solipsistic about Operation Overlord. 'It really wasn't all about you,' my mother pointed out. But I'm not going to, because the act of remembrance is profoundly personal, and it is all about me. I think my dad and all of them wanted it to be about me, just as I want it all to be about my son.

All my life I've been aware of the war humming in the background. I was born ten years after it was finished, and without ever seeing it. It formed my generation and the world we lived in. I played Hurricanes and Spitfires in the playground, and war films still form the basis of all my moral philosophy. All the men I've ever got to my feet for or called Sir had been in the war, just as all the men from my grandfather's age had been in the Great War. They're down to a handful, and soon the veterans of the Second World War will be too. What will I do without them? It was the event whose gravity has informed the orbit of everything in public life, politics, diplomacy, social science, culture; it made the United Nations, the welfare state and the European Union; and it ended the age of empire. It'll be odd and sad not to have these men as a touchstone, a fixed point of reference.

I watched parts of the coverage of D-Day on CNN, whose broadcast and commentary was incredibly good, though I should admit to having a lusty fondness for Christiane Amanpour. It was particularly nice to have a woman's voice, rather than those over-sonorous men who invariably get wheeled out to do dead soldiers, with that memorial rhythm that sounds like a rolling gun carriage with one oval wheel. I'm sure this is how epic poetry was born: men tumpity-tumping old battle honours.

For me, the highlight was President Bush's rattling good speech. The band of brothers who wrote it for him had obviously imbibed every episode of *The West Wing*, and it made the French chappie sound like a cheese-eating surrender monkey. By contrast, our own dear monarch sounded as if she was winding up a dog show. She was, though, the only head of state who had actually lived through D-Day and served in uniform, so I suppose she had the right to say whatever she wanted. But it is a feature of our royal family to perfectly judge an occasion, then quite purposely understate it. There is a certain type of blimpish, smug bar bore who imagines that this is the very height of eloquence and oratory; that the finest thing you can say is a muttered, embarrassed platitude. It's such a dull English affectation.

I must say I was dreading the BBC's big drama, *D-Day* (BBC1): it sounded like a buffet of cringeworthy first-hand reminiscence, dramatised. Television really shouldn't attempt large-scale action; film does it far better. And the dramatising spoken narrative is all too David Starkey and his blessed Queenie Elizabethans. But, as so often in this game, I was wrong. It was a marvellous combination of remembrance and drama. The action scenes were kept micro-focused, and the cutting of original film with dramatisation was neatly done. It was compelling both as history and a memorial to the day, and no other television network or platform could, or would, have made it. This was an example of the best sort of public-service broadcasting: popular, intelligent, informative and gripping, without being remotely patronising or intellectually compromised. Get rid of the licence fee and you'll never see its like again.

A broadsheet obituarist once pointed out to me that veteran soldiers die by rank. First to go are the generals, admirals and air marshals, then the brigadiers, then a bit of a gap and the colonels and wing commanders and passed-over majors, then a steady trickle of captains and lieutenants. As they get older and rarer, so the soldiers are mythologised and grow ever more heroic, until finally drummer boys and under-age privates are venerated and laurelled with honours like ancient field marshals. There is something touching about that.

The Trench

Let's make this week's review a little test. You watch television. You like quizzes and conundrums. Right, the question. Is the new series *The Trench* (BBC2): (a) an inventive and accessible way of looking at the First World War; or (b) an unutterably crass and tasteless trivialisation of a monumental human tragedy? Just in case you didn't catch the first episode, the format consists of a purpose-built, historically accurate trench dug in northern France, and a group of volunteers from Hull who spend a fortnight living the life of 1916 Pals. There is a plot based on regimental diaries.

Right, off you go.

To help you come up with an answer, let me paraphrase some of the explanations given by the Tristrams who made this pro-gramme. It uses familiar popular formats, like those of *Big Brother*, *Survivor* and *The 1900 House*, to illuminate a serious subject, thereby attracting an audience who might well be put off by a man with a moustache lecturing them. It is essentially the same as any other historical re-enactment, such as the Sealed Knot or civic pageants. By putting contemporary people in historical situations, you get empathy, and on television – as, indeed, in a great deal of contem-porary culture – empathy is everything. Finally, the end justifies the means. If a new generation comes to a greater understanding of the Great War, then that's a good thing.

Okay, now here's a précis of the other side of the argument. If the programme's justification is to make an otherwise disinterested audience aware, then why is there no historical context? If viewers need to be shown what a latrine looks like and how puttees are worn, then they might also need to be told why the First World War was fought, how it came about and who turned up. The only context here is emotional and personal. There is no attempt to place *The Trench* in anything but a distant and nebulous past. The audience's only link is through Oprah-style feelings.

But there are human experiences we simply cannot empathise with, because of their magnitude, their time and that tricky old context. To attempt to pasteurise them into Experience Lite both traduces the facts and makes the re-creation worthless and self-obsessed. The argument that this is no different from any other historical re-enactment is the most vacuous – a battle without bullets, shells and bombs, without death and fear, is like a cookery programme that uses everything except food. This isn't a dressing-up-box version, or kids playing Spitfires and Messerschmitts in the playground, or car salesmen dressing up as Roman legionnaires at the weekend.

Just extrapolate the format forward. If *The Trench* is deemed a success, will the next version be to get twenty Polish Jews and mock up a concentration camp so that the couch-bound viewer can get a deeper, more emphatic, accessible understanding of the Auschwitz experience – using, of course, *Top of the Pops* smoke for gas, as they did in *The Trench*? Up to a couple of weeks ago, I would have said that would have been beyond even satire. Look, I'm going to stop trying to be even-handed here and man my barricade. I thought *The Trench* was one of the single most depressing and defiling things I have seen on television, not because of anything that appeared on screen – in fact, it was all rather tedious and trite – but because of the lousy, self-serving, morally bankrupt excuses that made up the justification for it.

My grandfather, like most of our grandfathers who fought in Flanders, never spoke of his experiences. Famously, they all took the truth of what the trenches were like to their graves. Since the war, historians, novelists and film-makers have tried to unlock that secret pact, but, despite all the words and informed guesses, the most truly moving thing about the Great War was the great silence that followed. Did they never tell to protect us from the truth? To protect themselves from the memories? Or because they had lived through something that was simply unsayable, beyond any empathy of comparable experience? For a very few, the Great War is still a living memory. But more than that, the shadow of its legacy stands on every village green. The consequences of the war still surround us, not just in the millions who died, but in the future generations that were never born. We are, all of us, standing in as other people. We have to be the children, grandchildren and great-grandchildren they never had. We are indebted. We owe them. We owe them more than to turn their short lives into an endurance game show, to repeat tragedy as vain farce.

Mary Queen of Scots

As far as the gay pageant of our island story is concerned, Scottish history comes down to William Wallace, Bannockburn, Bonnie Prince Charlie and then a long skirl on the pipes as the Jocks go in to do English imperial dirty work. Oh, and, of course, there's Mary, Queen of Scots. Mary is traditionally cast as the Joan Collins character in the Elizabethan dynasty. The Tudors were the most efficient and long-lastingly effective propagandists this country has ever had. Elizabeth didn't just stitch up Mary like a Loch Fyne kipper, she made sure she came out of the regicide smelling of English roses.

In fact, Mary's reign was far more exciting and riotous than her cousin's Stalinist spying and purging. I only mention this because you would never know it from watching *Gunpowder, Treason and Plot* (BBC2), a grit-and-wig affair that got up to slog it out for the title of very worst historical drama ever made. Where to start? Let's begin with the plot bit. This is the story of Mary's return to Scotland as queen and Elizabeth's scheming to undermine her. It's also the story of a Catholic queen in a religiously divided nation and a woman alone in a viciously tribal society. It's the story of a Renaissance princess transported to the last outpost of the European Dark Ages, and a patriotic papist confronted by one of the towering fundamentalist reformers of Christianity, John Knox. If you can't make a great drama out of that, you have no business behind the glass of a television set. And they couldn't. This was *Rab C. Nesbitt* meets *McBlackadder*.

As far as television costume drama is concerned, there is only one type of Scotsman: a chippy Glaswegian, an Old Firm nutter. In this case, most of them were Rangers nutters. Mary was brought on as the new manager for Celtic. The plot-laden dialogue was so God-awful and God-awkward that the actors looked as if they were swallowing cod-liver oil. Poor Daniela Nardini, playing the part usually reserved for Diana Rigg, seemed particularly distressed with her utterly impossible lines. All the men were essentially the same man, with the exception of Mary's Italian friend, 'Little'

David Rizzio, who reminded us that he wasn't a Scot, but was cultured, by continually clutching a huge shaven poodle, talking like Inspector Clouseau and having a birthmark. All the other men had multiple scars, so if you stood them side by side, they looked like a fold-up map of the Road to the Isles. All this would have been forgivable, or at least forgettable, if the drama had been remotely dramatic. But they managed to make this highest of romances as turgid and leaden and visually impaired as an episode of *Brookside*.

Finally, there was Mary herself, played by some imported bit of easy-on-the-eye French totty, devoid of thespian talent. Never once did she seem to have the slightest idea what the words struggling to escape her bee-stung lips meant, or, indeed, who all these appalling men in scars were. She was the lucky one. All in all, it was an episode of *I'm a Regal Celebrity ... Get Me Out of Here!*

Wild West

They said television would kill all sorts of things: wireless, film, conversation, novels, sex. It didn't. Television did kill something else, though. It killed history: Herodotus, Gibbon, A. J. P. Taylor-style history. Since 1955 we've had a continuous babbling brook of television and it is all current affairs. In a hundred years, if anybody wants to know what the 1960s were like they can just call up an episode of *Father, Dear Father* or *Magpie* and it will tell them more about the politics, aspirations, social behaviour and fashion of the time than a whole library.

There are a hundred cameras running twenty-four hours a day, every day, and they will go on for ever and ever. No thought, no joke, no tear is too insignificant to record. No history, just endless current affairs. I expect in the distant future they will look at us in the same way we look at old photographs. I have a bottomless fascination with pictures of people who died before my grandmother was born; they are from another planet. Just looking at the state of all those nineteenth-century men's chins makes you wonder about the women's armpits.

Two of the best things on television in recent years have been history and have used loads of old photographs: *The Civil War*, an exhaustive survey of America's fratricidal coming of age, and *Eyes on the Prize*, the story of the civil rights movement. They were by far and away the most provoking, moving and informative series for years and they were both American. Time was when the idea that intelligent, serious documentaries could come from the land of unbridled commercialism would have been laughable. Surely some mistake, how could the tasteless, cultureless, ill-educated Yanks with their three-minute attention spans make serious documentaries? If you want flash and laughs by all means go to the New World, but if you want depth, gravitas and resonance you need the men in corduroy. The chaps with bad teeth and a degree from universities that were old before Columbus set sail. Well, it ain't necessarily so.

What must have been so galling about the American documentaries for the Tristrams here was that they weren't made with modern flashy technology and loads of expensive special effects, they were made with the things we are supposed to be good at: the old journalistic disciplines of exhaustive research and an ordered mind. That and bloody good rostrum cameramen. Having said that, the latest offering from WGBH Boston, *The Wild West* (C4), is a severe disappointment. It looks great, the editing, the subtle mix of live action and stills is riveting, perfectly set to music. It's just the history that's bunk.

The series has come down with a terminal case of political correctness. It's the story of the opening up of the Great Plains, or as they invariably say 'the forging of a nation', and the subjugation of the Indians. History is, of course, always written by the victors, but boy, do this lot feel like war criminals. The Indians are referred to whenever possible as Native Americans, which in itself is evidence of the sort of moral knots this programme finds itself in. Why would these savages want to be natives named after Amerigo Vespucci, a man who was an invader? The Indians want to be part of the most powerful and prosperous country in the world, but they also want to stand apart as noble victims. Various survivors in aviator spectacles called Margaret Running Bath and Gordon Loan Pay and

Display wagged angry fingers down the years, piling on the guilt. The redskins can do nothing wrong. They are cast to epitomise all the touchy-feely, hug-a-tree, at-one-with-the-oneness virtues. The voice-over reached great depths of whispered solemnity whenever the savages were referred to. It was one of those American voices that sounds as if it has cake crumbs in its throat and its teeth have been marinated in treacle and brandy. It's really annoying. Look, the Indians had no concept of ownership of land, right? Then how come they're still bleating about all the stuff that's been stolen from them? Huh, get out of that without moving.

Martin Scorsese, in his blissful personal journey through American movies, obliquely titled *A Personal Journey with Martin Scorsese through American Movies*, dwelt a lot on the western movie and how it changed in particular, how the films had come to be metaphors for America's view of itself. They've gone from *Stagecoach*, where the Indians are just target practice, and *The Searchers*, where the savages are the embodiment of perversion, mendacity, lawlessness and just plain un-American foreignness, to *Dances with Wolves*, where the Indians are a mix of Timotei models and Relate therapists.

It's all stuff and nonsense. The immigrants did what immigrants and entrepreneurs do, and they did it with astonishing endurance, hard work and ingenuity. The Indians were a ragged, cruel irrelevance, rolled over by history, not white men. The unspoken assumption of the Wild West is that America would be a better place if it had languished in the Stone Age with a population of half a million tent-dwellers and a billion buffalo, cutting each others' throats in a spiritual way. There isn't a country in the world that couldn't find a parallel to the opening out of the west in its own history. In fact, compared with India, China, Russia or even Britain, the civilising of the western states was astonishingly quick and painless. If you compare the casualties in the Indian wars to the American Civil War or the Crimean, they're negligible. It's sad, no, it's pathetic, that America is so unnerved, insecure and uncomfortable that this series has to apologise so humiliatingly for the amazing fortitude and vision of its pioneers.

Military history is to the study of history what science fiction is to novels. It's where all the loonies and single-issue fantasists end up. Chaps who don't just inquire into it but live it. *War Walks II* (BBC2) started last week with Professor Richard Holmes, the Sister Wendy Beckett of blood and guts. Holmes collected a rich crop of medieval nutters, blokes who spoke fluent saga and looked like Beowulf's hearthrug.

Mosley

I'm wearing Oswald Mosley's dressing gown. It came as a bit of a shock. There was I lounging on the sofa, there was he lounging on the Riviera in the same dressing gown. It was horrible. I've always assumed that my clothes were essentially apolitical in a liberalish sort of way. There is a pair of Lycra Speedos I have my doubts about, but I don't mix with them much. They all seem to rub along together all right, the Indian cotton with my dress shirts – but here, all of a sudden, I discover my dressing gown's come out of the closet plotting Lebensraum and wanting to deport my underpants to a charity shop.

Why anyone wanted to make a four-part series about a fascist bathrobe is beyond me, but then that's costume drama for you. By the end of the first episode of *Mosley* (C4), we still hadn't been introduced to the star of the show, the famous blackshirt, what we had instead was a lot of terrible stuffed shirt. Making a drama out of a dressing gown actually made more sense than trying to make one out of Oswald Mosley. Excuse me, but why glorify this wholly repellent and faintly ridiculous man with a vast series, because even though I'm sure in later episodes we will get a wrist-slap for the nastiness and boy-scout bullying of British fascism, the spit and polish of the detail and all this wardrobe stuff is very glamorous. Mosley is handsome and twinklingly lecherous in a Clark Gable way, because of the conventions of costume drama. If you didn't know any better, you'd be rather taken with him. 'He isn't any worse than Mr Rochester, is he, really?' Well yes, really, he was. But this isn't real, this is cosy costume-and-carriage land, where everything glitters and shines, where everything will be all right in the end, and this is no place for Oswald Mosley.

This lovingly over-decorated production makes him attractive and debonair, even aspirational. I'm sure it's not what the writers meant, not what the producers meant, but what they've got is what the wardrobe meant. The history is told in a heavy, plodding manner. Everything has to be explained: in fact, there is so much explanation of who is who and what is what, there's no time for character development. People meet in grand rooms and declaim large chunks of O-level British constitution as if it were the sort of thing they said all the time. Even in bed they can't waste time not explaining unlikely bits of foreign policy: 'Oswald, let's not talk about splits in the Labour Party and the Black and Tans now.' No, let's not.

It would all be amateurishly funny if the shadow of the gas chamber didn't lurk just outside the frame.

Americans have a collective creation myth, and Steven Spielberg's DreamWorks has produced a new, panoramic version of it, *Into the West* (BBC2), with all the traits that have made DreamWorks' television output so memorable: a sweet tooth for sentimentality that makes it look like a bulimic diabetic drowning in toffee, a desire to accumulate and exhibit clichés and truisms the way old ladies collect small china cats, a belief that the prime purpose of actors is as hod-carriers for plot bricks, and that performances should be measured by their ability to hit a cue and deliver a line slowly, with the minimum of confusing or extraneous facial and limb movement. Also, that all emotion that can't be experienced by a prepubescent boy with a split-cane fishing rod and a dog is unnecessary or too embarrassing to examine.

Channel Islands

What have the Channel Islands ever done for us? A couple of really expensive potatoes, a few flowers and fatty milk. That's about it. We know what the Channel Islands did for the Germans, mind

– they lay on their backs and made moaning noises. And so ITV rather hopes that they'll do much the same for them. The new series *Island at War* (ITV1) is a huge investment for the channel. In fact, it is probably costing more than it did for the Germans to invade.

Calling it *Island at War* isn't really historically quite accurate. Island hanging out white flags and profiteering doesn't sound quite as snappy, but it's closer to the truth. The question still lingers: do we care about the Channel Islands? Television is exceedingly regionist. As a nation, we've always been ambivalent about them, as indeed they have been about the rest of us. What do you think of when you think of the Channel Islands? Tax haven for secretive arms dealers and shysters in blazers, medieval laws about what colour you can paint your front door, cheap booze and fags, boredom, putting greens and snobbery. The occupation of the Channel Islands has never loomed large in our collective mythology of the war. We cared far more about gallant little Malta and tragic Singapore. It's rather as if, since the Channel Islands insisted on keeping the mainland at arm's length in peacetime, we in turn couldn't exercise much concern about them when they got a jackboot in the Jersey royals.

Well, you might ask, why should any of this small-minded prejudice matter in TV land? It's all just a backdrop. The drama's the thing. Well, yes, up to a point, but for this sort of drama, empathy is everything. What ITV1 is trying to do is cross *Heartbeat* with that mawkish, highly successful drama, called something like Old Tom, that had John Thaw taking in an evacuee. The danger is, it will end up being *Emmerdale* crossed with *'Allo 'Allo*.

The first episodes of big dramas are always problematic. There are just so many introductions to get out of the way – it's like the receiving line at a stranger's wedding. An introduction that had cost a lot of money; nervous commissioning editors and accountants like to see value on the screen. So there are dozens of extras traipsing around in the background of every shot, all accoutred and gutted with obsessive detail. Everything has to be precisely right, and you know that every teacup, tin and advertisement is utterly authentic. The effect, though, isn't one of effortlessly wafting you back in time, but rather an eye-catching waxwork-museum diorama. Too much information distracts rather than adds.

Altogether, this first episode didn't have the plot legs to carry the great carapace of its production values. It had to sit down every couple of minutes to catch its breath. This didn't feel like an island gripped by the terror of invasion. It looked like people worrying about the clothes they were wearing and the sorts of things that people in soap operas and nostalgic dramas always seem to be worrying about. This means they look out of the window and sigh a lot before uttering bits of sub-Alan Bennett dialogue.

Island at War may pull itself together and get a sense of direction as it goes on, but the first episode was a terrible car-boot sale. And if you think it doesn't look much like the Channel Islands, you're right. It's actually the Isle of Man, which is pretty much Scotland – presumably because the Channel Islanders have some weird rule about acting in public or that nobody outside the Bailiwick is allowed to own a camera. The final thing that annoyed me was the music, that all-purpose moody nostalgia noise that sounds like an orchestra talking to itself. I know how much this means to ITV1, so I wish it well as I wave it goodbye. But at the moment, the Germans are winning.

The Vikings are like dinosaurs. The audience already has a head full of preconceptions that, though perhaps wrong, are vivid and engaging and the reason they tuned in in the first place. The great fault of *Blood of the Vikings* (BBC2) is that it has been handed over to archaeologists. Archaeology is just as boring as it looks. Archaeology is to history what post-match pundits are to football. If archaeologists made porn movies, they'd show you stains on the bed and then comb the sheets with a toothbrush, looking for exciting hairs, to prove the existence of sex. And then they'd build a clay model.

The only historical discipline even more boring than archaeology is retrospective genetics. This show managed the double, proving that (a) the Vikings had children who, in turn, had children, who, down the generations, might have ended up running a sweet shop in Forfar;

and (b) they were very tidy. They didn't leave much behind them. They didn't build the Taj Mahal, invent the aircraft carrier or paint the Sistine Chapel roof. Indeed, the Vikings may have been the first minimalists, destroying abbeys as a style statement. Interminably, we were told that everything we liked to believe about them was false, and there was no evidence to prove anything else. So, after an unconscionable amount of time watching desperately hairy men dig sodden holes with brickies' trowels, we were left wiser but knowing less, which is an almost impossible trick.

David Starkey

Dr David Starkey laid his claim to the throne of eccentric experts of all the land of television, this sceptic isle set in a sea, etc., etc., with a three-part C4 documentary on Henry VIII. The genealogy of TV egghead sovereigns is long and noble, and drenched in blood, spit, uncontrollable limbs, bad breath and loony hair. And, most important, funny voices. It all started in the mists of radio with the semi-mythical Sir Mortimer Wheeler, and then there was A. J. P. Taylor. High points included mad king Magnus Pyke; TV's Boadicea, Barbara Woodhouse, with the viciously spinning bosoms; and emperor of the galaxy, the late-night Darth Vader, Patrick Moore. In recent years, the throne has been occupied by the absentee Brian Sewell, who is always away on crusades. The young pretender Starkey landed on the shores of Sunday night, planted his standard and shouted: 'Kiss my pinkie ring.' Or perhaps it was: 'Kiss my ring, pinkie.'

Anyway, he claims his right from his electronic father, Lord St John of Fawsley, the old pretender. Starkey has all the qualities we've come to expect from a hereditary telly eccentric: hair that ought to have separate billing, a wardrobe that makes you think music hall isn't entirely dead and, most importantly, a general demeanour that wouldn't survive ten minutes in a Gateshead pub on a Friday night. Starkey chose his ground well. Henry VIII is a good place to start a campaign. Unlike so much history, the audience doesn't have to ask 'Who's he, then?' They already know he's

Keith Michell. All over the country you knew a million housewives were saying: 'Whatever happened to that nice Keith Michell?' 'Shush, dear. This weird little regal bloke is about to tell us.' Well, if only he had. Starkey is a perfectly good historian but, better than that, he's a gossipy, opinionated, censorious and deeply self-satisfied one, which makes him a natural. He presents his subject not as a supplicant or curator but as a nosy interior decorator.

Unfortunately, his director lost his bottle and didn't trust Starkey to do what comes naturally – have a bitchy, lemon-tongued rant. This programme was larded with more bogus absurd bits of business and props than *Blue Peter* during Advent. Every statement came with a little underlining illustration for the hard of thinking. At every name that was mentioned, an unlikely Angels & Bermans fitter would appear as a ghost. Oh, and here's Erasmus and Sir Thomas More discussing the scatter-cushions for Utopia. And there were jigsaw puzzles to explain the Wars of the Roses, and a cheese … I'm not quite sure what the cheese was for except that France was soft cheese and Blighty was hard cheese. The whole episode suffered from a terminal case of remedial literalism. Starkey had to drag the props around like a headsman's axe (we'll get plenty of those next episode).

The worst bit was the tacky attempt to claim current newsiness by drawing parables with our own royal family. But let me tell you, as a man who has drawn parables out of thin air, you can make analogies out of anything, but comparing Henry VIII in full jousting armour to Margaret Thatcher in a tank isn't history or current affairs, it's *Have I Got News For You?*, and it makes Starkey look like the unmarried man's Angus Deayton – which is a simile worse than death. I'm afraid Starkey is going to have to pull something pretty spectacular out of his bag if he wants to get any closer to the throne than Derby. On present form, the fight for the Crown will be all over in a volley of grapeshot vowels when Brian Sewell gets home. He's going to be the Simon de Montfort of the eccentric box. And that's quite enough mixed metaphor history for now.

Hitler

Adolf Hitler is the King Lear of the small screen: the monumental part you get to do when you are a character actor who has grown too characterful for rural doctors and detectives with drink problems. They can't complain there's no meat in Hitler, no scope, no challenge. He's the big one, the Man, a surefire Bafta nomination. Have you noticed that, as a rule, hammy actors play Churchill, but only good Method actors play Hitler? But Churchill is invariably portrayed more believably than Hitler. It's in the nature of evil. He's so bad, we have to assume he's mad; but if he's played as just mad and bad, his success at being able to organise a world war becomes inexplicable. Actors always leave out the two things memoirs always stress: he was mesmerising and had enormous charm. Nobody wants to make Hitler lovable.

It was Ken Stott's turn to step up to the Reich last week, in *Uncle Adolf* (ITV1). He kept his Scots accent, which made Hitler sound rather like Gordon Brown, and he behaved like an old-time union leader. The story here was the dubious gossip about his relationship with his niece, who committed suicide because, we are told, Uncle Dolfi kept bumping off her boyfriends and weeping on her bosom. Stott couldn't bring himself to do the charm or the sexiness. He'd clearly studied all the newsreels and had the walk and the hand movement. He just couldn't fill the suit with a real person. Women threw themselves at Hitler; they begged to have his children. But with no charm or sensuality, this story was just a pantomime with a dirty ending. And that's the problem with Hitler on the small screen. More often than not, he becomes Abanazar, and if you don't give him real humanity, you don't make him believable; and if you don't make him believable, you remove the moral point of doing him at all.

Romans

You may have noticed that history isn't really about the past, but is the dressing-up-box version of the present. At the beginning of

Blair's reign as great protector, all the history on television seemed to be Tudor: David Starkey waving his cabochon at men in tights. The intrigue and energy of the Elizabethan court reflected New Labour. Now the wheel of history has turned back to the Romans. There is, in the collapse of classical order, the end of empire, the migration of barbarian intolerance and schism, an echo of the fear in the present. So the BBC (inevitably, in conjunction with the neocons' religiously righteous Discovery Channel) has launched its big autumn drama, *Ancient Rome* (BBC1). The first episode focused on Nero, the emperor whose ambition was to be god and perform his one-man show on stage. He was a sort of Barrymore with slightly less megalomania, which is rather how Michael Sheen played him. Sheen does a nice turn in mania, megalo- and hyper-. He has a face that can go from intelligence repose to stark-staring, satanically bonkers at the twitch of a lip.

The big problem with Roman emperors is that none of us has actually seen one. We can only guess, and actors can't help but guess big. They go way over the top, get operatic, when they get laurel wreaths and porphyry. Our own dictators and tyrants look like Relate counsellors by comparison. Despite having Suetonius, a mass of contemporary commentators and the greatest of modern scholarship devoted to any age, the Roman Empire still seems closer to *Star Wars* than to modern Europe or the America it's so obviously meant to illuminate. Like most sword-and-sandals jobs, *Ancient Rome* couldn't bear the ungainly weight of its own production values. Nobody has ever managed to make a toga or that miniskirt armour look remotely comfortable, elegant or practical. Personally, I think the demise of the Empire could well have been due to a gigantic fashion disaster, and it's time someone made a series about it. *Handbags in History. Pants Past.*

Docudrama

What is real? Why are we here? What does it all mean? Is there a point? Are there many points, or are they perhaps not points at all but little knobbly things? Is life uphill or downhill, or just flat, with a lot of sleeping policemen?

Frankly, I haven't got the energy. Let's just stick with what is and isn't real. Leaving aside Kant, something I've always been able to do with consummate ease and agility, reality holds few terrors for me. I can, in the immortal words of P. G. Wodehouse, tell the difference between a ray of sunshine and a Scotsman with a grievance. Or indeed any other variety of Celt.

Which brings us to reality on TV, which isn't quite so straightforward as reality that's not on TV. Here's a little practical example of what I mean. Get up now and go and find Robert Kilroy-Silk. Smile in a warm, friendly sort of way, then punch him on the nose. Now go and find Robert on television – despite my best endeavours, this is still relatively easy to do. Wait for a close-up, same smile, and punch him on the nose. If you followed the instructions carefully, you will have noticed a distinct difference. On the one hand, you were suffused with a sense of public-spirited righteousness; on the other, you're probably dribbling blood. That's the difference between reality in life and reality on television.

And so we come to Bloody Sunday (ITV). Television, being a medium with a Nostradamus-like obsession with almanacs, has felt obliged to re-create it in the mulish genre Tristrams like to call docudrama. The thing with mules, of course, is that they're infertile. Bloody Sunday was an episodic re-creation of some events, made using all the techniques of news-gathering – camera angles, movement, natural lighting, staccato editing and incomprehensible sound – that are supposed to give the impression of reality. It isn't real, it's television. Television isn't real. Docudrama is as artificial and contrived as the Teletubbies (I'm sorry, they aren't real either).

This would be fine if there wasn't a heavy implication that docudrama tells you the way it really was, that this is what the news would have looked like if it had had a bigger budget, a better director, a crew of gaffers, make-up artists, wig-adjusters and continuity girls, and they'd been able to do the tricky bits over and over again. Docudrama starts off by telling you the facts, but it isn't what it appears. What it really is is Sealed Knot television, dressing up re-creationists who end up making nostalgichistorokitsch. It has all the insight of the warehouse clerk who believes that if he gets his belts and buckles right, he'll know exactly what it felt like to be Prince Rupert of the Rhine.

The truth and the facts aren't necessarily the same thing. Telling the truth is the object of all art; facts are what the unimaginative have instead of ideas. Collating facts buries the truth in a chaff of irrelevance; facts are to the truth what grit is to a pearl. This film was a handful of gritty pebbledash that pretended to be a necklace. The inherent fault of this docudrama, as with the Stephen Lawrence and Hillsborough re-creations, is that fact-stringing allows for no fictive licence, so the drama part is always overwhelmed by the docu bit. Where the plot and pace demand more interest or rounder characters, the realism insists that the bean-counting facts won't allow it.

The makers of *Bloody Sunday* tried to leaven this by casting recognisable actors in key roles, so the audience could fill in the bits the script couldn't manage. There was James Nesbitt, that nice Irishman from *Cold Feet*. He must be a good guy. And there's Tim Pigott-Smith in a uniform – he's always bad. At one point, the nice, cosy, softly sexy Irishman says: 'This is our Amritsar.' And we all go: yeah! Pigott-Smith probably did that too, he was the wicked Brit copper in *The Jewel in the Crown*.

My criticism of this film isn't that it's revisionist left-wing tosh or plodding republican propaganda. Any of these things would be perfectly legitimate positions for a television drama to take. Frankly, I don't care if they dress the paras up in SS uniforms and have them eating babies. I don't care if they change the location to the Bahamas. I don't care about these things because I already know they are not remotely real. This is television. What I do mind is being lectured by some Tristram who thinks he's got the definitive word on the past simply by getting the wigs right.

Bloody Sunday wasn't a useful observation on Northern Ireland, nor did it illustrate damning evidence from the current inquiry. It wasn't even diverting. It was pompous, crass and sentimental, an awkward waste of effort, talent and my time, that suffered from the chronic disease that has bedevilled Ulster for generations: selective literalism and self-serving fact-stockpiling.

Now compare *Bloody Sunday* with another historical drama on this week, *Conspiracy* (BBC2), the reconstruction of the secret meeting, held in Germany during the Second World War, that formalised the Final Solution. Made by the BBC for HBO, it had a heavyweight star cast led by Kenneth Branagh and Stanley Tucci. This was a very old-fashioned film, using all the well-worn conventions of war flicks, biopics and courtroom dramas – it might have been called Twelve Angry Germans – and it began with all the clichés of that collective genre. Characters had to archly introduce themselves to the audience: 'Ah, General Heydrich, did you have a good trip from Bohemia, where you're in charge of rounding up Jews? Have you met Herr Thingy, whose work on the laws of race you must be familiar with?'

Essentially, this was a board meeting of Nazis'R'Us. A lot of men sitting round a table talking. There was precious little action, and a lot of what they said was mundane and repetitive, but it slowly grew to be compulsive. The actors weren't trying to be newsreel dummies, they were allowed to act, and the facts on which this was based were simply there to serve a greater truth about how simple it is to deform civilisation and humanity. It was the very prosaic mundanity that gripped. We saw the slow bureaucracy punctiliously creep step by step, with an accountant's logic, towards the unthinkable. The banality of evil is in the detail. All society needs is one wickedly false premise to construct a seemingly rational and empiric excuse for Auschwitz. There were arguments as to how Jewish a Jew had to be. They searched for euphemisms, mulled over widows' property rights and the technical unfeasibility of mass sterilisation.

Carefully mixed with the dramatic device of lavish gluttony and small talk, here was the bonhomie, the fear, the office politics, the jockeying for power. And it was all so believable and predictable and pitifully human. The facts were peeled away by a faultless script. This wasn't a mere Tussaud's reconstruction. It was a dramatic autopsy. Branagh, with a chilling mix of chummy bonhomie and silky cunning, gave a consummate performance as Heydrich, as did Tucci as Eichmann.

Conspiracy just about managed to pull off an ending that in any other context might have collapsed into bathos. As he's leaving, Eichmann puts on a Schubert record. The limpid, yearning violin fills the empty house where the deaths of millions have just been decided. It poses that hoary old question: how could they? How could the Germans be responsible both for this most beautiful music and most terrible crime? The camera ponders for a long moment before Eichmann says tartly: 'I could never stand his Viennese sentimentality.'

Of course, the question is a non sequitur. Some people make culture, and some organise train timetables. The trouble begins when the latter think they're the former.

Trooping the Colour

'The postilion, resplendent in the dress uniform of Her Majesty's limo attendant, is Staff Seargeant Willard Winkie, who has been sitting on the third horse from the left since 1962. They pass the honour guard mounted by Shirley Battalion, the Scots Guards, whose proud colours boast 105 battle honours, names drenched in blood that send a clarion down the ages: Gerrards Cross, Morden, Upminster, Chalk Farm, Ipswich Bypass. The barouche picks up speed past the horses of the Royal Blues band playing the regimental slow march, Agadoo. The great kettledrum shire horses Tesco and Lilywhite ...'

Trooping the Colour has always been an act of faith. It is the BBC's thing, its national service of thanksgiving. It may not be able to organise a middle-class soap opera in a country that is one huge middle-class soap opera, it may have spent the entire licence fee on management rebirthing seminars, but, by God, it can do a decent pageant. The sonorous rise and fall of the presenter's voice, like lapping tapioca, the minutiae, the gold braid detail, it's all too, too comforting, too, too snuffily reassuring.

But this year I had doubts. It struck me that actually this is all absolutely stark-raving doolally. All this stuff, all this frogged and polished litany. It's actually like watching 3,000 manic obsessives banging every railing round the park. It's unhinged. What finally did it for me was a piper's spat. We were shown the piper in all his glory, swagged and swathed like a Liberty window, and then we were shown his spats. 'There are twelve buttons on each spat, making a total of twenty-four. He has another eighteen buttons on his jacket as a constant reminder that the regiment was raised in 1824.' Sorry, come again? He uses his clothes as a ready reckoner for useful dates? This is bonkers. All this tradition stuff has lost contact with life as we know it, Jim. This is treatable. I'm as willing as the next man to get lumpy and dewy over the boys in bearskin, but, frankly, when it comes down to choking back the emotion over buttonholes, it's time to say enough is enough. This tradition stuff is getting out of hand.

What is so worrying is how events on which the ink is still wet slip on to the tasselled pennants of obsessive thin red hindsight. The battle honours go: Agincourt, Arras, Alamein, Goose Green, Kuwait, Divis Flats. Now, I remember half of them and there wasn't a man in spats in any of them. No sooner have they played the last post, and the collateral damage has been pushed away to sheltered accommodation and grief counselling, than it all becomes a bit of needlework on a flag. I'm not sure what I'm really complaining about. There must be some way of dealing with military tradition that treads the line between jingoism and disgust. I've just lost the ability to believe that a lot of blokes in gardening boots with endangered species on their heads, doing the chorus line bit from *Riverdance* and counting their buttons, is quite the way to do it.

Travel

Whicker

I remember it as if it were yesterday. 'Hello, New York ... This is the BBC in London, hello. It's still only midday in New York, maybe they're out to lunch. Hello? No, we seem to be having some trouble. Bob, perhaps I can come to you and you can explain how come they're still out to lunch when we've just finished our tea?'

The first 'isn't-it-a-small-world' satellite transatlantic television link, it must have been some time in the early 1960s. It took hours and there was an awful lot of static and fog and somebody I fondly remember as being Richard Dimbleby, but it could have been Cliff Michelmore shouting, 'This is the BBC from London' into the ether like a man dropping a name to an ethereal bouncer trying to get into an astral nightclub. It all seemed so exciting, so memorable, so important. And now, in no time at all, it is just 'Who's he?' stars live from Hollywood picking up awards because they are too lazy and important to turn up at the Dorchester. Familiarity breeds contempt.

Laying out the wonders of the world on the nation's Axminster is the oldest and biggest of all of broadcasting's purposes. Lord Reith carved it in tablets of stone: 'Nation shall speak peace unto nation.' That seems such a quaint Woodrow Wilson league-of-gentlemen nations' idea now. The way to global brotherhood was to invite people from around the world in for something hot on a tray and we would learn to love them, or at least to stop wanting to bomb them. Of course, it had quite the reverse effect: the foreigners seem all the weirder. They are odd little johnnies with disgusting habits and bad teeth.

This is partly because it is the odder little johnnies and the nastier habits that make jolly interesting television. The job of honorary tour guide to the nation used to be Alan Whicker's. Nobody could show up an odd johnny like Alan. He did not have to say much, although what he did say was usually worth listening to. He just had to stand next to some johnny foreigner and they would look shifty, their habits nasty. He became a legend and a cliché. *Whicker's World* is still captivating to watch, not just as a period piece of fashion and manners, but for the tantalising, teasing subtlety and nuance of his interrogation, combined with the terrible tabloid alliteration. Whicker was one of the first television journalists to realise the possibilities of having a style: the glasses, the blazer, the moustache and the highly inimitable delivery all made him a brand that he exploited at a moment when the rich and famous were flattered and amused by television. He, in turn, flattered and filleted them. Nobody would get anything like the access he had today. I don't believe in golden ages, but *Whicker's World* did embody all the early promise and possibilities of popular television in a distinct and original medium, and when you see the third series of *Travel Reps from Ibiza Get Sunburnt Tits*, well, you think, perhaps we've lost something. Perhaps we could do with just a touch more blazer and a smidgen less thong.

Simon Sebag Montefiore went in search of his roots in *Travels With My Camera* (C4), looking for the Sebags in Morocco. He found a solitary cousin selling tourist knick-knacks. 'For you I have Sebag. Only Sebag in Morocco. Very rare Sebag. Honest. Trust me. Good quality Sebag. No rubbish.'

It must be said this programme had great charm and not a little unintentional humour. Sebag's French, for a start. 'Voilà!' he said, over and over, with the utter conviction of a young thruster who knows a horizon when he sees one. And there was the rucksack. The mother of all rucksacks, he told us. The heavyweight rucksack made a number of guest appearances. What could this weighty reticule contain, a breathless viewer wondered. Slowly, like Gypsy Rose Lee in reverse, all was revealed. It contained all the costumes and props from *The Desert Song* and most of *Lawrence of Arabia*. As Simon motored further into the desert, he slowly went native, coming out in Mauritania as a cross between Beau Geste's dream date and a

boy-scout Rommel. 'Voilà!' he shouted, with extravagant arm move-
ments, to bemused natives. It was all in the finest tradition of the
English adventurer; and, of course, the best thing about being hung
with a huge double-barrelled byline is that he'll be able to do it all over
again next summer, when he can drag the dressing-up box in search
of the Montefiores. I do hope they're Italian ice-cream vendors from
Liverpool. They'd simply adore him up there. 'Who were you calling
a Montefiore, Jimmy?'

Travellers

Denis Norden – why? Answers on a postcard please. Who is he?
Why is he? Who are his people? And, more mysteriously, what
was he before he was Denis Norden? Nobody can have been born
Denis Norden. You can't imagine anyone saying 'I was at school
with Denis Norden' or 'Denis Norden took my virginity'. Perhaps
the next volume of the Wyatt Diaries will shed some light. 'To the
American Embassy for dinner. Everyone much excited by coming
Cabinet reshuffle. Quentin tells me Margaret has gone into purdah
and will only take counsel from Denis Norden. The old éminence
grise regales the table with anecdotes of comic fluffs on children's
television. All the women entranced, he exudes an animal sexuality. I return home in a bad mood, oddly jealous.'

How did Norden ever get on television? Was it a moment when
someone said: 'You know, what we need is a fresh, vital, witty,
crowd-pulling, sexually atavistic It bloke'? And some Tristram
said: 'Well, there's this Norden chappie sitting in the corridor with
a clipboard full of killer puns and flaccid double entendres. He has
the delivery of a cold Skoda on a November Monday. He'll do.'
Norden is Raymond Baxter without the roar of the trusty Merlin.
He is one of those flightless, mould-coloured, myopic bird thingies
that David Attenborough finds on the top of antipodean mountains
and says is the last one in existence.

There is a heavenly irony in the little corner of television's junk
shop that Norden has made his own, those compilations of soft
outtakes and impromptu slapstick. The biggest blooper of them all

is that Norden is on the box. Collapsing sets and actors forgetting their lines aren't anything like as incongruously amusing as the fact that a suburban accountant walked through the wrong door and became, if not a star, then a permanent black hole on television. Denis is the last proponent of a style of entertainment that to all intents and purposes died with the Home Service: non-threatening whimsy.

Last week, Norden left tongue-tied newsreaders and windy outside broadcasts to whimsy all over award ceremonies in *Denis Norden's and the Winner is* ... (ITV). This is a truly bonkers idea. Trying to find the good bits in award ceremonies is like trying to find the edible bits in manure. They're desperate when they are current, but utterly boggling when shorn of expectation and competition. In fact, it was such a surreal idea, the writers of *Big Train* must be kicking themselves they didn't think of it first. And yet, and yet. It was made oddly compulsive by the human Teasmade chuntering and inserting his old chestnut stuffing between the clips. Norden is like those annoying jingles you can't quite get out of your head. I can't stop thinking about him now, I keep imagining scenarios. Denis Does *Dallas*. Denis Accepts the Nobel Prize for Chemistry.

There was another one on last week: Peter Ustinov. What was Peter Ustinov? In my search to compile a list of TV personalities who are universally and unanimously loved, I mooted Ustinov (at the moment the only name that's unopposed is David Attenborough). But I found strong resistance among young women. 'Isn't he the man who makes farting noises?' Yes. 'What else does he do?' Do you know, I couldn't think. He did make a couple of black-and-white war films playing greasy foreigners. They were pretty ghastly. And for a moment he was the Unesco version of Robert Morley. But after that I think it's all been the twilight zone of Royal Command Performances and hotels in totalitarian states, where he does cars they don't make any more, like an automotive Percy Edwards. I must say that the slight ability to sound a bit like a Hispano Suiza and an Austrian hurdy-gurdy don't really seem to be much of a foundation for a career of international stardom – or life as a tax exile in Switzerland. But there you have it: Peter Ustinov is an international star. They always say so, but they never mention what for.

Then there is the matter of his ancestry. No belted earl can bore quite so panglottally about his lineage as Ustinov. To my certain knowledge, he has forty-eight mothers, sixty-five fathers, well over a thousand grandparents, and collateral cousins, uncles and half-nephews too numerous to count. They range from Norwegian belly dancers to mulatto xylophone-tuners, Moldavian duchesses and a Chipping Norton fishmonger. I think herein may be the answer to Ustinov's popularity. His audience is made up entirely of relatives who feel compelled by ties of blood to buy tickets and laugh politely at his oral flatulence.

Last week he started on a very odd little series, *Planet Ustinov: Isles of Paradise* (C4). It was precipitously hooked on to a book written by Mark Twain a hundred years ago. Why a mongrel resident of the cantons who can pass wind in thirteen languages should be retracing the steps of a dead American journalist was never vouchsafed to us. But I imagine the reason was rather closer to home. Some Tristram said: 'You know, it's a terrible shame that Michael Palin can only be in five places at once. The books made a great deal of money, it's a pity we can't clone him.' And a pert little researcher replied: 'But you could use one of his fathers – Peter Ustinov is sitting in a deckchair outside Geneva pretending to be a New Orleans funeral. Why don't we send him to Fiji?' And so they did.

Which was brave, because Ustinov can barely walk from the sun lounger to the drinks trolley unaided. Most of the programme was dedicated to the technical difficulties of perambulating. There was a moment when he confronted a Hindi-speaking parrot. It could have been awkward, with bird and man endlessly, competitively, running through their repertoires. However, wisely, the parrot remained mute. But you could see it thinking: 'Who on earth taught that fat, featherless geezer to speak?' Sadly, the promised tropical splendour of the South Seas looked like 1930s St Petersburg in a thunderstorm, but then everywhere Ustinov goes ends up looking and sounding like 1930s St Petersburg in a thunder-storm.

I don't know if Jools Holland is the result of a lonely night Ustinov once spent with an Angoran hotel trouser press, but I wouldn't be at all surprised. Televisually they are related. Where to start on annoying things about Jools Holland? Well, we could begin with being called Jools. Which is, on its own grounds, enough for a slow garrotting. But I think the most annoying thing is the voice (I blame his father). Although Holland must now be well into his forties, his voice is still truculently twelve. When is Jools's voice going to break, is there some sort of medical problem, has something got stuck? He is slouching round the world in the opposite direction to his dad, with even less reason. Perhaps they'll meet up in Guam and make ghastly mouth music together. Jools started in Hungary for *Beat Route: Budapest* (BBC2). This being a young person's programme, he had the obligatory open-topped sports car and showed us some of the worst hotel cabaret acts in Eastern Europe, Hungary producing busking itinerant hotel violinists the way Harlem produces basketball players. The programme was a spectacular of mediocrity and tired travel-film clichés, with a great deal of ancient stuff about Transylvania and vampires. Transylvania having nothing to do with Buda or Pest, and indeed not being in Hungary at all but in Romania, didn't seem to matter. This was a nadir in the television cult of lazy, self-regarding, charmless youth amateurism, and the only redeeming feature is that it must have been marginally more embarrassing to transmit than to watch.

Norfolk reared its flat inbred head in the first episode of *Travels with Pevsner* (BBC2). Pevsner is one of those works that people like me drop knowledgeably into conversations but haven't actually ever seen. It's a uniquely British – well, English – piece of lunacy, and so, naturally, it was taken on by a German. The eponymous Pevsner cycled past every house in the country and wrote the sort of specialist gobbledegook that makes wine tasters seem essayists of Orwellian clarity. Things such as: 'Bronco Magna. Best yew-blodged moley house in the county. Interesting candy-twist splans and an exceptional fiesta-grieved spindle window with flying boon-lobs. On the truncated west mitchet are decorative terracotta poove vents set in a rustic splay-and-fondle pattern. These are a later addition.'

Palin-tology (1)

There is an old writer's truism that says all stories can be reduced to a brace of formulas: the journey, or a stranger comes to town. Of course, as with all rules, there are exceptions – *Coronation Street*, for example, where nobody ever comes to town and nobody ever goes anywhere. The journey is a great favourite with television. It gives an instant flexible structure to a programme. Except too often they start off and you expect to see one of those Second World War posters at the airport that reads, 'Is your journey really necessary?', as the umpteenth wannabe Columbus departs for Havana to share a mohito with the world's most interviewed barman. 'So this is where Hemingway drank?' 'Oh yes – and Clive James, Clive Anderson, Jeremy Clarkson, Carol Smillie and something called Jools Holland.'

The mention of Hemingway brings us naturally to Michael Palin. No, it doesn't – well, only in the wacky, anything-goes world of television does it. A thousand dons could play literary couples for a thousand years without ever matching Ernest Hemingway with Michael Palin. Indeed, Palin is to Hemingway what Ffion Hague is to Linda Lovelace, only less so. Because I've been away, I missed the first episode of this journey, and maybe a connection was explained then. However, in last week's episode of *Michael Palin's Hemingway Adventure* (BBC1), it seemed to hinge on the fact that Hemingway's grandfather came from Sheffield and so did Palin.

Journeys are, of course, Palin's thing. Soon I expect him to follow Amelia Earhart and call it Palindrome. He seems to have misunderstood the rubric that all stories are journeys by imagining that all journeys are stories. They're not, and this one in particular isn't. A blue-plaque schlep around Hemingway-Fell-Over-Here sites brings us no closer to Papa, the places or Palin. Indeed, his palpable dislike of all the blokeish impedimenta made the whole deal even more inexplicable. If you don't like boxing, hunting, fishing, war and bullfighting, why take on Hemingway? The sight of Palin holding a shotgun in the manner of Sister Wendy Beckett being handed a vibrator made you realise he'd have been far better off following in the footsteps of Richmal Crompton or Beatrix Potter. Celebs' *Reader's Digest* tours may be a nascent genre, and we can look forward to Ainsley Harriott's Proust, Kilroy-Silk's Mishima (actually, I'd pay to see that) and Jim Davidson's Graham Greene.

This is all indicative of the most pressing problem facing television at the moment: too many presenters and too few formats. Winning formats are incredibly rare, performers aren't. Presenters are like elephants; they make a terrible mess of their environment, tearing things up and trumpeting. Hemingway would have known what to do with them – turn them into wastepaper baskets and billiard balls.

Palin-tology (2)

Michael Palin has the most useful stamp in his passport: better than a diplomatic carte blanche, better than being an international weapons inspector, better than being Kofi Annan. It's his face. It is a face from *Monty Python*, and nothing will open more doors and provoke more smiles and warm greetings around the world than being a Python. Palin may be politely fed up with having to be regaled by gumbies in hotel lobbies or drunk men in late-night bus terminals singing the Australian Philosophers' Song in a second language. But he must know that this, the longest snake in the world, is the ladder that got him where he is today. Which is absolutely anywhere he wants to be.

His latest series, *Himalaya with Michael Palin* (BBC1), has gone somewhere gruelling geographically but even more fraught politically. Up there are some of the most dangerous, incendiary borders and provinces in the world. Palin started in the Hindu Kush, the tribal-border badland between Pakistan and Afghanistan. Even the SAS has trouble getting in there; it's virtually impossible to get a visa from Pakistan. This is where American special forces are gingerly looking for Osama; this is where the Taliban come for rest and recuperation. But Palin found a polo match. This is the first time I've actually known some of the places he's gone to. Like Peshawar, a city I remember as having more than two million Pathan refugees living in biblical squalor. It also had some of the most radical, rabid imams, mosques and mujahedin. It is a hugger-mugger bubbling pot of intrigue, smuggling, poverty, filth and some of the best food in Asia. Palin found a dentist in what appeared to be a Peshawar garden suburb, an exotic and gentle outpost.

Palin is becoming an attractive cross between Katharine Hepburn and Candide. I don't mind that he makes a rough bit of the world look like Perthshire with altitude, full of nice, friendly people. Palin himself is patently nice and friendly. These films are classy television, beautifully shot. I can't work out how many cameras he takes. They're also inventively researched, and he is an engaging and sympathetic guide. So what if they paint the world with a cheery, rosy glow? Most television and journalists make the world look terrifying and murderous, which actually it isn't. Palin is a decent voice in a global cacophony of intolerance and incomprehension and fear. He's a nice good thing, an ambassador for out there.

Now, if I said 'Judith Chalmers' to you, what image does that conjure up? A pair of orange-peel thighs and one of Thora Hird's sunhats sitting under an umbrella saying: 'We've found that the pedalos were 15 Zamoran dollars cheaper one-and-a-half miles down the beach. Although the locals are very friendly, we felt it was a wise precaution to strap your passport and traveller's cheques to your colon. Cheers! [Hold something long and fruity up to the camera.] Or, as they say here, "Hup-ya-bum".' We have also been offered tours with Magenta DeVine, but she turned out to be another Judith Chalmers, without the dark sensuality.

Alistair Cooke

The best thing on television last week was thirty years old, which is a very long time in TV years; compared to television years, dog years are positively geological. There is precious little from 1972 that you could show today without selling it as nostalgia, or humour in a vein that wasn't intended, but *Alistair Cooke's America* (BBC4) was button-bright, intelligent, personable and engaging. But what was pleasing about this series was that it hadn't simply, by some technical change or editorial luck, managed to appear ahead of its time. It quite plainly hadn't been made yesterday, but it still managed to be authoritative as opposed to senile.

One of the things that struck me as being different was the amount of time allotted to single shots and straight-to-camera dialogue. I think there's a sort of universal directive today – after twenty seconds to camera, they start torturing the director's children unless he cuts to something else, ideally moving and set to pop music. Cooke regularly talked to camera for a couple of minutes, but then that's what he's good at. And there were tracking shots on real rails. Today, cameras are so light and versatile, they swap a formal rhythm for intuition and immediacy. The size and technical limitations of equipment back in the 1970s meant that the look and pace of programmes had to be decided before the shot was made, by the lighting cameraman and director, not, as today, by an editor and a computer, and after every angle has been covered.

But the main reason *Alistair Cooke's America* hasn't dated is that the subject is as germane as it ever was; indeed, there's an uncanny resonance with 1972. That was the time Nixon decided to wrap up the Vietnam War. Most of Europe was dramatically and implicitly anti-American. If the government and Conrad Black think the BBC is anti-American now, they obviously weren't watching television in the early 1970s. But here we are again, another war, another bout of Yankophobia.

Cooke is the embodiment of the special relationship, and he made this series in part to show the endearing and more enduring side of the New World; to explain that countries and people are greater than the sum of their politics. The story of America is the great *Iliad* of the modern era, and it has never been told more winningly than by Cooke, or made more convincingly and elegiacally than by Michael Gill, who was my dad.

There used to be a car advertisement with a French girl who extols Froggy things and an English boy who boasts of Brit stuff. It finishes up with her saying something like: 'Paris, the most romantic city in the world', and our boy leering: 'Prove it.' Anyway, someone liked it so much, they turned it into a series, without the Brit bloke. Most travel shows on telly tend to be of the nineteenth-century gentleman-adventurer type, about places you're pleased to look at and even more pleased you don't have to spend a fortnight in. But last year there was a good insider's guide to Venice, and now we're being shown *Paris* (BBC2), which is very annoying, mostly because we're being shown it by a Parisian, and nothing in the whole wide TV world of fact or fiction is as creasingly, colon-scouringly irritating as a French bint with her smug up.

This one has that 'I'm smart and sexy simultaneously, n'est-ce pas?' look. The programme is the sort of tourist guide you get on the in-house channel in international hotels: short on interest, long on soothing PR adjectives. With that laughable accordion jazz the French simply won't admit is ghastly, we were shown the Revolution's declaration of the rights of man. Our guide told us, with a patronising smile, that this document had changed the world, that the French had invented the age of reason and, with it, human rights for the rest of us. 'It makes me feel very proud,' she added, with all the vaunting modesty a Parisian can muster. The truth is that the French bill of rights comes thirteen years after the American one, which it copies virtually word for word. In fact, Thomas Jefferson was the ambassador to Paris at the time, and he helped them to write it. We were also told that the nasty old guillotine was not really French at all but the invention of those barbarous Italians. Next week, Pigalle, birthplace of Martin Luther King, where he wrote his famous 'J'ai un rêve' speech; and Montmartre, home of rock'n'roll.

Science

Richard Dawkins

How! Hold your palm up like an Indian and repeat in a deep voice: 'How!'

Remember *How!*? It was a children's science programme with a team of uncles and aunties explaining simple bits of physics and chemistry. Through the smoke I can still see their faces, but their names have been worn away with time. Except the late, great Jack Hargreaves. I pity those of you too young to have been bathed in the magic – there is no other word for it – of Jack Hargreaves in his prime. He was the Olivier, the Paganini, the Nijinsky of the small screen. When he was on, you couldn't take your eyes off him. Hargreaves was a man who was made for television out of bits of old baler twine and sheep fur. He was the lofty prototype of a thousand thousand frantic, enthusing television explainers. Actually, forget the mere performers. Hargreaves was television's Aristotle. He would ask lugubriously: 'Would you like to make a high-impact, low-fall-out explosion in your living room?' And, all over the country, kids would nod avidly at the screen. Then he would say: 'Well, best do this with the curtains drawn, because the noise might frighten the neighbours. First, get a large porcelain bowl, something made of gold, a silk dress and a photograph album, and then some sugar, bleach and a bottle of whisky ...'

How! made a huge mess, and, for a generation of us, that is what science was: small explosions and a huge mess. And thirteen mildly dull things to do with baking powder. We graduated to *Tomorrow's World*, where science was plugs and technology presented by geeks and was mostly about clearing up the mess that scientists had prepared earlier. Now, every so often, a Professor Brainstawm gives an illustrated lecture on television, where he makes bangs and smells and coloured smoke, and where vegetable marrows implode. We all know science is really bad five-year-olds' party entertainment, but not any more. Bring on the new improved great explainer, Richard Dawkins. Dawkins is the Keith Floyd of the Petri dish. He is *The Science Man*, written by Malcolm Bradbury. Despite the trust-me comfy sweaters and neatly tended hair, he is a science fundamentalist, a man who believes not just in the spirit of *Origin of Species*, but thinks every damn word is atheist holy writ. The men in white coats who look after him in Oxford have gently ushered him away from Bunsen burners and needles and electronically millinered monkeys and given him the easy chair of Big Bang and Stinks PR. So, naturally, he has evolved into a six-inch-high, two-dimensional talking head.

His thesis in *Break the Science Barrier with Richard Dawkins* (C4) was that science has a bad time of it in our culture. That art and imagination get all the attention. Just to show us what we are missing by frittering away our lives being merely entertained, he introduced us to a couple who have had that rare eureka moment, the lab version of seeing the Virgin Mary. One lady had found a star. That's interesting, dear, we need a new star. What's it like? 'Well, you can't see it, it is an ex-star, but you can see this squiggle on a long bit of paper, which is a drawing of a radio signal you can't hear.' My, that's attractive, maybe we could have it put round a pelmet or something. What have we learned from this defunct, ex-deaf non-star that we can't see? 'Well, for a start, we know it is there, which is really, really exciting.' Yes, well, I can see that, or, rather, I can't see that. 'And it helps us to see [or not to see] what the end of the world will be like.' You mean the end of the world won't be a poetic bang or a whimper? It will be a lot of squiggles on a bit of paper, not that anyone will be there to shout the final eureka? Gosh, that is useful, and golly gosh, is that the time? I've got to go and see a man about some fruitflies.

The next great discoverer was a chap who spent his entire waking life face-to-face with deformed fruitflies. Well now, that is more entertaining than opera, novels, the National Gallery and *EastEnders*. Oddly, actually, it was very like *EastEnders*. So what did the fruitflies do? 'Well, they live in this glass bottle and

I pull the wings off them.' That's nice. 'Yes, and then I found this one with a deformed eye.' Let's have a look. Oh, crikey, that is deformed. 'Anyway, we bred lots of them with deformed eyes. And from this we may, just may, perhaps, be able to find out a little more about cancer.' Heavens, I can't wait to see it on *Casualty*. Dawkins did everything he could, short of exploding, to crank up the excitement, but frankly, it wasn't very exciting.

Realising he needed a big show stopper, he turned on religion. This is a favourite old easy-to-hit target for Dawkins. Just to make it even easier, he chose to go for extreme-Southern Genesis literalists and faith-healing quacks. Most religious people in this country would be equally horrified by them, but Dawkins tars all religion with the same empirical swab. The unintentionally amusing thing about all this is that Dawkins sounds just as frothingly inflexible and blinkered as the Alabama pulpit-thumpers.

Finally, he was reduced to blaming education, and his audience, for not being interested enough in science. Well, this was tacky. Everyone, from Shakespeare scholars to vicars, blames education for everything. And even an amateur-theatrical assistant stage manager could have told him that blaming the audience is the last resort of the intellectually bereft. Science is never going to be as interesting, exciting or popular as the liberal arts. No amount of wishing or argument will make it so because it is not designed to be. The purpose of art is to entertain. Science may entertain with sad magician's tricks, but they are a by-product, not its function. Art is limited only by imagination; science is constrained by experiment results and the tedious, plodding stepping stones of empiricism. Dawkins made the very artistic and prima donna-ish mistake of confusing popularity with importance. Science may not get the respect he thinks it deserves, but he can take cold comfort from the knowledge that religion is also a minority interest and does not get the respect it deserves, either. What appears on television just is more exciting than what goes on in the back of it. If Dawkins would like a practical *How!*-style demonstration of what I mean, he should go to his kitchen. To all intents and purposes, cookery is scientific experiment, biology, chemistry and physics. He and I can both follow the same recipe, but I bet my cake is better than his. That's art, luvvie: theatre, magic, fairy dust, imagination, lights, music, applause, my public. There are stars and there are stars, darling. Some are dull, repetitive squiggles on paper, and some are fabulous, witty, thought-provoking, incredibly popular squiggles on paper.

Walking with Cavemen (BBC1) is a BBC co-production with the Discovery Channel, so it's made for thirteen-year-old Californians, and the cavemen have no genitals, never fornicate and don't kill anything. It's fronted by Professor Winston and his moustache, a man who does for natural science what Rolf Harris does for art, but with a bigger budget. There ought to be a word like anthropomorphism for inflicting the emotions of Mills & Boon on our distant progenitors. Even when a bit of science does manage to slip past the soundtrack, the computer and the bathos, it's reduced to meaningless, fortune-cookie hominid homilies. But the best bits of all are the actors in the monkey suits. This is beyond Japanese horror movies for kitsch naffness. The unintentionally redeeming feature of this series is that it turns out to be very funny. Winston up a tree staring into the eyes of a little nylon Lucy Africanus made me laugh like a gibbon. What they've actually made is a very self-important, very expensive version of *The Muppet Show*, with Latin.

Gunther von Hagens

Art and education are the two great alibis of entertainment in this country. Whenever some louche performer gets nicked in possession of a dodgy bit of burlesque, he just says: 'It's not what you think, your honour, it's educational.' Or, alternatively: 'Lay off, you philistine Establishment lickspittle – can't you tell art when it's gyrating its nipple tassels at you?' The art defence, it must be said, has been abused by cynical men. It's worn thinner than a fat girl's G-string. Certainly, on television, it's difficult to explain things away in terms of art. What's art got to do with the box? You don't pay your licence fee to have it wasted on art. Education is the fig-leaf of choice when telly needs to get a bit of how's-yer-father into a discerning nation's living room.

So, *Anatomy for Beginners* (C4) was swagged and swaddled in a modest merkin of education, like those how-to-have-sex videos. We got a very personable Harley Street-style doctor in a pristine trust-me coat, who said plummily reassuring things about radii and cerebellums. But he was only the beard. The real joy, what we'd come to see, was Gunther von Hagens, Fritz the Ripper, a spooky Kraut who has filleted and plasticised cadavers, turning them into exquisite, Germanically bad-taste trophies that pretend to be both art and education.

Here he was cutting up a fresh body (of an acquaintance), ostensibly to show us how it worked. But from the moment he began to flay the skin and arrange it over a sort of trouser-press affair, telling us in his Peter Sellers Hunnish accent that it had to be done neatly, standing exactly like an adulterer holding up his pants with his willy still in them, he had also stripped away any pretension of informing or educating. This was basically a straightforward freak show, set to stun and revolt in a comfortable sort of way. It belonged in the tent next door to the mermaid in a bottle and the dog-faced woman. That's not a criticism: television is the natural progeny of the Victorian cabinet of curiosities. But it was hypocrisy. As with the sex videos, the pretence of public service made this much more bizarre and voyeuristic.

We were offered the addition of a naked live man, a lost, coy Chippendale who had muscles drawn on him by a lady body artist, like face paint at a children's tea party. But nothing was as weird as the German professor, who is a cross between Frankenstein and Joseph Beuys in his fedora. He is a splendid specimen of a fictional character straight from an Edwardian adventure story, probably written by John Buchan.

We can only begin to guess at his motivation for fiddling about with corpses. It isn't education, nor is it art, and I don't believe it's simply entertainment or exhibitionism. He is a double rum cove. The studio audience of 'medical students and body donors' was included only for horrified reaction shots. The corpse wore a mask of plaster of Paris, making it even more bizarre. This was to 'protect his identity' – as if he could care. I expected Richard Hannay to run on and pull it off to reveal the true king of Ruritania.

Why should Channel 4 have got its knickers in such a genre twist over this programme, and why are we so horrified and threatened by dead bodies? This should have been the most familiar and mundane programme. We all own one, have lived in it all our lives, and everyone we've ever known is either dead or dying. The revelation of a patella should by rights be greeted with yawns, not gasps. Yet our understanding of our inner lives is so completely divorced from its physical reality, there is nothing of the experience of life to be found underneath in the mechanics of our bodies.

Everything that is emotionally, intellectually and metaphysically vital is separate and apart from the meat and offal: we are, in the most profound sense, only skin deep. If you want to cut up dead bodies on telly, it's the devil's work; but if you want to cut up live ones, it's the new Bafta-winning Lynda La Plante.

$E=mc^2$ (C4) was a joyous piece of television. Rarely does a programme this pompous and ponderously faux-wise take such a fabulously slapstick platform. The premise was a neat one: to tell the story of Einstein's famous theorem by tracing the series of scientific discoveries that led up to it. A good idea, except that they had also, at the same time, had the not-so-bright idea – in fact, the calamitous idea – of making this a co-production with the French. Deciding to make television with the French is like deciding to make an aeroplane out of mud, or canapés with Texans.

What should have been a small, intelligent, talking-head documentary about physics became a costume re-creation that grew to be a wonderful homage to Monty Python – blissful little dramatic reconstructions, with lots of wigs, where some quite good actors got to test the extremes of their ability to withstand corpsing as they delivered lines of chronic, unintentional hilarity. It left me breathless with pleasure: 'Nobody expects the splitting of the atom.' All this was accompanied by that terrible, by-the-yard Walking with Dinosaurs-type music, a portentous soundtrack with big hair. Mind you, there was a secondary pleasure in knowing that the French were going to have to sit through this, and that it was going to be the best thing on their set this season. My opposite number in France, if there is such a Gallically oxymoronic thing as a French television critic, will be saying what a triumph $E=mc^2$ was, and how it injected a little taste of French intellectual rigour into the flabby, moronic mental mush that is English-speaking broadcasting.

Quiz Shows

Quiz Show Host

Might I ask you to just stop what you are doing and spare a charitable thought for a sad and neglected group of modern life's victims. In these troubled times there are so many deserving causes clamouring to make demands on our philanthropy that it is all too easy to put aside the less attractive sufferers. But please offer the balm of your concern to a truly pathetic huddle of the mentally diseased. I'm talking about know-alls, clever dicks, smart-alecks. The correct medical term for their condition is buzzermania. Delusional men who think they have all the answers. It is endemic among quiz show hosts and comes from working year in, year out with small pieces of card.

Quiz show hosts grow to believe they actually are clever because it says so on the card in front of them. Bamber Gascoigne now knows so much, he can't fit in front of a camera. He hires himself out as an encyclopaedia, and he's leaving his body to a reference library. Magnus Magnusson has become Obi Wan Kanobi. Of course, Jeremy Paxman suffered acutely before he ever got near a starter for ten. But perhaps the saddest of them all, the most deluded with illusions of solomonism, is William G. Stewart. You don't know who William G. Stewart is? Well, I do. He inhabits the sound-down, rubber-knicker, no-sharp-objects land of remedial daytime television. He hosts a programme called *Fifteen to One*, which ought to be the Princess of Wales in a muddy bath with the England rugby squad, but isn't. It's a bog-ordinary school quiz of general knowledge questions.

I've met William, or Bill, as we media folk know him. Bill and I shared a dressing room once. I played the Princess of Wales. He is very proud of his knowledge, is Bill, and he's very generous with it. 'Who won the Nobel Prize for flower arranging in 1937?' I

don't know, Bill. 'I do. What's the Hebrew word for toilet paper?' I
don't know, Bill. 'I do. How many pints of custard can you get in a
kangaroo's pouch?' I don't know, Bill. 'I do.' The questions echoed
after me down the corridor. 'OK, here's an easy one. Where should
we put the Elgin Marbles?' On the back of your neck, Bill.

Bill moved to the cool clear watershed this week with a patronisingly bizarre *Without Walls* lecture on the Parthenon frieze (C4).
Bill knows the Marbles should be in Greece, and he hectored us as
only a man who has all the answers on bits of card can. In the hard
light of grown-up telly, it was pathetically obvious that here was a
bloke who confused knowledge with intelligence. He has bundles
of the former but is virtually bereft of the latter.

The Melina Mercouri argument for handing the frieze back to
the Greeks is well known. A mixture of irrelevant history dates,
times, number of saws used, etc., with a lot of breast-beating emotional pap – our soul, our spirit, our very being – etc., studded with
a few insults – your stunted, cold northern sensibilities, perfidious
Albion, a nation of thieving museum-keepers, etc. This isn't, as a
bod from the BM said, 'cultural fascism'; at least fascism has an
internal logic. It's cultural Zorbaism, emotionally incontinent bullying. If there is just one thing that on every level patently belongs
to this country, it is the Elgin Marbles. There is no argument, just
whining. We have a better claim to them than to the Falklands
or the Crown Jewels. Elgin acquired them entirely legally. If the
Greeks were daft enough to have misplaced their country at the
time, that was hardly his fault; and considering how many antiqui-
ties they themselves have flogged to anyone with a dollar or two, it
probably wouldn't have made much difference.

As for the spiritual home, London, Paris and Berlin have far
better claims to being the cradles of the essence of ancient Athens.
Classicism is at the heart of our culture in a way that it patently
hasn't been in Greece for 2,000 years. It is an integral part of our
living civilisation, from architecture to art to literature to music,
law and chess pieces. There is no question: the Marbles have found
their true home in Bloomsbury. If you still have any doubts, go to
Athens, go and see how much the Greeks really care about their

precious heritage. Go and marvel at the Acropolis and see the reverence and splendour of the city they've built around it. Wonder at the beautiful yellow fog they shroud it all with. Athens vies with Bucharest as the weeping pustular colon of Europe. Bill tearfully pointed out that Elgin ripped one of the caryatids from the Temple of Apollo. Horror. He failed to mention that the Greeks have had to rip out the rest because they're rotting. The one in the British Museum is now better preserved than anything in Athens: she's the only girl with a face.

I've gone on about this because who owns culture is an argument that has been made redundant by the electronic media and television. Television is as much part of twentieth-century civilisation as the Elgin Marbles were for the fifth century BC. But we will never ask for our tapes back of *The Jewel in the Crown* or *Upstairs, Downstairs*. Broadcasting has retaught us that culture doesn't reside animistically in things. It is in the ability and imagination to make things. And great art is a celebration of our species, not our passports. It belongs to whoever is moved by it. The Greeks confuse a carving with culture because they have misplaced the intellect and the imagination that made them. In the 3,000 years since the glory that was Athens, their only contribution to the edification of the world has been what? Demis Roussos and the doner kebab, which they nicked from the Turks, anyway.

Deal or No Deal?: a game show that demands the mental skill and dexterity of a fridge magnet, that has contestants as plain and unexciting as a chiropodist's waiting room, and a studio audience who would defy Tommy Cooper and Jessica Rabbit to warm them up. It also has zero viewer participation or empathy, and if all that wasn't enough, it's got Noel Edmonds. And the last thing it has is that it is utterly compelling, the most brilliant format for a game show since Michael Miles's *Take Your Pick*. Most game shows boil down to the binary excitement of winning or losing: this one has an internal tempo that builds and twists like a Hitchcock plot. It's just that, instead of Anthony Perkins, we get Noel, with his mum's hair on his head and her bikini wax on his chin. I've had to forbid myself from watching any more. It's like putting heroin in the TV remote in the middle of the afternoon.

Bob Holness

Africa, huge and mysterious. Africa, baked, thorny, shimmering crucible of humanity. The cruel unforgiving veld laid out like a hot flapjack, scorched and creviced, till in the far distance it breaks on the monstrous granite Drakensberg Mountains. We followed the leopard's spoor for hours, silent, single file, the Shangaan tracker, the white hunter, the Blonde, and me looking like Sanders of the River. Then a native village, a squat huddle of round, thatched cottages oddly reminiscent of Surrey. It was not going to win Best Kept Village prize. The inhabitants stared with the same blank indifference as the landscape.

I had lost track of everything except this damned leopard. I hadn't heard a wireless or seen a newspaper for a week. I had no idea what day it was, where I was; just Africa, endless, timeless, etc., etc. Through the strange syncopated chirping, honking, thumping, growling sounds of the veld wafted a weirdly familiar noise: 'CNN world report continues after these messages.' And lo, there, under a jacaranda tree in the centre of the tribal meeting place, where for centuries chiefs had dispatched impi to slit Michael Caine's gizzard, was a vast, timeless, hot, Japanese television set. Ted Turner had tracked me down, yea, even to the ends of the earth.

Now if I were Laurens van der Post, or even Clive James, the presence of the box might launch a thousand pithy, adroit metaphors, similes and bony epigrams. But the truth that struck me was very little, yet oddly comforting. The thing about this television in the back of beyond was that, though it was on, bringing Bosnia and the Nikkei index to the bush, nobody was actually watching it just like at home. As British Airways continually likes to say, there are more things that connect us than divide us.

I did watch a bit of South African television. They take it terribly seriously, arguing a lot about access and responsibility and balance. But they argue in the press, not on screen, because nobody really does watch it. It's still in the 1950s by our standards, very starchy and self-conscious, cheap and earnest. They have the seemingly insurmountable problem of two national languages – like Wales with elephants. All the people with power speak Afrikaans, all the people with table manners speak English. Instead of sensibly giving one channel to each, they use both simultaneously. I watched an early-evening news-magazine programme, spellbound. Here were the familiar handsome Him and cool, sexy Her trying to crank up the F-factor chemistry, being rather hindered by the fact that he spoke English and she Afrikaans. 'So, Helen, you've had your hair done differently, I like it. Now, President Mandela is going to have some tough things to say to Congress next week, isn't he?'

'Ja, Desmond, yo hunky biltong dik-dik, lager volk van der Merwe, lekker biki shambock kaffir.'

'Ha ha,' Desmond grins at camera, shuffles paper. 'More of that later.'

It was the most van der Bonkers thing I have ever watched on the box.

Back home and back to real, grown-up, sophisticated, First World television. Bob Holness. Need I say more. Culture shock with perfect creases. Mr Holness, a man who uses Sketchley instead of a bathroom, is fronting a ground-breaking new quiz show, *Raise the Roof* (ITV). The Unique Selling Point of this, above all other quiz shows, is that the lucky winner gets to move into the ground that has been broken: the prize is a house. OOOOOoooooh! Worth at least £100,000. Bigger OOOOOoooooohs! Well, it is worth a hundred Gs at the beginning of the programme, but given the property market at the moment, they would probably take it off your hands for £95,000 by the time the credits roll.

Bob Holness is a safe pair of game-show hands. In fact, he has an extraordinary pair of hands. I don't know if you have noticed game-show hands, but dexterous digit work is a central mystery of their craft. They all do strange, deft, semaphore things. Bob is simply the best. I can't take my eyes off his extremities. It is pure palmistry in motion. He used to do a show with school kids – a sort of Grange Hill University Challenge. He held the cards as if they were medical slides, stained with dengue fever. He has lost none of his touch on *Raise the Roof*. The latchkey is produced with a flourish, like Lafayette handing the key of the Bastille to Jefferson. In fact, it was the key to a perfectly hideous bungalow on a golf course in Florida. The quiz bit is arthritically pedestrian. At one point the two contestants sit in the yawningly familiar sound-proof boxes and answer the same question. So it goes: 'Terry, what is the meat filling in a pork pie? Take your time.'

'Pork, Bob.'

'Trevor, what is the meat filling in a pork pie. Take your time.'

'Pork, Bob.'

'And the answer to What Is The Meat Filling In A Pork Pie is pork.'

After five rounds of that I was pretty close to needing the solitude of a bungalow on a golf course in Florida myself.

Bruce Forsyth has resurrected *The Price is Right* (ITV). This was Leslie Crowther's show. Leslie did it rather well, whipping the audience into paeans of ecstasy. The idea is to guess the cost of things. A Forsyth isn't worth anything like as much as a Crowther. He doesn't have the hands, for a start. Frankly, I have never been able to get close to seeing the point of Bruce. He is unfunny, annoying, patronising and hideous. Now I grant you, many television personalities have managed successful careers with only half those talents, but Bruce wraps them all up with a sort of barely suppressed smiling anger. A cynic might say a Forsyth is a man who knows the price of everything and the value of nothing. I read in the newspaper this week that he has a fan club who wear bits of carpet on their heads when they meet. I don't know why I bother going to Africa to seek out strange and exotic folk.

The Great War

Half-a-dozen years ago, I launched a small expeditionary force in an attempt to liberate the BBC's archive. It didn't come to much. We laid siege and put down a barrage of threats, entreaties and flattery; they, in the time-honoured Reithian manner, sat behind the impenetrable Verdun of the licence fee and did nothing. I got bored banging on about it, the editor got bored printing it, and so we all went home.

My point had been that television is wasteful. It is a one-off, one-time entertainment provider. Repeats are a dirty word in broadcasting circles; in every other form of performing culture, they are a measure of excellence. Nobody says: 'Oh, God, there's nothing good on at the opera any more, they're showing *Don Giovanni* again.' This throwaway culture means television audiences – and, more important, programme-makers – undervalue the product and the medium. And it means that TV has no sense of its own history. Few drama directors today will have seen Peter Watkins's work, or early Dennis Potter, or *Play for Today*. Only in sitcoms, which are repeated as a sort of life support, is there any sense of a heritage. So, directors and writers constantly reinvent the television wheel; they remake mistakes and can't learn from the canon. Television has the superficial look of being very now, but, in fact, its genres move in slow circles.

The BBC archive is the equivalent of the British Museum, the British Library and the National Gallery. It is the greatest repository of the defining culture of our times. Unless you go to great and expensive lengths, however, you can't see any of it. What's more galling is that it's yours. You own it. You paid for it.

The series I sent my expedition to rescue was *The Great War*. Made in 1964 as a co-production with the Imperial War Museum and the Australian and Canadian national broadcasting channels, it had a mammoth twenty-six hour-long episodes, and essentially invented the historical documentary. It was the forerunner of Jeremy Isaacs's *The World at War* and, I'd imagine, Ken Burns's *American Civil War*. Uniquely, it has hundreds of eyewitness accounts, men who had never been filmed before, and, of course, never will be again. Despite the continued and growing interest in the First World War, it has never been repeated. The BBC's excuse was copyright difficulties. I always felt it was much more to do with the prevailing broadcasting climate and a fashion that nobody wanted to bother with repeats. I got quite angry, then depressed, and finally I thought, my life's too short to fight lonely battles on behalf of people who couldn't care less.

Anyway, that was then. Last week I had to go to Broadcasting House, and I popped into the BBC shop. Lo and behold, there was *The Great War*, reissued as a boxed set of videos or DVDs. Obviously, copyright wasn't such an insurmountable problem. It sat on my desk for a weekend. I worried that all my boastful bluster on its behalf might turn out to be wishful hindsight. I was, after all, only ten when I saw it. Today, it might look cranky and clumsy and imperious.

I'm late writing this because, once I put it on, I couldn't drag myself away. It is staggering, stunning, mesmerising. And because of all of the television that's come after it, it gained a mournful, monumental gravitas; it has become a war memorial, beautifully narrated by Michael Redgrave, and principally written by John Terraine and Correlli Barnett. Even given its extraordinary breadth and wonderful editing, the miles of original film footage and the remarkable, choking interviews, it's the script that really makes it a classic. Succinct, authoritative, moving, committed, cliché-free, with copious references and quotes that are always germane and poignant, it's an extraordinarily clear and committed view of a notoriously complicated story. This is the measure not just for history on television, but for all factual programmes.

Naturally, in the accompanying booklet, the BBC apologises for it as a period piece. It asks 'one of the up-and-coming generation of history producers' what he thought. Well, he thought that, nowadays, cinema vérité techniques (dressing up) are essential for military history programmes, though he patronisingly admits it's one of the BBC's treasures, and adds helpfully that his girlfriend was unimpressed. I spend half my life in a foxhole defending television against accusations that it's dumbing-down, but, you know, sometimes I just have to throw my hands in the air and give up. If you like great TV, this is the best, most compulsive thing you'll watch all year. This is television's *Citizen Kane*. Don't wait another forty years before seeing it.

Afterword

I just know that the day after John Logie Baird invented television, a woman in serious shoes knocked on his door and said: 'Turn that thing off. Have you any idea how damaging it is to kiddies' eyes, verbal reasoning, language development, attention span and social skills? And anyway, there's nothing on but rubbish.' And there was another one last week: television prevents two-year-olds constructing sentences, apparently. The compilers say parents should turn off and take their toddlers shopping as an aid to conversational skills.

It's beggaring that anyone can still be bothered to print this stuff. Certainly nobody who's ever taken a two-year-old shopping would. Of course, it's always on behalf of children. Nobody ever writes a report that says: 'I'm a forty-year-old who has grown up with unrestricted TV and I'm near-sighted, selectively deaf, incapable of maintaining even the simplest conversation. I'm bankrupt because I can't resist the commercial breaks, socially inept and my attention span is …'

And I've yet to see the authoritative committee that points out that 90 per cent of everything we all know, we glean from the telly. That it's a friend to the lonely and a nanny to the young, or that television is a cohesive meeting point for our dispersed, insular community, or that the shared experience of past television is one of the most bonding and inclusive things in society. Or even that television has done more to promote liberal values of tolerance to minorities and the alienated than anything else, or that it's made a generation aware of the rest of the world, or that, uniquely among cultural media, television has not only invented its own genres but has nurtured and encouraged other cultural activities as well. Sport, for instance, would be a very poor shadow of itself if not for the box. Most importantly, nobody has ever bothered to write a paper that says television allows access to all aspects of the nation and, indeed, the world, for people who might otherwise be excluded. Children don't risk anything like as much as they gain from watching the box.

You probably don't remember public service announcements. These were short films that were shown late at night. They had a wordy safety message paid for by the Ministry of Don't Do That. Things like: don't leave a chip pan on when you go on holiday; don't keep fish-hooks in a baby's pram; don't put lit cigarettes down the back of the sofa before going to bed; don't invite strange men in to help you polish the silver.

My favourite, now something of a cult classic, was: don't go to sea in a boat with a hole in it. As a child, I used to try to imagine to whom this would come as useful and original information. I tried it out on my father as he left for the office. 'Dad, don't go to sea in a boat with a hole in it.' He imagined I was being elliptically and metaphorically sagacious beyond my years, and sent me to boarding school. The other one I liked was: don't bury broken bottles in the sand on a beach. All that's left of this comforting nanny *oeuvre* is the annual drink-drive commercial.

Public information films died because they were obvious, useless truisms, but also because most television is a public information broadcast. Those who complain, usually from the Parnassian heights of print journalism, that TV is dumbed-down and peddles dross to the lowest common denominator, citing *Big Brother* or *Celibate Love Island*, miss the point. Reality TV is the exception; it's a tiny proportion of television's output. Most of broadcasting tells you things, and it's TV's great gift to impart information. The real criticism should be that it doesn't differentiate enough. It doesn't know the value of the stuff it pours out in a constant warm stream. We absorb what's useful and interesting.

In barely a generation, the information from television has changed the way we see the world and everyone in it. That's no small achievement. Television really does make a difference. There are obvious individual examples: *Cathy Come Home*; the newsreel of the Vietnam War in America; the Ethiopian famine; the rebellion in Biafra. On a broader level, the environmental movement would still be five beardies up a tree if it weren't for television. Charities and pressure groups, from pillar-box conservation to animal welfare and cancer research, glean power and funds from tiny exposures on the box. It can bring down walls, save lives and right wrongs.

It can also tell you how to put a water feature on your patio.

Dates

Fictions

Cops	Prime Suspect	October 27 1996
	Poirot	February 18 1996
	Cop Shows	December 4 2005
Doctors		June 16 1996
Children	Teletubbies	May 25 1997, March 15 1998
	Puppets	September 18 2005
	Cartoons	October 10 1999
	Just William	November 20 1994
Costume Drama	Middlemarch	January 30 1994
	Georgians	December 1 1996
	Trollope	April 25 1994
	Victoria and Albert	September 2 2001
	Russians	May 14 2000
	Nostalgia	February 8 1998
	Thomas Hardy	July 12 1998
	Rhodes	September 22 1996
Poliakoff		January 26 2003
Soap	Soap Opera	February 13 2000
	Coronation Street	December 3 2000
	Crossroads	January 19 2003
	Middle-Class Soap	June 4 1995
	Monarch of the Glen	March 5 2000
The Waltons		July 28 2002
Comedy	Laughter	September 26 1999
	Comedians	February 10 2002
	Liverpool	May 12 1996
	Friends	May 23 2004
	English Sitcom	July 26 1998

	American Sitcom	June 7 1998
Dennis Potter		December 26 2004
Actors	Actor	September 24 1995
	Maureen Lipman	October 31 1999
	Dawn French	November 2 1997
	Richard Briers	April 23 2000
	Paul Scofield	30 March 2008
	Actresses	October 6 1996
Sci-fi	Star Trek	September 11 1996
	Buffy the Vampire Slayer	January 24 1999
	Xena, Warrior Princess	July 20 1997
Golden Rose of Montreux		May 3 1998
Cathy Come Home		November 2 1997

Facts

Batman TV		August 25 1996
Sport	Sportsmen	December 19 1999
	Tennis	June 29 1997
	Winter Olympics	February 15 1998, February 24 2002
	Snooker	October 31 1999
	Robot Wars	February 6 2000
	Summer Olympics	September 24 2000, July 28 1996
	A Game of Two Halves (1)	July 21 1998, June 27 2004
	A Game of Two Halves (2)	July 24 1994
News	Breaking the News	June 22 1997, March 26 1995
	War (1)	March 30 2003
	War (2)	October 7 2001
	Dunblane	March 24 1996
	New Orleans	September 11 2005
	GMTV	June 5 1994
Aids		December 10 1995

Class		March 10 1996
Reality TV	Fame	September 29 2002
	Trading Races	February 3 2002
	Popstars	February 11 2001
	Celebrities	September 8 2002
	Big Brother	May 28 2006, June 1 2003
	42 Up	July 2 1998
Cookery	Cooks	June 12 1994
	Fat Ladies	October 13 1996
	Christmas	December 23 2001
	Jamie Oliver	September 24 2006
	Fanny and Delia	October 18 1998
Philosophy	Philosophy (1)	August 15 1999
	Philosophy (2)	April 2 2000
Music		October 13 1996
Art	How Art Made the World	May 15 2005
	Rolf Harris	November 25 2001
	Sister Wendy Beckett	July 7 1996
	Surrealism	September 30 2001
Presenting	Carol Vorderman	July 23 2000
	Terry Wogan	June 8 2003
	Louis Theroux	February 23 2001
	Richard Whiteley	July 3 2005
	Joan Bakewell	November 25 2002
	John Motson	June 7 1998
Un-facts		March 23 2003
Nature	David Attenborough	September 16 2001
	Survival	August 17 1993
	Congo	February 4 2001
	The Great Auk	June 20 2004
	Cruel World	July 15 2001
Politics	Ballot Box	October 2 1994
	Budget	December 3 1995
	Michael Heseltine	September 17 2000
	Election 1997	May 4 1997
	Tony Benn	July 21 2002

Index

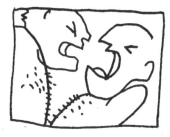